FLAT-COATED RETRIEVERS

Today

Joan Mason

HOWELL
BOOK HOUSE

New York

HOWELL BOOK HOUSE
A Simon & Schuster Macmillan company,
1633 Broadway, New York, NY 10019.

MACMILLAN is a registered trademark of Macmillan, Inc.

Library of Congress Cataloging-in-Publication data

CIP date available on request

ISBN 0-87605-124-7

10 9 8 7 6 5 4 3 2 1
Printed and bound in Singapore

CONTENTS

ACKNOWLEDGEMENTS

Chapter One: ORIGINS OF THE FLAT-COATED RETRIEVER   6
Shooting in the early 19th century; Retrievers; The "Canadian" dog; Inter-bred retrievers; The Shirley family; The "making" of the Flat-Coated Retriever; A featured breed; 'Young' Will Simms; The turn of the 19th century; Original aims; Flat-Coat type; The Riverside kennels; Aldridge's sales; Changing concepts: Flat-Coats at Crufts; The winds of change; The dual purpose retriever; Declining fortunes; The gamekeeper's choice; The end of an era.

Chapter Two: REVIVAL OF THE FLAT-COAT   19
The Atherbram kennels; Claverdon and Pewcroft; Influential kennels of the 1950s; The Sixties; The situation in the US; The Flat-Coated Retriever Society of America; Field trials in the UK; The Seventies; The Eighties; The Shooting Dog Certificate; "The working group".

Chapter Three: CHOOSING A PUPPY   31
The puppy-finding trail; Dog or bitch?; Approaching the breeder; Assessing puppies; Preliminary arrangements; The day of collection; Early training.

Chapter Four: ESSENTIAL BASIC TRAINING   38
Learning through daily activities; Vocabulary and voice tone; Simple early field training (Equipment; Home work; Introduction to gunshot).

Chapter Five: CARING FOR YOUR FLAT-COAT   43
Ingredients for a proper diet; Complete foods; Homemade foods; Manhattan mix; Special needs; Exercise; Grooming; Beds and bedding; Housing; Alternative housing; Old dogs.

Chapter Six: HEALTH MATTERS   51
Immunising inoculations; Inherited conditions (Hip dysplasia; Progressive retinal atrophy); First aid kit; Temperature; Common ailments (Anal glands; Cuts; Digestive problems; Constipation; Ears; Eyes; Feet; The skin; Patella luxation; Peritonitis; Pyometra; Teeth; Worms); Disposal of faeces; Administering medicines.

Chapter Seven: THE BREED STANDARDS   58
British Breed Standard; American Breed Standard; Clarification (General appearance; Temperament and character; Head and skull: The skull; Egg Heads; The muzzle; Nose; Eyes; Ears; Mouth; Neck; Shoulders; Forequarters; Body; Hindquarters; Feet; tail; Gait/movement; Coat; Colour; Size; Faults).

Chapter Eight: SHOWING YOUR FLAT-COAT   71
Types of shows; American shows; USA dog show procedures; Ring training in the UK; Preparing your dog; The big day; Hints; Are judges born or made?; Positive judging; The final thought.

4

Chapter Nine: THE WORKING FLAT-COAT   82
The shooting field; Field trials; Working tests; Working trials; Obedience and Agility;
Hunting with the Flat-coat in the US; American field trials; Agility in the US; Flyball;
Canada.

Chapter Ten: BREEDING AND MATING   101
To breed or not to breed?; Requirements in a breeding bitch; The stud dog; Choosing a
stud dog; Colour; Methods of breeding; Making arrangements; Breeding age; The in-
season bitch; Reluctant bitches; Scientific help; Stud dog management; Pre-mating
preparation; The mating; The tie.

Chapter Eleven: PREGNANCY AND WHELPING   109
The in-whelp bitch; Worming; Feeding; Whelping beds/boxes; The "shopping list";
The labour; The weak puppy; Colostrum; Tidying up; Complementary feedings;
Dewclaws: Visitors; Initial "nest" cleanliness; Puppies' progress; Early feeding;
Bedding; Toys; House training; Registration; New homes; Owner's package.

Chapter Twelve: CONTEMPORARY BRITISH KENNELS   118
Belsud; Bordercot; Cannimore; Casuarina; Claverdon; Cleovine; Collyers; Courtbeck;
Darillens; Downstream; Emanon; Eskmill; Exclyst/Wyndhamian; Fenrivers; Fenstorm;
Fossdyke; Gayplume; Glidesdown; Gunmakers; Hallbent; Hartshead; Heronsflight;
Kenjo; Marlcot; Oakmoss; Puhfuh; Rase; Ravenhall; Riversflight; Rondix; Shargleam;
Shiredale; Stonemead/Bramatha; Tarncourt; Tonggreen; Tomstan; Torwood/Lathkill;
Varingo; Waverton; Westering; Windy Hollows; Withybed; Wolfhill; Woodland;
Wizardwood; Scottish kennels (Braidwynn; Branchalwood; Colona; Glendaruel;
Kilbucho; Lacetrom; Longforgan; Pendlewych; Rainscourt; Vbos).

Chapter Thirteen: THE FLAT-COAT WORLDWIDE   141
France and Belgium; Germany; Holland; Switzerland; Denmark; Sweden; Norway;
Finland; New Zealand; Australia.

Chapter Fourteen: THE FLAT-COAT IN NORTH AMERICA   165
A-Z of leading kennels in the US: Altair; Amani; Athercroft; Bertschire; Black Gamin;
Bolingbroke; Casablanca; Curlee Hill; Destiny; Dexmoor; Duckacres; Flatford;
Grousemoor; Hardscrabble; Hihill; Hy-Times; Jo No Re; Kistner; Mantayo;
Meadowrue; Omega; Petersfield; Quillquest; Rockledge; Sassacus; Springvalley;
Sterling; Summerhill; Twin Oaks; Canada (Parkburn; Prarieflight; Inglis; Flat-Coats in
Ontario; Fleetwing; The Flat-Coated Retriever Society of Canada).

Ch. Heronsflight Pan's Promise. Owned and bred by Joan Mason and Rosemary Talbot

Acknowledgements

The overall enthusiasm generated during the putting together of this book has been a very real incentive. Every contribution, large or small, has had its own importance in giving a comprehensive view of the breed. Many thanks to those who made time in a busy world to write about their own particular field of interest. You will come across their names as you read on.

My thanks to the Hon. Amelia Jessel who provided the line drawings; to Rosemarie Wild for allowing the use of her easily understood illustrations on colour transference, taken from her book *The Flat-Coated Retriever and Chesapeake Bay Retriever,* published by Muller and Ruschlikon; to Sally Anne Thompson for allowing the use of her photograph of Ch. Bordercot Guy, also to Roger Chambers and Gerwyn Gibbs who have allowed the use of their photographs; to Randle Cooke who allowed the inclusion of excerpts from his grandfather's scrapbooks and to Gwen Knight for the use of her 'training in a nutshell' from her booklet *Training your Flat-Coat.*

Appreciation also for two who gave practical assistance: Caroline Langman who managed to keep a supply of hard-to-get typewriter cassettes to hand, and Anne Smith who undertook the onerous task of "tidy typing".

Page One photograph
The Windyhollow's Flat-Coats: Ch. Kulawand Woodnymph of Windyhollows, W. Mirage, W. Phantom, Riversflight Ganol of Windyhollows, Torwood Pegasus, Tripontium Minerva and W. Tornado.
Photo: Gibbs.

6

Chapter One

ORIGINS OF THE FLAT-COATED RETRIEVER

About two miles from where I live stands an impressive Gothic manor house set back across parkland from river and road. It comes as no surprise to learn that the house is reputed to be haunted by a lady dressed in grey. For our purposes it would be more appropriate if the ghost was a black dog, for this is Ettington Hall, for generations the home of the Shirley family, without whom it is unlikely there would have been the Flat-coated Retriever as we know the breed today. Indeed, in the latter half of the 1800s, the breed was known as the Shirley Retriever, but we need to find out how this came about.

It is interesting that we can look at, say, a Pharaoh Hound or an Ibizan Hound and find they are relatively unchanged from drawings in ancient Egyptian tombs, yet, when we look at the retriever breeds, there are a lot of suppositions and theories as to what might have taken place in the course of their development.

SHOOTING IN THE EARLY 19TH CENTURY

Prior to the mid 1800s, shooting dogs had been mainly of the setter, pointer or spaniel type which were suited to shooting with the flintlock or muzzle-loading guns when, in general, shooters walked up their game. Only very occasionally was there driven game. It was only with the advent of the breech-loading shotgun that the need arose for a dog with speed, game-finding ability,

Canis familiaris from The Illustrated Natural History by the Rev. J.G. Wood, 1865.

stamina and a tender mouth to find and return dead and wounded game safely to hand. The introduction of the cartridge, as opposed to pinfire breech-loading, further intensified this need. The pattern of shooting changed also; whereas early in the century a few hundred pheasants would be raised on an estate, these now numbered thousands. It became usual to travel long distances to shoots and thus came about the very fashionable late Victorian, and then Edwardian, shooting parties.

They were for the seriously rich – not only the host but those attending as guests. The "knock-on" effect of changing to the breech-loading shot gun and then the cartridge was quite amazing. Due to the far higher numbers of birds being reared on large estates, there was a need for more keepers and beaters and, no doubt, indoor staff as well to care for the needs of guests. So the humble cartridge did, indirectly, give rise to employment for hundreds of people but, of course, at great expense to the estate owner. For the ladies who accompanied their husbands an extensive wardrobe was required, with three or four changes of costume each day, and it was absolutely de rigueur not to wear the same outfit twice!

RETRIEVERS

The retrieving breeds had always been of somewhat mixed origin – in other words, anything that would retrieve was a retriever! In consequence there were certain differences in type, and the name given to the type tended to be based on coat, so that in the same litter might be found one dog described as a Labrador, with a sibling called a Wavy-Coated Retriever (Horton Max, one of the famous dogs of his time, was a case in point). To show a little more clearly how intermingled these retrievers were, Zelstone (1880) was the grandsire of two yellow retrievers from whom, by selective breeding, further yellow retrievers were bred and, eventually, Golden Retrievers which bred true – although this is putting it in decidedly over-simplistic terms. But Zelstone was also the sire of the highly acclaimed Ch. Moonstone (Wavy Coated Retriever) who, in turn, was grandsire to Ch. Darenth. To bring this nearer to the present day, Dr Nancy Laughton's Claverdon Jorracks Junior was in direct descent, and many of you will either posses, or have seen, descendants of his in present-day pedigrees.

THE "CANADIAN" DOG

There could well have been regional variations also, indeed almost certainly, because even now one can come across "pockets" of Flat-Coated retrievers, particularly in parts of Scotland, with breeding and bloodlines specific to the area and virtually unheard of elsewhere. The common factor in the development of the Retriever breed (it was not yet split except by differences in type) was the bringing-in of dogs of Canadian origin, mainly of the Lesser Newfoundland or St John's Bay Retriever type. There was a steady plying across the Atlantic of ships carrying timber from Canada to various British ports. It was commonplace for dogs to travel on these ships; indeed some were virtually "ship's crew" as their strong swimming abilities were used for some water tasks. The dogs frequently accompanied their owners ashore and were seen by local folk, and gamekeepers were quick to recognise and appreciate their inherent characteristics. In consequence there became a demand for these dogs for crossing with existing working dogs. Their excellence in water, and good scenting ability combined with a rare courage as "night dogs", when the keeper had to walk the lonely "rides" to look for and apprehend poachers, made them invaluable.

I have letters from the late Stanley O'Neill who, with his wife Kathleen, bred the influential Pewcroft Flat-Coated Retrievers, in which he mentions seeing these dogs when, as a youngster, he accompanied his father, who was a superintendent of fishing ports. Stan mentioned the dogs as varying in colour from sandy through brown to black, frequently with tan or some white. They

*The St John's or Lesser
Labrador Dog, Canada, late
19th Century.
Property of Joan Schwartz.*

were all prodigious swimmers but it was the black dogs which were in most demand. I had a thought as to whether the "sandy" dogs may have been from the Chesapeake Bay area?

Quite certainly, the dogs which were bought were used for crossing with setters and the existing retrieving dogs such as the Wavy-Coated Retriever; so the Canadian dogs were quite influential when the Flat-Coated Retriever was being evolved. I suppose this fact gives some validity to the claim of the Canadian Kennel Club a few years ago that the Flat-Coated Retriever is indigenous to Canada and thus counts as a native breed. Who can blame them for wishing to have some claim to such a delightful breed? But I think we have to accept that the breed as we know it originated at Ettington Park.

INTER-BRED RETRIEVERS

It is as well to remember that at that time and indeed, to a lesser extent well into this century, it was common practice to inter-breed any of the retriever types (they were not yet breeds), the only criterion being that of having good working ability. In this century, when the retriever breeds had been granted separate recognition, the Kennel Club would register progeny as "inter-bred" and this was only rescinded in April 1971. The latest such registration I could find was a litter of Labrador-crossed Goldens in Scotland in October 1969. It has to be said that earlier the main crossing was more frequently between Labrador and Flat-Coat. For all essential purposes this type of registration no longer exists, the retriever breeds being regarded as totally individual.

As a matter of interest, many of the older Swedish pedigrees contain Mimosa of Halstock whose great-grandfather Warroch Diamond (inter-bred) was sired by a Golden, Mika of Yelme, from a Flat-Coat, Strowan Black Beauty.

THE SHIRLEY FAMILY

This family, as I have said, owned Ettington Park, an estate which lies some six miles south of Stratford-upon-Avon in Warwickshire and which had, and used, Wavy-coated Retrievers of high repute. The family is one of the oldest in England, being descended from Saswalo, a Saxon Thane who held the manor of Ettington before the Norman conquest (1066 AD). The present house was built on the site of the original Saxon house, and a family chapel has been preserved in the ruins of the Norman church which stands beside the house. Although the estate still belongs to the family, no Shirley has lived there since before World War I when the then Colonel and Mrs Shirley moved to Ireland to live on an estate the family had owned since the time of Queen Elizabeth I. The manor house is now leased to an hotel group.

As we have seen, the mid-19th century was a time of change for sportsmen, particularly in the shooting field. At that time the Wavy-Coated Retriever was much favoured. It was a sturdy-boned dog, very powerful, with a broadish head, a definite "stop" and carrying the profuse wavy coat from which its name came – in other words, a dog showing very clearly the influence of the Lesser Newfoundland dogs, wonderful water dogs, courageous and honest. But despite these attributes the dog did not fill the needs of the new pattern in the shooting field.

The Wavy-coated Retrievers at Ettington included Ch. Moonstone, recognised as one of the most noteworthy retrievers. In a Kennel Gazette dated June 1886, Ch. Moonstone is offered at stud thus:

Ambrotype, circa 1860. Purchased at auction in London. Property of Joan Schwartz.

"Moonstone. Champion. (14,181); fee 10 guineas, sire of Mahdi, Myra, Goldstone, Blackthorn and Cypress. Kennelman J Gibbs. Ettington Park, Stratford-upon-Avon; G.W. Railway Stratford-upon-Avon (6 miles) London and N. Western Railway, Ettington (2.5 miles). Telegraph Stratford-upon-Avon (6 miles)."

Ten guineas was a large sum in those days – equivalent to a year's wages for an under-kitchen maid in a large household. Zelstone, Moonstone's sire, was also offered at stud, for 7 guineas; he was owned by a Thorpe Bartram of Essex.

Throughout its history the Flat-Coated Retriever has been fortunate in attracting dedicated followers, many of whom were also extremely wealthy. First and foremost of these was Mr Evelyn Shirley, a great sportsman who was founder of the Kennel Club in 1873 and became its first president at the age of 29. He recognised the need for a different type of gundog and, with a group of like-minded enthusiasts, decided to try and breed the "perfect" shooting dog, using as a base the excellent Wavy-coated Retrievers that had been bred by, and belonged to, his father.

THE "MAKING" OF THE FLAT-COATED RETRIEVER

The aim was to breed a dog similar to the Wavy-Coated Retriever but less heavily built, with greater agility, a more refined head and a coat that would be waterproof but not so heavy and dense. In addition, the dog needed to be a good game finder, that is possessing a good "nose" and soft mouth combined with a responsive biddable temperament to return dead and wounded birds to hand. Although Shirley bought some stock from another Retriever enthusiast, Bond Moore, Flat-Coat type was, in fact, moving away from the "boxy" outline favoured by Moore which became typified in the Labrador Retriever. Almost certainly setter blood was introduced to give the more elegant, flowing lines with, possibly, some sheepdog outcross, presumably for responsiveness. It has also been said that a Borzoi cross was made but I always find this hard to imagine, although the statement was made by an authority of the time, Major Harding Cox. The aim presumably

A Marquis of Carmarthen Retriever.

was to fine down the skull and head but according to Harding Cox the results were not pleasing, which is hardly surprising.

Whatever was introduced in the evolution of the breed, it can only have been after careful consideration because type became reasonably well-established in a relatively short time. Indeed what was achieved was a shooting dog with that "touch of class" ideally suited to accompany a gentleman to a fashionable shooting party. In fact, by the end of the 19th century, the Flat-Coated Retriever was the accepted shooting dog among wealthy and dedicated sportsmen.

By the end of the 19th century the breed had gained many more devotees who were seriously engaged in breeding good stock – people like Mr L. Allen-Shuter, Major Harding, Mr J. Hull, Messrs Cox and Shipton and Mr H. R. Cook of whom we shall hear more later.

A FEATURED BREED
The frontispiece of *Our Dogs* (price 1 penny) for June 26th 1897 shows the Flat-Coat bitch Longfield Ivy owned by Mr James Brown of Heaton Chapel. Inside is a glowing report on the bitch who was sired by Mr Shirley's Rightaway from Longfield Bess. The *Country Life* issue of May 10th 1902 has a long article on Mr Allen-Shuter's dogs, with several photographs including Horton Rector, a son of Darenth. No mention is made of another son of Darenth's, bred and owned by Mr Allen-Shuter, Horton Max, who was regularly shown and won Labrador classes!

The fact that these two quite diverse papers featured Flat-Coats at this time was proof indeed that the Breed had "arrived". The opening paragraph of the article on "Mr L. Allen-Shuter's Flat-Coated Retrievers" reads as follows: "The popularity of the Flat-Coated Retriever has increased so greatly during the last few years that the Breed has become one of the very strongest features of most of the great dog shows. As a field dog, moreover, the Flat-Coated variety is most popular among sportsman as he is an extremely tender-mouthed dog for the most part, is brimful of intelligence and possesses a most amiable

Darenth (Hopeful – Donna): Bred and owned by Mr L. Allen-Shuter.

disposition. In addition to these extremely high qualifications, this breed has an excellent constitution to recommend it, a result being that puppies are easy to rear, and develop into nice serviceable animals, so that they can retrieve a hare over a gate without any difficulty or mauling." And that was just the start!

'YOUNG' WILL SIMMS
Some seventy years after that article appeared I made a momentous visit to "young" Will Simms; he was ninety-two at this time. "Young Will" was the son of Old Will who had been keeper to Evelyn Shirley. Quite by chance I learned that "Young Will" lived within a few miles of me and, in view of his advanced age, a visit sooner rather than later seemed indicated. I was directed to Blue Wood and told to drive along a green lane until I reached a clearing which was where Will and his wife lived. I followed instructions but, on approaching the clearing, could see no sign of the expected cottage. What I did see was a double decker bus almost hidden in the trees; alongside was an open-sided shed covered in Russian vine under which was parked an elderly car. The bus

proved to be surprisingly snug and warm, as was the welcome I had from Will and Mrs Will. Will was a big man who completely filled his saggy armchair; and he was well equipped, as down one side was a packet of biscuits and down the other a bottle of whisky. He had so many tales to tell, one being how his father found Ilmington Ranter tied to a wagon in a farm yard in Ilmington and bought him from the farmer. He also said that his father had no time for Labradors and would say: "Flat-Coats are gentlemen's dogs, Labradors are for tinkers (gypsies)"! When I left, Will insisted on giving me two *Kennel Gazettes*, one dated August 1884, the other June 1886; I still cherish them, although the paper is so brown and fragile I hardly dare touch them.

THE TURN OF THE 19TH CENTURY

From the suppositions and theories on breed origins of all the retriever breeds certain facts emerge. By the approach to the 20th century the retriever family had divided into recognisable separate breeds. The Curly-coat, for so long a firm favourite with gamekeepers, had maintained a certain independence; in 1902 the Kennel Club gave recognition to the Labrador; to the Golden with its colour firmly established and its own delightful personality; and to the Flat-Coated Retriever as being *the* shooting dog for the fashionable shooting enthusiast. The consolidating of the original divisions into individual breeds was achieved solely by careful and selective breeding, the concept of which is as important today as it was over 100 years ago. Only by selective breeding can type, temperament and general characteristics be consolidated and the dog breed true.

ORIGINAL AIMS

A fact which tends to be overlooked even now, and perhaps more so during the past ten years or so, was the original aim in breeding a Flat-Coated Retriever. Those of you who have read this far will surely say: "It was because the need arose for a competent retrieving dog with stamina, particularly good scenting ability, a biddable character and the ability to find game on his own by using inherent skills in the shooting field." Right, with "shooting field" being the operative words. So why does this tend to be overlooked or forgotten as it is, particularly by those whose interests lie almost entirely within the competitive world of field trials? A good field trial dog is not automatically a competent worker in the shooting field, in the same way that a dog who is an asset in the shooting field may show little talent in the more regimented atmosphere of field trials. On the whole, Flat-Coats are best suited to, and can excel in, the shooting field, their true

Southwell Peter, circa 1910.

An early, heavier type Retriever.

environement. Having said which, I am immediately going to appear to contradict myself, because toward the turn of the century Flat-Coats featured greatly in field trials of the time and performed with merit. Frequently the classification would specify "for retrievers, smooth, wavy or curly coated". At the International Gundog League's Trials in 1904, of nineteen runners one was described as a Labrador, four as Flat-Coated, four as Wavy-coated, eight as "smooth" and one as "unknown". The sire of one of the "smooth" dogs was Black Quilt who was a Flat-Coat and the sire of one of the "Wavies", Wimpole Peter, was also a Flat-Coat, so the descriptions do not necessarily denote the ancestry.

FLAT-COAT TYPE
Flat-Coat type was emerging as far more flowing in outline, showing the elegance and "touch of class" that is so evident in the wonderful Maud Earl paintings. Quite certainly these characteristics came from the introduction of setter blood made for precisely this purpose. The setters were thought to be the black setters found in Wales. Mention is made of Gordon Setters, which of course is possible, but it hardly seems likely that they would have had the required fining-down influence.

Even today one can see the setter influence in the manner of scenting and pattern of work in the shooting field. Conversely one still comes across the Labrador influence which came a little later in the century. One can look round a show ring and find dogs which show definite Labrador tendencies. Match-box outline, blockier skull, shorter muzzle, shorter rib cage – the difficulty being that often these dogs are well put together, frequently move steadily, and appeal to "all round" judges, who often find Flat-Coat type difficult to assess.

THE RIVERSIDE KENNELS
In many respects one of the most significant happenings in the last decade of the century was the establishment of Mr H. Reginald Cooke's Riverside kennels at Nantwich in Cheshire: he was to dominate the breed for an incredibly long time. He lived to be 91 and when he died in 1951 he had been involved with Flat-Coats for practically seventy years. While recognising his contribution, it has to be said that for one person to have such mastery, indeed monopoly, over any breed cannot be entirely beneficial.

The Reginald Cooke "scrapbooks" is surely a misnomer because they amount to, I believe, thirteen remarkable bulky volumes – an incredible record kept by Cooke of his dogs and their pedigrees, with letters, press cuttings and photographs. For many years the Flat-Coated Retriever Society (UK) has held nine of these books. Extracts were printed in the Year Books for 1973, 1974 and 1977 and make fascinating reading. The actual amounts of money involved are quite surprising, particularly to those of us who have fondly extolled the virtues of the breed as being non-commercial!

A visit was made to Riverside, Mr Cooke's home near Nantwich, in 1903 by one who called himself 'Viator', presumably to indicate one who travels, but I have no idea whose nom-de-plume this was. It is worth reading 'Viator's' comments both on Riverside and the dogs, in full, as follows.

"The enormous strides taken in the last few years by the wavy Retriever have been due to the efforts of recent lovers of that useful and ornamental variety of sporting dog. Principal amongst these comes the name of Mr H. Reginald Cooke, who owns the leading kennel of this variety. It is true Mr Cooke has a unique opportunity for producing winners, for at Riverside he is the fortunate possessor of a snug little property, which comprises ample stabling accommodation for a hunting stud, and also room for twenty-five or thirty dogs, who are disposed of in a range of specially

Reginald Cooke (Riverside). Photo courtesy: Randle Cooke.

designed kennels, as complete in every detail as money can make them, and as many loose-boxes as may be needed. These, with a comfortable cottage for the head stableman and kennel manager, Slater, form an establishment second-to-none for the purposes for which it is intended. The moment one enters the spacious stableyard, one in imagination sees the word ORDER writ in large letters all over the place. Mr Cooke believes in doing things well and in Slater he has a dependable man who is as anxious as he is himself in this desirable direction; never was a place kept in a more scrupulous state of order and cleanliness, and no-one would imagine that seven horses and nearly thirty Retrievers were kept in such a little ground, and every animal in show form and fit and well. The kennels are very well built, with concrete yards and railings of good height, with an elevated roof over all. The sleeping accommodation is A1, with a passage at the rear, and no effort is wanting and no expense spared to keep everything 'decently and in order'."

I so like the phrase, "a snug little property", which must surely be the understatement of the year!

'Viator' then goes on to describe the dogs themselves.

"Seated in the comfortable saddle-room, Slater brought the dogs before us. At hand were the pedigree books and list of prizes, which greatly facilitated our work. First came that great veteran, Ch. Worsley Bess by Barton Zulu-Trinket, bred by Mr G. Cooke, and born March 1894. To look at this grand bitch, no-one would dream she is the age she is. A big one, with quality, describes her in a nutshell, a wonderfully intelligent head that has not gone coarse, great bone, clean shoulders, and undiminished muscular power are her great and leading features. She is fit to win anywhere now. She is the dam of Ch. Paul of Riverside, Baden Hero, Squib etc. Ch. Wimpole Peter followed; he is by Black Drake-Racket, and was bred by Mr F. Rem. This fine dog cost Mr Cooke £105 when a puppy; he is not only good-looking, but a capital worker; he moves freely and straight, has grand legs and feet, small ears which he invariably transmits to his off-spring, a good eye, nice skull, and has power, yet shows quality before the eyes, his head has kept well, and as a stud-dog has more than proved his grand excellence.

"The third champion to be led forward was Ch. Bring 'Em, by Black Drake-Squib, and bred by Mr G. Baddam. This is a beautiful type of bitch, particularly good in head, eye and retriever

Reginald Cooke's Ch. Kiss of Riverside, 1935.

character; her body properties are quite above the average, her ears are a thought big, and her skull may be smaller – the only faults in an otherwise beautiful Retriever.

"The fourth champion to be reviewed is Ch. Black Quilt by Ch. Morton Rector – Ch. Black Queen, bred by Mr Harding Cox. This is a grand-headed dog, with the right type of foreface and skull, powerful legs and feet, with good ribs, chest, and plenty of propelling power; he moves and gallops freely and well; he has a suspicion of twist in his coat, but is a real good all-round dog, who is doing well at stud. He cost £200 and is worth the money, as his all-round excellence makes him a dangerous opponent for the best of his variety.

"Champion number five is Paul of Riverside, by Ch. Wimpole Peter – Ch. Worsley Bees, a marvellous bred one, with a grand head and small ear, clean, good bone, and capital feel, head and eye, capital body in quality, full of prominent lines. This is a high class dog of the greatest merit; his coat is good and flat, shoulders and action before and behind absolutely perfect, a dog that wants beating and his record shows it.

"The last champion is Ch. Gipsy of Riverside, by Wimpole Peter – Maid of Llangollen. She is nineteen months old, and was bred by her owner. This is a really great bitch, with a long, level and beautifully chiselled head, wonderful quality all through, grand shoulders with deep ribs and any amount of power behind. Quality and quantity is exemplified here, and the right type from nose-end to tail-tip, no wonder she has gained the honours she has.

"So much for the champions "in esse", but there are many "in posse". Amongst these is Black Mab, home-bred, by Wimpole Peter – Mountain Dinah. She is a beautifully formed and fair-headed bitch, with nice bone, legs and feet, a very good worker.

"A very remarkable dog is Sandy of Riverside, a recent purchase, by Mountain Sam – Tyncefn Jet. This dog, when thoroughly wound up, will practically make the best dog in the kennel.

"A notable dog, and a rare worker, is the Field Trial winner, Broom Faskally, a dog who on one or two occasions has had very hard lines at trials. He is by Wimpole Peter – Dunlin. A rare-shouldered dog is this, with wonderful body and good, sound bone; he is made all-round like the worker he is, and has a big reputation amongst the keepers in the neighbourhood.

"Besides these there are a lot of brood bitches out on breeding terms and endless good puppies, some of which we saw. The kennel even now is not nearly at its best, and may be expected to hold its own for a long time to come."

Obviously to see and review such a marvellous lot of dogs was a real treat to "Viator".

ALDRIDGE'S SALES

In the same extracts from the journals there is an account of one of Aldridge's Bloodstock Sales, that of June 9th 1905, of dogs for the moors; the facts one learns are illuminating to say the least, and Reginald Cooke is again directly involved.

"The attraction, of course, was the dispersal of the High Legh Retrievers, the executors of the late Lieut Col. Cornwall Legh sending up the whole of the stock of the well-known kennel; and although there was absolutely no bid for the first lot (Pirate) while the second (High Legh Druid) realised but eight guineas, the competition was brisk enough when High Legh Blarney, a well-known winner in the ring, was benched. The son of Black Quilt – High Legh Moment was in beautiful form, and put in at fifty guineas, he was quickly run up to 200 guineas, at which figure he passed into the possession of Mr H. Reginald Cooke, who must now have a wonderfully strong kennel.

"Mr Cooke's head kennelman outstayed all opposition, the hammer falling amidst manifestations of approval at the plucky purchase. Some were heard to say it was a fancy price, no dog being worth it; but when one considers the value of a good stud Retriever such as this, the figure does not represent twelve months' stud fees, whilst Black Drake, cut off in his prime, brought in over 1000 gns at stud. In High Legh Blarney I think Mr Cooke possesses the best Retriever living today. High Legh Moment was bought in at 96 gns, Dorcas likewise at 55 gns. This is not the first occasion upon which Mr Cooke has paid 200 gns for a Flat-Coat, Black Quilt having cost him this sum, and must have earned considerably more."

The extract for July 14th 1905 is also of interest: "There was an all-round improvement in the prices at Aldridge's sale last Friday, but once more there was a better demand for Retrievers than for Pointers or Setters, the record price of the season, 205 gns, being reached for one of the former, a useful-looking, Flat-Coated bitch by Faskally Broom. She is in her second season, and was described as a very high-class no-slip Retriever, exceptionally good in the water and absolutely steady on all game. She had won prizes at the Gamekeepers Show."

CHANGING CONCEPTS

Even when re-reading these accounts I find it quite amazing how concepts have changed. I can't think of anyone I know who would be prepared to send a dog to a sale with no knowledge of who the new owner would be. But to some extent, and to some people, dogs were regarded as another branch of livestock, as is obvious when, as we have seen in the previous report, it was publicly printed that Ch. Darenth earned around £1,500 in stud fees, which was quoted to justify Reginald Cooke paying 200 gns for High Legh Barney. In other words, it was regarded as usual to send dogs to a collective sale in the same way as a horse. Of course this is still common practice with working sheep dogs. With this emphasis on Reginald Cooke we have to remember that there were still other equally dedicated Flat-Coat breeders but, perhaps, without quite the resources available to him. We have just read of the dispersal sale of the noted High Legh retrievers on the death of Lieut Colonel Cornwall Legh. On July 8th 1904 there was a dispersal sale at Ettington Park of the entire kennel following the death of Evelyn Shirley. There was great interest but prices were strangely low, with a total of 300 gns for over 30 retrievers. Such a brief, stark statement with which to mark the end of an era.

FLAT-COATS AT CRUFTS

In 1905, Flat-Coated Retrievers had separate classification at Crufts for the first time. There was an entry of eighteen for the judge, Mr F. Gresham, to go over. Best Bitch and BoB went to Cooke's Judy of Riverside, Best Dog to Allen-Shuter's Royal River. It has to be said that at this time, and for a considerable time to come, the Kennel Club allowed a very real laxity on qualification for entry in a certain breed: it was still left largely to the exhibitor to choose which breed the dog most resembled!

THE WINDS OF CHANGE

We saw earlier that Flat-Coats did well in Field Trials at the turn of the 19th century at a time when trials were limited and not enormously popular. But gradually a change was coming about, with a greater and more widespread interest in competitive field trials. Labrador breeders and, considerably later, Golden breeders, recognised the fact that for competitive field work different skills were needed, so some breeders started to breed with field trials in view. Flat-Coat breeders did not follow this trend and in this sphere were left behind. I'm talking of around 1910 onwards. The consequence to Labradors and, in time, to Goldens, was the eventual splitting of these breeds into two types, "show" and "work", both types gaining and losing in the process. The "workers" tended to lose "type", whilst the "show" lost a certain amount of inherent ability (*all* in some instances) and, sadly, there were cases of suspect temperament, even though the dogs were aesthetically pleasing. In essence, therefore, Flat-Coated retrievers were the only remaining dual purpose retrievers. I am not including Chesapeakes, because at the time under discussion they had not come into this country in any significant number.

There were consequences to Flat-Coats as well. They did not reach the heights in the show ring nor did they excel in Field Trials, owners not having turned to professional trainers and handlers, preferring on the whole to train and compete themselves. In fact they enjoyed their dogs and, with a few exceptions, remained typical Flat-Coat enthusiasts, content to be amateurs!

THE DUAL PURPOSE RETRIEVER

With the mention of the "dual purpose" concept, perhaps this is as good a time as any to discuss this "hot potato" remaining to this day.

What then is meant by "dual purpose"? Certainly in cattle the concept went out of favour and became unfashionable and was thought uneconomic. The dual-purpose cow was one such as the Dairy Shorthorn or the Red Poll: either breed would give a reasonable yield of milk but also had acceptable meat value. The reason I mention this apparently irrelevant bit of information is the word "reasonable", i.e. reasonably efficient for either milk or meat production but less efficient than the animal bred solely for high milk yields or for quick weight gain.

Dual purpose, in relation to a retrieving or working breed, means a dog bred both for conformation and working ability: that is, recognisable as belonging to the breed it represents but retaining the ability to do a particular job of work adequately. If just one aspect is concentrated upon, this will be strengthened but, quite possibly, at the expense of other attributes. In other words, if breeding is solely for working ability, as has already been mentioned, other qualities are lost; equally, if breeding is carried out with the sole aim of winning in the show ring, it does not take too long to end up with a ring full of brainless beauties. I personally find either of those options unacceptable and, while recognising the drawbacks, wholeheartedly support the continuation of maintaining the dual purpose abilities in the breed.

Breeding has to be done with great care and be highly selective. Rushing to the latest top winning dog or, overseas, using the latest foreign import is not the answer. Those of us who try to maintain dual purpose characteristics are, in effect, breeding in the hope of producing a dog with the inherent ability to do a competent day's work in the shooting field (with equally competent training, of course), and also fit to be shown, if so desired, with credibility as a representative of the breed. Sounds quite easy, doesn't it? After all, the breed standard, as we shall see later, stresses "no exaggerations". In other words the conformation of the dog fits the job for which it was intended.

The difficulties arise with the attributes I think of as "imponderables". It is these which need knowledge and skilful breeding to maintain and, at times, improve upon. They are, in fact, the qualities which need to be inherent: the dog must be born with them, they cannot be taught – for example, a good "nose"; that is the ability to scent out game. The dog also needs to have enthusiasm to hunt up but at the same time be responsive to the handler. A soft mouth to return game undamaged is of importance, but there are times when a "hard" mouth is developed through circumstances. These abilities are all essentials in a dual purpose dog and if we lose these inherent characteristics, we lose the Flat-Coated Retriever as we know it. Remember I am talking about Flat-Coats in the shooting field and not in competitive field trials – a different ball game and one to talk about later, along with "single purpose" breeding.

DECLINING FORTUNES

This is not a "history" of the breed, but it seems important to have some knowledge of what has gone before to help understand the character of the Flat-Coated Retriever. It all adds up to make a retriever that is totally individual and unlike any of the other retriever breeds. You either have the temperament for them and are dedicated for life, or they send you mad.

We have seen that from reaching the heights of fashion and popularity, by the first World War the breed was slipping; it is so true that the higher you climb the steeper seems the slippery slope down. Obviously, as with all breeds, the 1914 to 1918 war was a time of standstill. It is perhaps surprising that one hundred were registered in 1919. With serving men returning home, registrations soared in the 1920s, reaching a peak of 440 in 1924.

The names found on pedigrees of this time include "Leecroft" (Ellis Ashton), "Peddars" (F. T. Allen), "Bryn Asaph" (R. E. Birch) and "Towerwood" (W. Skerry) to name just a few. It hardly needs saying that the Riverside dogs continued to be prominent. Another name that was to have enormous influence in the future was that of the Atherbram dogs, bred by Will Phizaklea, who founded his kennel in North Warwickshire in the early 1920s.

THE GAMEKEEPERS' CHOICE

At this time although there fewer wealthy patrons of the breed, many gamekeepers had remained true, recognising the breed's worth as a reliable game-finding dog well-suited to their needs. It has to be said that at this time after World War I there had been further inter-breeding between Labradors and Flat-Coats – strangely enough (although I would say, understandably) with the aim of improving the Labrador rather than the Flat-Coat. Incidentally, even in 1924, when we saw that four hundred and forty Flat-Coats were registered, nearly one thousand three hundred Labradors were registered over the same period, a trend that has continued.

Miss Phizaklea with four Atherbram Flat-Coats (1930s).

A group of Mrs Hemm's Adlington Flat-Coats (plus a Collie) 1943: Rastus of Adlington, Oliver of Adlington, Chloe of Adlington, Chita of Adlington, Dawn of Adlington, Muffin of Adlington, Jane (the Collie), Miss Jombo of Adlington and Ch. Kala Rat of Adlington.

THE END OF AN ERA

Despite there being dedicated Flat-Coat owners, the number of registrations continued to fall by about forty each year, so that, by the end of the 1930s, registrations were down to about 80. One can only suppose that breeding was in the hands of relatively few breeders which would result in a concentration of those particular bloodlines and indeed individual dogs – very apparent when one examines pedigrees of that decade. Names on pedigrees still include Leecroft and Towerwood, W. Simms (Tosca), E.W. Bryant (Ponsbourne), Will Phizaklea (Atherbram) and Southam, who did not have an affix but where all names started with "Sp", and Colin Wells, a then emerging Flat-Coat owner, whose names all started with "W". There are also Mrs Hemm of the Adlington affix, Mrs Barwise (Forestholm) who later concentrated on Livers. A highly significant kennel was that of Stanley O'Neill and his wife: the Pewcroft dogs have had enormous influence on the breed which extends to the present time – true dual purpose Flat-Coats.

The continuing domination of the breed by Reginald Cooke quite assuredly had an inhibiting effect on other Flat-Coat owners whose resources were less ample than Cooke's. Admittedly he would pay high prices for promising puppies, very tempting to keepers in particular in view of the low wages at that time. He also appears to have "gathered" any adult animals that seemed likely to have good prospects. The thought comes to mind that he was, in fact, a "collector" of Flat-Coated Retrievers as the stock bought was varied and not confined to certain bloodlines.

In 1951 Reginald Cooke died at the age of 91. Incredibly, right up to this time, the Riverside dogs had continued to hold their own in the show ring and at field trials; Joy of Riverside winning the All Age stake in 1949, 1950 and 2nd in 1951, the year of H.R. Cooke's death. It is strange that there is no further mention of the Riverside dogs that I can see.

I have three splendid little books by Reginald Cooke. The first is *Short notes on choosing and breaking a Retriever*. Note the term then used, as for horses, "breaking" as opposed to training. Then there is *A few more short notes on Retrievers* and finally a tiny three-page booklet *Short suggestions for judging at Retriever Trials* – a gem, it should be compulsory reading for all who field trial. Reginald Cooke certainly holds a unique place in the history of the Breed.

With the outbreak of the Second World War in 1939, many keepers followed their masters into the services. Once again there was minimal breeding and an overall reduction in numbers which was to have repercussions later.

Chapter Two

REVIVAL OF THE FLAT-COAT

Throughout its history, as we have seen, the Flat-Coated Retriever has always attracted dedicated enthusiasts who remained constant even during the breed's less fortunate times. Two major world wars left the breed with a nigh-on catastrophic reduction in numbers so there was a great need for people prepared to give time, money and expertise to its revival.

The late 1940s proved to be the birth of a new and exciting era with the return home of military serving members such as Stanley O'Neill, Harry Wilson and Colin Wells of the "W", later "Woodland", prefix along with other gamekeepers. Resumption of more peaceful pursuits saw the re-establishment of these kennels, very largely by stock from Will Phizaklea's "Atherbram" kennels, so influential over such a long period.

THE ATHERBRAM KENNELS
The Atherbram prefix, founded in the early 1920s is perhaps unique in that it has been held by a member of the Phizaklea family for several generations. The original holder was Will Phizaklea who farmed in North Warwickshire. The name Atherbram was a combination of "Ather" from the town of Atherstone and "bram" from Bramcote, where Will and his wife Winnie lived for some time.

Mention has already been made of the important role played by Atherbram stock when the need arose to re-establish pre-war kennels. Very many present-day pedigrees will be found to carry Atherbram bloodlines. In consequence the Kennel was highly influential both here and, later, in the USA when foundation stock was sent there.

In 1948, when the Flat-Coated Retriever Association and the Flat-Coated Retriever Club amalgamated, Will had the honour of being the founder President. Both Will and Winnie took an active interest in all the aspects of the breed. Winnie's interest continued after Will's death and in 1957, when vice-president of the Flat-Coated Retriever Society, she presented the Atherbram Cup to the Manchester Championship show. As Will and Winnie had no living issue, after Will's death the affix passed to a niece, Peggy Payne who, at that time, had her own affix "Sharpethorne", which she then relinquished in favour of the noted "Atherbram". She also had some of the dogs and, in 1953, won four firsts at Crufts with Atherbram Windy. Peggy later transferred the affix to her daughter Annabel, but for various reasons Annabel was only able to continue with the dogs for a few years and, in 1982, passed on the Atherbram name to her cousin Hilary Hughes, the present holder.

Hilary says that her mother Monica, who was Peggy's sister and is now 86, remembers clearly, as a child, going to the family home, Clifton Hall near Tamworth in Staffordshire. On shooting days the Phizaklea brothers would all come in to tea in front of a roaring open fire with wet, muddy dogs, mainly Flat-Coats and spaniels. Hilary herself remembers visiting her aunt and uncle at Hill Farm, Shuttington. There were several duck lakes; all the Atherbram dogs were excellent in water and Will was constantly asked to have dogs in to train on his ducks. Hilary remembers watching Will with his dogs and says he was a very quiet trainer, with a wonderful understanding of dogs' minds. Interestingly, she remembers only one dog living in the house: this was Ch. Atherbram Jet, and she was even allowed to have her puppies in the house!

After Winnie died, the Coal Board demolished Hill Farm so it now exists only in memory.

CLAVERDON AND PEWCROFT

Of enormous importance in 1944 was the founding of Dr Nancy Laughton's "Claverdon" kennel with the purchase of Ch. Claverdon Jet and, later, Revival of Ettington. The influence of Dr Laughton's expertise in the breed has been and, indeed, is far reaching. A mere five years after founding the kennel, Dr Laughton was second in the Flat-Coated Retriever Society All Age Field Trial with Ch. Claverdon Jet. First and third places went to H. R. Cooke's Joy of Riverside and Nobby of Riverside. Looking at the Field Trial awards, Dr Laughton's name is among the most consistent, along with Colin Wells and Harry Wilson.

During this post-war period, Stanley O'Neill and Kathleen O'Neill were able to re-apply themselves to the Breed. Stanley had considerable breeding skills, what he would have termed "nous", a north-country term for "knowing how". He worked unceasingly to keep bloodlines going to implement the sadly depleted gene pool and admitted that, at times, dogs were used that would not have been considered had there been greater choice. Their Pewcroft dogs were truly dual

Dr Nancy Laughton's Ch. Claverdon Jorracks of Lilling.

Stanley and Kathleen O'Neill with some of their Pewcroft Flat-Coats.

purpose and some years after Stan's death, the late Harry Wilson, that stalwart of Field trials, presented the Pewcroft Trophy to the Society to be awarded annually to the best Flat-Coat achieving in both Field Trials and the show ring.

Stan was of Irish/Yorkshire parentage and it showed. He suffered fools badly (as did Harry Wilson) but his knowledge of the breed was vitually unsurpassed. A prolific letter-writer, he was informative, amusing, at times scurrilous but always knowledgeable. The contribution made by him and Kath to the breed was enormous. The bloodlines proved to be prepotent so that, even today, the type can be clearly recognised.

Understandably, registrations increased in the late 1940s but followed a fairly erratic pattern throughout the 50s and 60s with a sudden peak in 1961 to over 200 from about 118 the previous year.

INFLUENTIAL KENNELS OF THE 1950s

During the 1950s several kennels that were to have long-lasting influence were founded. Barbara Hall had owned Flat-Coats for over twenty years but was yet another whose progress had been restricted by the war. In 1953 she decided to make a fresh start and did so with the purchase of Pewcroft Prim (Denmere Prince/Ch. Pewcroft Pitch) who formed the base of the **Blakeholme** Flat-Coated Retrievers. Read Flowers had a litter sister, Pewcroft Proper, on whom he founded his **Fenrivers** Kennel. Both Read and Barbara used Ch. Waterboy on their bitches. One of the bitches, Asperula from Proper, went to the Hon. Amelia Jessel and was the foundation of the **Collyers** Kennel. It is quite interesting that a son of Denmere Prince, Denmere Bruce, also was mated to Pewcroft Pitch. One bitch puppy went to Walter Hutton (**Yarlaw**) and became Ch. Pewcroft Prop of Yarlaw who so nearly became a Dual champion; another, Pewcroft Putt, was retained by O'Neill. The particular interest is that O'Neill mentioned Denmere Prince as one of the dogs he only used through force of circumstances, yet in fact the progeny proved to be of value and had very worthwhile influence on the breed.

Other noteworthy kennels of this time, and for some time to come, included Georgina Fletcher and "Tinker" Davis's **Rungles** kennels founded on the bitch Happy Wanderer, dam of the very beautiful Sh. Ch. Rungles Lady Barbara.

Margaret and Dennis Izzard's **Ryshot** kennels were based largely on the **Forestholm** dogs of Phyllis Barwise, whose strong Liver influence remained for many years. Several of the early Swedish imports, particularly livers, came from the Ryshot Kennels. Then, following Margaret's

A Field Trial in 1949 (left to right): Joan Wells Meacham with Flash of Ibadon, Phyllis Barwise with Shot of Forestholm, Winnie Phizaklea with Ch. Claverdon Jet and Gwen Knight with Claverdon Celeste.

ABOVE: Read Flowers' Ch. Fenrivers Golden Road.
Photo: Ann Edman.

LEFT: Ch. Ryshot Velvet, owned by Margaret Izzard.
This bitch enjoyed great success in the 1960s and
early 1970s.

death, the good bitch Ch. Ryshot Copper Ring of Fire went to Jeanette Lindquist (now Mornen), who knew the bitch from her stays with Dennis and Margaret. It had given Margaret great joy during her final illness when June Squire handled "Fire" to gain her needed third CC.

One of the best remembered Ryshot bitches must be the black Ch. Ryshot Velvet who had great success in the 1960s gaining 21 CCs, 10 RCCs and 17 BoB. Dennis and Margaret's son Brian now has his own "Bryshot" Flat-Coats.

World-wide, one of the most significant breeders must have been Patience Locke who founded her **Halstock** Kennel in the late 1950s, although there is a marvellous photograph of Patience as a small girl, dressed in a white coat and fur-trimmed muff and bonnet standing on the steps of her father's house with his Flat-Coats at her side.

Patience started the Halstock line with a combination of Pewcroft, Claverdon and "W" (Woodland) bloodlines, which she then combined with some Rungles blood. Patience and John perhaps bred a little more than was usual at this time but the breeding was done with care and skill. Stock from this kennel was exported to Scandinavia and one has to acknowledge that Patience never exported a dog unless she felt it would benefit the breed in the country of import. A typical example was when, in the 1960s, Halstock Javelin was exported to Ed Atkins in the United States of America and proved to be both a splendid ambassador and an asset to the breed.

Peggy Robertson had already achieved success with her Golden Retrievers when she included Flat-Coats in her programme. Primarily a show kennel, several useful litters were bred, the main importance being the export of two **Stolford** Flat-Coats to Margaret Evans in New Zealand in 1972 with obvious influence on the breed there. Margaret Evans had emigrated to NZ with her Vanrose Goldens.

One remembers especially Rosalie Brady who "finished" Mrs Mopp for Peggy and later

*Colin Wells with Ch. Wave FTW,
Norfolk, 1960.*

Rosalie's wonderful record with Ch. Bordercot Stolford Doonigan who, although registered in husband Gerald's name, was steered to such great heights by Rosalie. In all, Doonigan gained 22 CCs, 16 RCCs and 13 BoB during the 1970s. As we have seen, Colin Wells, originally **"W"**and later **Woodland,** had re-established himself in the breed on returning to his peacetime occupation of gamekeeper. A very strong male line was established, which was maintained right through Colin's long and active involvement with the breed. I have to mention that even writing 'Colin' I have a twinge of hesitation. At that time Colin was always "Mr Wells" or, presumably, to his employer, His Grace the Duke of Rutland, "Wells". Certainly one did not presume upon his christian name. It was years before I felt free to call him "Colin".

The incredibly prepotent male line stemmed from Ch. Waterman, followed by Ch. Waterboy, Ch. Workman, Ch. Woodlark and so on. With three dogs and Claverdon Tawny Pippit, Colin had BoB for ten years in succession at Crufts. These were first and foremost working dogs, but with the type and conformation to reach the heights in the show ring.

Having singled out males, one then immediately remembers the splendid bitch Ch. Woodpoppy, whose daughters included the late Paddy Petch's foundation bitch, Woodwren, and Brenda Phillip's (**Exclyst**) Woodlass, not actually Brenda's first Flat-Coat but the one from which most of the Exclysts stem. During these years of the late 1950s into the 1960s, Colin Wells was also having very creditable runs in field trials, Ch. Waterboy in particular performing prestigiously. It does bring home quite forcibly the fact that skilful breeding is not so much a matter of depth of "pocket" i.e. money as of skill and that gut feeling on what will work and what won't. This unfortunately is something one either has or has not – the human "imponderables".

After Colin retired as head keeper at Belvoir Castle (a typical English quirk of pronunciation, Belvoir is pronounced "Beaver"), his son Ron became head keeper in his stead; a very responsible and demanding position on such a vast estate with very high-class shooting. I visited Colin some little time before he died in 1994. The visit was magic. So much knowledge, he could talk of people who are only names to most of us. I came away feeling I knew nothing. We lose so much when such a person dies. I believe Ingemar Borelius did once try to take recordings, but really one would need short and frequent visits which, as a person gets older, may be too wearisome and the recorder inhibits the natural flow of reminiscences.

THE SIXTIES
Many of the kennels that became involved with Flat-Coated Retrievers in the 1960s and early 70s are still active today, so more information is given when discussing present-day kennels in a later chapter.

Joan Mason's Ch. Heronsflight Black Bell of Yarlaw: A truly dual purpose bitch whose worth can be assessed by present-day descendants.

Alphabetically:-

Courtbeck	Helen Beckwith
Downstream	Peter and Shirley Johnson
Exclyst	Brenda Phillips
Glidesdown	Bill and Wyn Garrod
Hallbent	Georgie Buchanon (now Pamela Stanley)
Heronsflight	My own (joined several years ago by my daughter Rosemary)
Rase	The late Paddy Petch
Torwood	Neil and Denise Jury. (now Denise Jury)
Wizardwood	Peter and Audrey Forster

These are some of the main names; unfortunately one cannot include all.

THE SITUATION IN THE US

In the November 1994 Flat-Coated Retriever Society of America Newsletter, there is a members' list of some 900 to 1,000 names – a fact that, at Crufts 1995, Joan Dever verified. This is forty-one years on and a far cry from 1953, when Flat-Coated Retrievers were re-introduced, or virtually introduced, into the United States of America. At that time the breed was at a low ebb in the UK with around 80 Flat-Coats registered that year.

Stanley O'Neill had partaken of a lengthy correspondence with the late Homer Downing resulting in Pewcroft Prefect (Doc) being sent over. Stan being a prolific correspondent, no doubt the letters continued; amusing, at times acerbic, but always knowledgeable. Two years later Will Phizaklea sent over the Liver bitch Atherbram Stella.

Further imports followed, largely from Dr Laughton's Claverdon Kennel, Rab of Morinda to Ed and Dorothy Moroff, Claverdon Gamble to Biz Reed, C. Duchess to a youthful Sally Jean Terroux who some years later, in 1966, obtained Witham, bred by Colin Wells and originally sent to Dani Lende. Following the success of Rab, the Moroffs also brought in Jet of Lilling, a bitch found for them quite fortuitously by Nancy Laughton. In 1957 there were 22 Flat-Coats but this included two litters.

History was made, again by the efforts of Homer Downing, on May 15th 1958 at Berea in Ohio, when the breed was given separate classification at the Western Reserve dog show. There was tremendous excitement over this event. Honours went to the Downings' Pewcroft Prefect and the Ratcliffs' Claverdon Belladonna.

The breed developed with further carefully considered imports. The young Ed Atkins brought in Halstock Javelin from Patience Lock in 1962. Over the years other imports included Claverdon Gossamer, Ch. Fenrivers Kalmia and later, Westering Warcry from Jane Smith, Yonday Swagman, Blakeholme Heronsflight Try and of course Ed Atkins' "share" of the jointly-owned litters bred by Brenda Phillips under the "Wyndhamian" affix from the Colin Wells bred bitch, Woodlass. The litters proved significant in their contribution to the American breeding programme. Interestingly,

LEFT: Dr Laughton, pictured in 1958, preparing to ship Claverdon Duchess to Sally Terroux in the USA.

ABOVE: Ch. Bamcroft Dandy UD: The first Champion Flat-Coated Retriever in the USA, and an outstanding Obedience dog. Bred by Homer Downing, owned by Sally Terroux.

whereas the "C" litter had the most far-reaching influence in the UK, possibly the "D" litter was most influential in the USA. The "C" litter was sired by Heronsflight Tercel and included Christopher, who remained with Brenda and proved to be a prepotent sire, Constructor who went to Valerie Bernhardt, and Cormorant who went to Margot Hallett and certainly made some contribution to the breed's credibility in Field events.

The "D" litter sired by Forestholm Donard greatly extended the bloodlines in the States with the bringing in of Wyndhamian Dash: a dog of considerable talent and a good producer, sadly he had an untimely death at only three years of age.

The most enormous debt of gratitude is due to these early supporters of the breed for the time, money and effort they put into building a solid foundation. While I have been looking at the pedigrees of the dogs mentioned (and making great efforts not to be side-tracked!), I have been so impressed by the sound, compatible bloodlines that were introduced. Ed Atkins deserves particular credit for this.

Quite assuredly, Vernon Vogel, until very recently historian to the Flat-Coated Retriever Society of America, has kept excellent records of imports and the breed in general. His on-the-spot knowledge must be far greater than mine, so I shall only mention a few other dogs. 1979 saw the import of Torwood Peerless (later Ch.) to Valerie Bernhardt – the dog who brought tears to my eyes in Denver in 1992, such a courageous old boy – and his litter sister Helen Szostak's Ch. Torwood Poppy, so like her "aunt", known in my family as "MBP" – Mum's Beloved Pansy.

Coming nearer the present day, Peter and Mollie Heide brought in some very successful dogs from Pat Chapman's Shargleam Kennel. More recently, Lena Haggelund's "O'Flanagan" Kennel and Ragnhild Ulin's Almaza Kennel, both from Sweden, are now represented in the USA, as is Leonie Galderman's (Holland) Swallowsflight Kennel.

THE FLAT-COATED RETRIEVER SOCIETY OF AMERICA

June Fuget is the newly installed President of the Society: as such she has most kindly written some comments on the Breed and the Society.

"The Flat-Coated Retriever in America remains modestly popular and relatively rare although registration statistics provided by the American Kennel Club (AKC) show an increase in dogs registered of approximately 60 per cent over the past 10 years. In 1993 there were 96 litters and 485 dogs registered. A steady growth of interest in the breed is anticipated and the Flat-Coated Retriever Society of America (FCRSA) is working diligently to protect the Flat-Coat from the problems of other breeds that become popular and are bred without regard for health, type and working ability. There are almost 1,000 members in the Society today and their emphasis is on maintaining the special qualities of the Flat-Coated Retriever in spite of the pressures of popularity and over-breeding.

"The Flat-Coat, more than any other retriever breed, has maintained the tradition of being a dual purpose dog that is both shown and hunted. A high percentage of our show dogs have AKC hunting titles and most of the dogs entered in the hunting tests are also shown in breed. Flat-Coats excel in the hunting test programme developed by the AKC but only a few are competitive in field trials which are dominated by the Labrador Retriever. There is also a high percentage of Flat-Coat owners who show their dogs in obedience and are very competitive.

"The Flat-Coat in America is still relatively healthy as compared to other breeds although deaths due to cancer is a growing concern. The FCRSA is sponsoring research at Ohio State University to determine if the Flat-Coat is affected by a specific type of cancer and if there is something that can be done to reduce the incidence of cancer, especially in our young dogs."

Valerie Bernhardt (Meadowrue) is health monitor to the FCRSA and holds a "watching brief" over hereditary defects or possible problems that might arise. It is felt that awareness is the best method of meeting problems; in this way the Breed's very good health record can, hopefully, be maintained.

Valerie has written a little on the progress of the breed from her own beginnings in 1971, as a Flat-Coat owner and breeder, not as health monitor.

"I joined the Flat-Coated Retriever Society in 1971 when there were only about 45 members in the whole U.S. What a close knit group we were at that time. We knew one another and every dog we each owned, and subsequently were well aware of everything going on within the Breed. In order to get competition in the show ring and to get points toward an American Championship we would travel great distances.

"Slowly through the 70s the Breed began to get noticed both as a working dog and show dog. With an annual meeting held in March in the Chicago Midwest Area, came supported entries, a class, a match and the goal to have a yearly Specialty.

"In 1978 this reality came true with the first independent Flat-Coated Retriever Society of America Specialty held on March 31st. The judge was Read Flowers and the entries were 96 in conformation and 32 in obedience. Since that time an independent Specialty has been held every year rotating from the middle of the US to the East Coast, back to the Mid West and then West.

"A Field event consisting of a singles championship and Working Certificate, Working Certificate Excellent tests was added to the Specialty events. In the late 80s came AKC Hunting Tests, a non-competitive event; so another day was added to the Field Events. In 1994, the American Specialty had an outstanding entry of 424 in Breed and 146 in Obedience.

"In the future the Society looks forward to adding agility events as well. Society-sponsored tracking tests are held every year sometimes in conjunction with the Specialty. The Society is dedicated to maintaining the working aspects of the Breed and recognises the need for Flat-Coats to use their brains! In 1992 after years of unsuccessful attempts the Society was accepted as a Member Club of the American Kennel Club. The AKC is a club of clubs and no individual memberships are accepted. I was given the honour of representing the Society as the delegate to the AKC, joining about 400 representatives of member clubs from across the US. This enables the Society to have a voice in voting on policies, and rule changes and in maintaining awareness on current dog legislation".

Mention was made earlier of the fantastic annual National Specialty organised by the FCRSA – championship show, educational workshops, Field events and the chance to meet up with other Flat-Coat fanatics. Talk, talk, talk, for nearly a whole week. I remember Don Freeman saying: "If a Specialty doesn't take a week to recover from, it wasn't a good specialty!" I think he actually said "a month" but that seems to be pushing it a bit.

FIELD TRIALS IN THE UK

Throughout the sixties field trials still attracted a band of stalwart supporters with the same names appearing in awards, albeit not always in the same order. Air Commodore Walter Hutton, The Hon. Amelia Jessel, Dr Nancy Laughton, Wilson Stephens, Colin Wells and Major Harry Wilson, who skilfully made up two field trial champions, Hartshorn Sorrel and Nesfield Michael. Harry Wilson had something in common with Colin Wells although not in the same context. Harry would take on almost any dog and by skilful training would achieve results, unless there was a total personality clash. Harry was tough with his dogs but they adored him – very different from the folks who blame their dogs for any lack of achievement, never themselves!

While the Society had always honoured its commitment to promote and support field trials and to some extent working tests, show activities were perforce restricted to classes at all-breed shows. The Society in fact showed a marked reluctance to promoting a show. Finally, an Open Show was arranged and took place on April 12th 1969. Joan Wells Meacham judged the 49 dogs who made an amazing total of 217 actual entries. BoB was Margaret Izzard's Ch. Ryshot Velvet.

The Hon. Amelia Jessel's Flat-Coats (pictured left to right): Collyers Peace, Ch. Collyers Blakeholme Brewster, Collyers Banda, and Amelia's foundation bitch, Ch. Asperula.

Pat Chapman with the legendary Eng. Ir. Ch. Shargleam Blackcap: Breed and Gundog recordholder.
Photo: Frank Garwood, courtesy of Dog World.

Brian Farr's Teal of Hawk's Nest: One of the outstanding Flat-coat sires of all time, even though he was only used five times.

THE SEVENTIES

The seventies proved to be a follow-on of the sixties in many respects, with existing kennels developing individual lines and consolidating their positions. Registrations continued to rise steadily to around 400. I remember Amelia Jessel, who was society secretary, mentioning an odd fact, which was that annual registrations seemed to be on a par with membership numbers. This in fact, remained true. I can only think that, however the membership increased, only a certain percentage undertook breeding; there seems no other explanation.

Quite the most memorable event of the late seventies was the making up of Werrion Redwing of Collyers into a Field Trial Champion – a very exciting happening not only for Amelia Jessel but for the breed as a whole. "Noonie" was sired by the Forster's Ch. Wizardwood Sandpiper from Collyers Juno. Another happening that was to have far-reaching influence on the breed was when a young lady called Pat Chapman, who worked in Jersey and had Golden Retrievers, came to the mainland to buy a bitch puppy from George and Joan Snape. George had mated his bitch Claverdon Flapper to Colin Wells' Kenstaff Whipster. To understand the full significance we need to go back a few years to 1967 when Nancy Laughton mated Claverdon Rhapsody to Captain Brian Farr's Teal of Hawk's Nest, possibly the most shot-over Flat-Coat of the time.

The ensuing litter, the Claverdon "F" Litter, proved to be highly significant including, as it did, Ch. Claverdon Fantasia, Jane Smith's Ch. Claverdon Fidelity, Fulmer, Flyer and Flapper. No-one would have imagined that Flapper would be a part of almost changing the history of the breed. Originally sold to a companion/working home, through a change in circumstances she had to be found a new home which proved to be with George and Joan Snape. In due course George mated Flapper with Whipster and it was from this litter that Pat Chapman chose her puppy, Yonday Willow Warbler of Shargleam. She had bought the foundation for her **Shargleam** Flat-Coated Retrievers. The rest you may say is history. More later on this influential kennel.

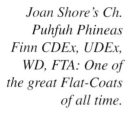

Joan Shore's Ch. Puhfuh Phineas Finn CDEx, UDEx, WD, FTA: One of the great Flat-Coats of all time.

Later in the decade, Jean and Peter Griffiths founded their **Riversflight** kennel with the purchase of a very promising bitch puppy from Denise Jury – Torwood Poppet (later Champion). Around the same time Ann and Richard Adams founded their **Withybed** kennel when they bought Shargleam Black Abby (later Champion) from Pat Chapman.

Black Abby was one of the litter born on June 26th 1977 from the mating between Yonday Willow Warbler of Shargleam and June Squire's Ch. Damases Tarquol of Ryshot. The litter of course included one of the most famous Flat-Coated Retrievers in the history of the breed – Eng. Ir Ch. Shargleam Blackcap, whose influence was to be so far reaching.

Society Open shows had become an annual event following on from the first one in 1969, moving to a different part of the country each year. They had proved so popular that on April 23rd 1977, the first Championship show was held with 146 dogs for judge Read Flowers to go over. The BCC and BoB went to Joan Maddox's Barnway Springles, with DCC to Paddy Petch's Ch. Rase Romulus. Ten years later, in 1987, Audrey Forster (Wizardwood) had an entry of 226 dogs: her DCC winner was Ch. Heronsflight Pan's Promise, with the BCC going to Jenny Bird's Wizardwood Black Magic of Shiredale. Despite the new names coming into the breed, registrations did not soar dramatically. In 1977 for example, the year Blackcap was born, there were 124 puppies registered. Ten years later there was a veritable explosion.

THE EIGHTIES

Wilson Stephens maintained, with some credibility, that no breed can survive a Best in Show at Crufts, and in 1980 at only two and a half years of age, Ch. Shargleam Blackcap went BoB under Mary Grimes, won the Gundog Group and then went Best in Show. However great one's reservations as to likely repercussions, it was tremendously exciting and at the time we were all willing him to win. Such a showman. It would be impossible to list all the new names that came into the breed. As time went on, many were "Shargleam satellites". Certainly for this decade, the show ring was dominated by Shargleam dogs, but to keep this in perspective one must remember that these dogs were shown at all the major shows. Most exhibitors show only at some of the shows and so their dogs are seen less often.

Field trials continued with varying degrees of success. Joan Marsden's Tarncourt dogs in particular did well in the early 1980s. Tarncourt Byron won the 1979/80 Society Open FT. Colin Wells' Woodland Whipcord won the non-winners stake. The following year Eric Baldwin's Collyers Rose

Mallow at Palgrave won the Open whilst Tarncourt Byron won the All Aged stake. Later in the 1980s Clive Harris had considerable success with Ch. Torwood Blue who, it was hoped, might manage to also become FT champion (Dual champion in fact) but this was not to be. Nonetheless, amongst other successes, Blue won the 1985 All-Aged Society stake and the 1987 Open stake, with Joan Marsden's Tarncourt Notable winning the 1987 All-Aged stake. In the same year Clive Harris's Paddiswood Affection won the Non-winners.

During the 1980s the Society introduced Area Members Working Progress competitions, with the dogs working on cold (dead) game as well as dummies (bumpers).

Claverdon Raffles of Collyers (Tarncourt Ranger – Claverdon Dollar) in winning form at Field Trials, 1994.

THE SHOOTING DOG CERTIFICATE

The real innovation of this decade in the field, however, was the setting up of the "Shooting Dog Certificate" scheme in 1981/2. The scheme had originated from Captain Birbeck, a long-time supporter of the breed, who felt there was scope for a test specifically for the shooting dog, not a working test nor the specialised sphere of field trials. Amelia Jessel worked on this idea and came up with the suggestion of a maximum of four dogs being tested under normal conditions on a regular shooting day. This scheme is still in operation, about four shooting dog certificate days a year are held, depending on demand.

"THE WORKING GROUP"

During 1985 a group was formed with the specific intent of breeding for improved working ability. At first it was thought that the group would be within the Society but in the event it was set up outside the Society as a self-formed/self-governing group.

The aims were admirable but some 10 years later there is little proof of any definite pattern having emerged. Joan Marsden, as we have seen, had some successes with her dogs but this may have been due more to her personal skills and dedication than to the involvement with the Group, of which Joan was one of the prime instigators. There was, however, an unexpected and I'm sure, unintentional, bonus. Although the group was very small, only some 12 or 15 folks originally, the fact that it had been thought necessary to set up a group with definite objectives, acted as a spur. In other words it made people think, take stock and consider what could be done to improve the working abilities within the breed. Towards the end of the 1980s there was a noticeable increase in the number of Flat-Coats taking part in A.V. Working tests. Far fewer than Labradors or Goldens, obviously, but it gave an indication that more owners were prepared to take their chance in tougher conditions and not remain within the more rarified atmosphere of "Breed" events – the only way to improve in fact. In 1989, 1,409 Flat-Coated Retrievers were registered with the Kennel Club – a somewhat frightening upsurge on which to meet the 1990s.

Chapter Three

CHOOSING A PUPPY

So you think you would like a Flat-Coated Retriever? From previous chapters it is clear that the Flat-Coat is a "purpose-built" model, so there are some very real requirements which, if not met, will result in misery for owner and dog. The Flat-Coat is not "the dog for everyone". Vets in particular are very given to recommending the breed, mainly when the client has had an unfortunate incident, with temperament possibly, in another Retriever breed. Great to think there is such confidence in the Flat-Coat's good nature, but it may be that the client's lifestyle does not suit a Retriever breed at all and a totally different type of dog is needed.

Let's get a couple of points out of the way. There are people who have had a Golden Retriever and feel they don't want to be drawing comparisons by having another Golden, so will have a "black" Golden. Or there are Labrador owners who decide to have a long-coated version this time. Both need to have the differences clearly spelt out. The Flat-Coat is not like either the Golden Retrieve or the Labrador, but is highly individual. From personal experience I have found that a

Nancy Schenk's Ch. Destiny One Gun Salute CDEx, WDEx, followed by Ch. Grousemoor Poppyseed Salute CD, WC, and Ch. Grousemoor Destiny Take Aim CD, WDX.
Flat-Coats are active dogs; they need plenty of exercise coupled with mental stimulation.

Ch. Andra of Camelot with her daughters Int. Ch. German Ch. VDH Ch. Amy of the Happy Den and Agnetha of the Happy Den pictured in Germany. Owned by Brigitte and Christoff Schneidermann. The Flat-Coat is one of the most attractive of breeds, but it demands a special commitment on the part of the owner.

previous Golden owner can adapt to a Flat-Coat better than a Labrador owner. The latter is particularly true with shooting men. To any dyed-in-the-wool Labrador man I would say "stay with the breed you know and get on with" – in my own mind thinking "possibly a boring man with a boring dog!"

Flat-Coats love people. This has its own drawbacks which actually need to be sorted out early in life; in other words the new puppy will need careful management so that this love of being with you the whole time can be contained. It is too late to try and do it when the dog is older.

The Flat-Coat is mentally very active and needs mental as well as physical outlets. This must be consistent. Not ten miles jogging at the weekend and then nothing for another seven days. Whilst physical exercise is necessary in the adult dog, there needs to be mental activity also, starting with socialising classes with the puppy. So one has to consider whether you have the time and inclination for this.

In other words the dog's inherent abilities and tendencies need channelling. Also, it seems a small point, but food is usually high on the Flat-Coat's list of "good things". They are thieves. Sounds no problem? – wait until you go with guests to the door to say "good-bye" and return to no cake and a slightly self-conscious looking dog! They also tend to eat anything disgusting that they find. A Swedish friend of mine insists that horse droppings are fine for them. Just as well. Taking all this into account one wonders why there are those of us who are totally committed to this breed. I must admit, however, that I spend an awful lot of time discouraging people from having a Flat-Coat. A certain temperament is needed on the part of the owner, a further trait in the dog being a clownishness which can assert itself at inopportune moments. Ask anyone who does Agility or some other activity. They know.

Having considered all these off-putting factors, if you are still inclined towards a Flat-Coated Retriever (I do detest the diminution to "Flatties", so all through this book you will have to bear with either the full Flat-Coated Retriever or, to me, the just about acceptable "Flat-Coat"). So, you still think you would like a Flat-Coat?

THE PUPPY-FINDING TRAIL

I would suggest getting in touch with the Kennel Club and asking for the name of the secretary of the Flat-Coated Retriever Society or Club in your country. The secretary can, one hopes, put you in touch with a reputable breeder who can give advice and possibly help with the whereabouts of a litter – again reputable. This is preferable to just getting a list of names direct from the Kennel Club. In the UK many people seem to get information by buying one of the two national weekly dog papers and then contacting the appropriate breed correspondent. I know I get very many enquiries from this source.

It is unusual for Flat-Coat puppies to be advertised – indeed the practice is frowned upon. The UK Society does have a litter-recorder, Shirley Johnson, who has undertaken this task since its inception and no doubt will for many years to come. She keeps a list of litters notified and then passes on names to enquirers. Admittedly not everyone uses this service. Well-established breeders have no need.

DOG OR BITCH?

Much depends on the reason for wanting a puppy. If the puppy is going to be a companion, it can be personal preference. Many people think that a bitch is more affectionate and biddable, but Flat-Coat dogs are very devoted to their owners and make excellent companions. It is worth keeping something of an open mind until you have met some of either sex. Obviously one's own surroundings and environment need taking into account.

APPROACHING THE BREEDER

When approaching a breeder a certain amount of care is needed and, of course, courtesy. A genuinely caring breeder will want to know as much about you as you want to know about the puppies. So be prepared for the fact that the breeder will wish to meet you and your family and, no doubt, ask some very pertinent questions before agreeing to let you have a puppy.

Do tell the breeder exactly the purpose for which you want the puppy – work, show, companion or possibly a combination of these.

The breed is basically very healthy and relatively free from hereditary defects and conditions but it is as well to ask if both parents have had eye examinations under the official Kennel Club/British Veterinary Association scheme, in order to ascertain that the dog does not have hereditary Progressive Retinal Atrophy (PRA) or cataract.

Also find out if both parents had hip X-rays. This checks on hip dysplasia. Again this is an official Kennel Club scheme. These checks are general to all breeds, not specific to Flat-Coats. In fact Flat-Coats rarely have any problems and it is unlikely that the dogs would be bred from if a problem existed, but the buyer needs to know. The system of hip scoring will be mentioned later under Health Care. While price should not be the first consideration, it is as well to ask for some idea of it during one of the early chats; also whether it includes any insurance cover and of course Kennel Club registration (this almost goes without saying).

The best age to view the puppies is another point on which the breeder can give guidance. Prospective owners of companion puppies love to see them when they are quite small, but if the puppies are possible show prospects, then the older they are the better. Many people favour six weeks, which I always feel to be a very in-between stage, particularly when assessing heads, but obviously decisions have to be made, as the puppies will shortly need to go to their new homes. When breeding is from long-established lines that are known to breed true in the main, many folk are prepared to take the breeder's recommendation, based on the knowledge of how one's own stock develops.

Going to see puppies is always exciting but there are certain points of behaviour worth remembering. Preferably do not take any dog you already own with you, but if this in unavoidable, do not let the dog out of the car without asking permission to do so, and also find out where the dog may go. Do not let your animal roam free.

It is very, very tempting, but do not pick up the puppies without first asking the owner. This applies whether the puppy is tiny or slightly older and is particularly important if you have children with you. Puppies are not play-things.

Do take note of the bitch and her behaviour, allowing for the fact that you are strange to her. Most Flat-Coat bitches actually love to have their babies admired and to be told how clever they are. But don't overwhelm her. Be quiet and take time.

ASSESSING PUPPIES
This can vary depending on what you hope to do with the dog, but there are certain basic requirements. The overall impression should be of a healthy, sturdy well-balanced puppy with confident demeanour. Again, allow for the fact that you are strange to the puppies. It helps to just sit quietly and watch them playing together, but the breeder is the person who will have had time to assess character and advise on which is best suited for your intended purpose.

When looking for a potential show prospect, the best way to make an assessment is to stand the puppy on a firm table with a non-slip top or with a thickish cloth cover. Stand the puppy up in "show pose". This gives an overall impression. Then start at the head and work back. Much of this is discussed in the Breed standard, but because puppies are not mature there are things which will change and others that won't.

As I have already mentioned, balance and proportions are all-important. The puppy who stands four-square with happy wagging tail and an interested expression starts with a bonus point.

Heads change enormously, the skull can go on changing literally for years. Starting with the head, smooth down the ears so that the skull shape can be seen; it should be flattish on top, not domed. Ears should be set level with the eyes and not be obviously large. Puppies are often said to "grow into their ears". Quite often they do but I would prefer the leathers not to give a spaniel impression. Eyes should not be yellowish in colour – actual colour is not easy to determine, but the eyes should be tight.

If the puppy is tired there may be some drooping of the lower lids but permanently droopy lower lids are best avoided, also very large round eyes. Expression is important: the puppy should be happy and interested. The muzzle should have depth, be in proportion to the skull and not be short and pointed (a "Mickey Mouse" look!). Upper teeth should be well over the lower. For some reason, the lower and upper jaws of Flat-Coats grow at a different rate, which means that the perfect close scissor bite at eight weeks can be undershot at six months. Not always, but a definite possibility. Check length of neck and angle of shoulder blades. Elbows should be well in and tight, not jutting out. The front legs should be straight with well-knuckled feet. Thin flat feet will remain so and will not improve.

The topline should be level running into the tail. Pups sometimes are a bit "proud of their tails", that is they carry them a bit high; unless the tail is almost vertical I wouldn't worry, but it is something that warrants time spent just sitting and watching the pup move around for a while. This also gives you the opportunity to judge how tightly constructed the puppy is and obtain some idea of movement.

The hindquarters need to be nicely angulated, not excessive; but they must be strong.

PRELIMINARY ARRANGEMENTS

By now, either you will have developed a preference for a puppy or a puppy will have chosen you. Whichever way, it is time to make arrangements for the puppy to take the big step of changing homes. Ask the breeder for a diet sheet, preferably in advance, so that the puppy does not have a sudden change of diet. Also a note needs to be made of dates of worming. Ask your own vet for advice on immunisation against hard pad, leptospirosis and parvovirus. Your local vet will know the hazards of your particular area.

If you haven't an indestructible small dog bed then a strong cardboard box with the front cut down makes a good puppy bed. Old woollens or "Vet-bed" (a type of simulated sheepskin) are cosy. Remember the puppy has been used to other little bodies all giving off heat, as well as the mother. It is quite a good idea to roll up some old socks or soft toys and place these in the bed. An old-fashioned crock hot-water bottle is marvellous wrapped in an old sweater. As you can see you need to go round gathering old woollen sweaters – preferably close-knit to avoid the puppy's nails catching. Warmth and snugness are the main essentials. The puppy is sure to be lonely, missing mother and the other puppies, and may tell you so quite vocally.

THE DAY OF COLLECTION

Even if you have a puppy carrying-box it is preferable to have someone with you who can hold the puppy. Supply old towels on lap and newspaper or kitchen roll for emergencies!

Collect the puppy early rather than later in the day. This gives time for the puppy to become at least a little familiar with the new surroundings. When collecting the puppy, hopefully the breeder will already have the KC registration papers, although sometimes these are delayed, plus a copy of the pedigree and, if the puppy has been insured, the cover note. Also, of course, the diet sheet and any other relevant information if not already given.

Insurance is a matter of individual choice and the options vary. Some breeders do not insure, but will do so if asked. This will not be not included in the puppy asking price, so is paid additionally. Other breeders insure for, say, one month and include this in with the puppy price. The buyer then has the choice of extending the cover after four weeks or not.

If the journey is long you may need to find a quiet place for the puppy to urinate. This is always slightly worrying and certainly should only be resorted to if a quiet and uninhabited area can be found, because this is an un-inoculated puppy, although one hopefully still carrying maternal immunity. On arrival home avoid too much excitement; let puppy look around and be taken just around the area attached to the house to learn the boundaries. A small milky feed is a good idea on arrival because the puppy associates food with "good things".

Do start as you mean to carry on, in other words don't pander to behaviour that you will later find unacceptable. Follow the existing type of feeding. If you wish to change, do this gradually; otherwise stress plus a change of food could cause an upset stomach. Until the full immunisation programme has been completed it is unwise – indeed one should not – take the puppy into public areas or allow the puppy to mix with adult dogs unless they are up-to-date with "shots", i.e. fully immunised themselves.

EARLY TRAINING

Never over-feed. It is far better to put down slightly less than you think necessary, so that puppy clears the dish. The puppy should not look distended after food. Never leave food down. If the puppy has not eaten up within a few minutes, remove the food and don't give anything further until the next feed is due. Then give fresh food but a smaller amount. Clean, fresh water must be available at all times. Your puppy has to learn that outside is for "piddles and poops", so immediately on wakening from sleep, when a puddle is usually instantaneous, the puppy should be taken outside. Also after food. When outside, encourage instant action and use a word which the puppy will learn to associate with relieving itself. Some people just say "be quick". In any case, give lots of praise when the puppy has performed. Overnight, it sometimes helps to have a thick layer of newspaper near the door (not where it will be trodden on) and often puppies will use this. As the puppy gets older the need no longer arises. If it is any consolation, problems of settling at night are usually short-lived. We have already discussed the need for puppy to be warm and snug. It is in fact more than that. The puppy, who has never before been alone own with no warm bundles to cuddle up to and no mother to set the rules, must feel safe.

Providing you know that puppy has been left comfortably, then try to ignore any noise. Usually after a few nights the puppy will settle down. For one thing the puppy will be getting used to a daytime routine and will be ready to sleep at night. Puppies sleep a lot. Should the crying continue, you can go to the door but do not go in. Bang the door and tell the puppy to "be quiet". In fact, to the puppy, it will just be a "not pleased" voice. During the day you should have been getting the puppy used to a pleased and praising voice, which is what the puppy wants to hear.

Remember the puppy's limitations at this stage. Do not go in and give cuddles as this will be fatal. Puppy thinks: I made a noise. Human came and cuddled me. Do it again. An old-fashioned remedy which worked for my sister's puppy is worth trying. The only problem is that you need an old-fashioned alarm clock that ticks loudly. Yes, I know, this is as bad as the crock hot-water bottle! A trip round the junk shops is indicated. Wrap the clock in an old sweater, the ticking gives the illusion of heart beats –in other words, another presence in the bed. In fact, with woolly sausage bodies, crock hot water-bottle, and clock, there will hardly be room for puppy! But it works.

Earlier I mentioned that Flat-Coats are so people-oriented that leaving them alone can bring its own problems, so this needs to be dealt with while the puppy is young. Nothing very drastic, but that is the whole point of doing it now. From the time you have the puppy home, start a little programme. Each day even if you are in the house, leave the puppy in the room where the puppy's bed is, with the door closed. The puppy should be put firmly in the bed, with a small biscuit, and a pat and be told "good dog, stay there". Turn, walk out and close the door. It actually does not matter if the puppy does not stay in the bed, but the puppy must stay in the room, or wherever, quietly. Start with a very short time, four or five minutes, then go in and if the puppy has been quiet, give lots of praise. Don't let out a shrieking puppy. Thump the door and only go in when the puppy is quiet. Increase the time every few days. This truly is an essential exercise. If it is not persevered with, it is easy to find you have a dog who is wonderful as long as you are there, but who will not be left. No-one can have their dog with them the whole time. Some people find cages helpful, both at night and if the puppy is left at times during the day. I think they have their uses but it is important that the crate is not over-used. Quite certainly this results in weak hindquarters and obvious lack of muscle development. If the dog is going to have to be kennelled at times, again, it is worth starting this at a fairly early age, providing of course that you have confidence in the Kennels. The dog can be left just for a day, then overnight, so that when a longer stay is needed the puppy knows that you will return. I don't think time, as such, registers very much, so that as long as the dog knows the pattern, which is that you, the important person, always come back, then the dog will not worry unduly. After immunisation is complete and at about four months it is a good idea to start socialising classes with very basic obedience, though quite often there are groups which specialise in even younger puppies – puppy parties, in fact. Whatever the classes you choose, don't let your puppy be pushed too hard too quickly.

Talking of Obedience, reminds me of an essential in the early home training. Having been given a name, make sure the puppy knows what it is. The other absolute essential is that *the puppy comes when called*. I cannot stress this too strongly. You can start in the house, in the garden or yard. When the puppy is a short distance away, call the name in a lively manner and, if you like say, "come", but the main importance is the name. If the puppy ignores the call, squat down and tap the ground making very enthusiastic noises. When the puppy comes, praise lavishly. There can be an occasional reward of a tidbit, but not every time. The encouraging voice is incredibly effective. If by chance you are totally ignored, you go up to the puppy very quietly, grab both sides of the neck (holding the loose skin and not hurting the puppy) growl at the puppy and, in a grumbly voice, say the puppy's name, accompanied by a little shake. Move back a tiny distance call the puppy immediately and then give praise when the puppy comes. The call *must* be in a pleasant tone. The other essential absolutely from when you take the puppy home, is lead training. If this is done immediately it avoids confrontations later when the puppy may be challenging your status as pack leader. I don't use a collar; a light rope slip-lead is good as it does not chafe the neck. Slip the noose (correct way round) over the head, slackly round the neck, pat your own leg and say "Heel" or "Come on pup" (using puppy's name) and just walk, fairly quickly and talking to the puppy the whole time. If puppy stops, you stop also, but having said "come on pup" and patted your leg encouragingly, set off again. In minutes the puppy will be trotting along happily at your side (*not* in front). The great thing is to avoid battle. Encouragement works wonders.

Hopefully you will already have been using the word "Sit". This can be started when the puppy sits down. As the puppy starts to sit say the word, otherwise apply very gentle pressure to hindquarters and say "sit". Once the puppy is confident on the lead it is a good idea to combine being on the lead with being tied up for a short time and told to "sit and stay", while you go on doing something near to hand. Just for a few minutes. These basic patterns can be learned by bringing them into the daily routine. Sessions should be short and always finish with praise.

By four to five months of age the puppy should be fully immunised; should have been wormed again as recommended; will come when called; walks well on the lead; and is enjoying socialising classes, which should help with car travel as puppy will be going to something pleasant. This type of simple training, worked in with day-to-day living, is invaluable, whatever you hope to do with your Flat-Coat as the young dog stage approaches.

Before leaving our puppy, just a word about retrieving. If you are an experienced gun dog trainer, then you will have your own methods. If, however, you are a novice who hopes to train your dog, it is easy to be too obsessed about retrieving. By all means you can "try" the puppy by throwing a rolled up sock or some such object. If the puppy picks it up, fine; if the puppy brings it back (remember my point about coming when called?!) even better. Incidentally, it is a good idea to do the sock-throwing exercise in a narrow hallway or passage if possible, then the puppy has to come back to you. Once you know the puppy will retrieve then it is far better to carry on with basic training, letting the puppy have an occasional retrieve as a treat.

Chapter Four

ESSENTIAL BASIC TRAINING

In the chapter on choosing a puppy, mention was made of the need for all puppies, regardless of future plans, to have socialising and basic behavioural training.

LEARNING THROUGH DAILY ACTIVITIES
To re-cap on the basics: From 8-9 weeks on the puppy learns during normal daily activities. No formal specific training is undertaken. Any training, for example lead training, should only be for a few minutes daily. The puppy must come when called. Remember the ecstatic praise! The puppy should walk on a slack lead at the owner's lefthand side. The puppy should learn to stay quietly when left alone for a short period – we are talking minutes not hours at this stage. The puppy learns to sit on command. The word "Sit" can in time be reduced to a quick "ss" noise.

In the same way that the puppy or young dog can learn "Sit", if you are going to show, then your dog can also learn "Stand". The puppy should also learn to stay quietly, hitched up, but at this stage only when you are near to hand, and only very briefly. Then praise.

If the puppy is eventually to be used in the shooting field you may also remember the advice not to get carried away with retrieving. This is one of the main causes of unsteady, unheeding youngsters. One retrieve a week as a "treat" – a sharpish, short, out-and-back.

Like all young things, puppies need to play and let off steam; free romping is fine but even then, make sure the puppy is never beyond recall. The puppy must never feel out of your control.

This "under six month" age, is the best time to introduce the puppy to water, preferably with an older dog who is a good swimmer, to act as coach, providing this is at the time of year when the water is reasonably warm. It need only be shallow. Again, short spells to begin with.

VOCABULARY AND VOICE TONE
As the puppy gets older, word recognition will increase. An adult dog who is accustomed to being talked to has a far wider range of understandable "words" than the animal behaviourists would have you believe. The puppy of rising six months will have an understanding of certain basic words, providing you have always used the same words for the same actions. The recognition of these basic words is essential whatever activity is intended for the future.

They are: Name – always get attention before giving any command. Come. Sit. Stay – at the same time holding your hand upright, at about shoulder level with palm toward the puppy. Wait – this can be an alternative to "stay" or in addition to it. I find, with an older "trainee", I use "Stay" when the dog is being left, and "Wait" as the command before the dog is to be sent on a retrieve, the word being spoken in a firm, growly tone with the syllables drawn out "W-a-i-t". At the same time I hold my hand, flat-palmed horizontally, at the level of the dog's head.

Get on – this is useful in the early stages when telling puppy to go and romp, particularly if spoken in a cheery tone with a semi-circling movement of the arm. Later, this helps when the dog is required to hunt up.

The tone of voice is very important, it conveys as much as the word. All commands must be clear, just as, later, hand signals must be clear and definite. Loudness is not the main essential. This should be kept in reserve for urgent need. Most of the time keep the voice clear but fairly low. Then, the puppy has to listen. A constant loud voice becomes so familiar that it tends to be ignored!

SIMPLE EARLY FIELD TRAINING

This is not a specialist gundog training book. There are some excellent publications on this which are helpful; but you always need to get out there with your pup to start more serious training. Again, two five-to-ten minute sessions daily can be enough for a six month plus pup.

There are now many gundog clubs, all are listed at the Kennel Club. These are excellent for getting pup used to having to concentrate when there are distractions in the form of other dogs. It is still essential to practise at home, reinforcing each step.

EQUIPMENT

A ROPE SLIP-LEAD: A length of smooth rope with a metal ring at one end and a loop to hold at the other. The neck noose is made by slipping the rope through the metal ring. It is useful to have a short lead for heel work and a longer one (six feet) as a training aid for sit and stay and that sort of thing.

CHECK-CHAINS: Some trainers prefer to have a metal check chain (largish links) and a clip-on lead. A sharper "reminder" can be given then with plain rope, although if the puppy has had early training with a slip-lead, this is usually quite sufficient. It is almost parallel with using a harsh bit on a horse: it can become a vicious circle. If the snaffle mouth is never ruined then the harsh bit is unnecessary.

WHISTLE: Two with different tones are very useful, but a bit difficult for the novice handler. If using one whistle, make distinctly different sounds, for example a strong blast to stop, a repeated, intermittent "peep" to recall. Work it out for yourself, but be consistent.

DUMMIES/BUMPERS: These can be canvas "water" dummies, but also have some covered in rabbit skin and others with duck wings (the wings can just be held on with rubber bands). Always have plenty, at least eight. Dogs learn to count, so vary the number of dummies being used and always leave one or two that you pick yourself. This is later on in training, it keeps the dog's interest and keeps the dog guessing. Later, you may feel inclined to try dummy launchers and more sophisticated equipment, but that is in the future.

You need a shoulder bag – like a game bag – for all these bits and pieces.

HOME WORK

You don't need an enormous amount of space for home training, in fact a restricted area in the early stages is preferable, making it easier to grab a youngster who gets a bit out of hand and needs a quick shake. A small fenced paddock is ideal but, failing that, a great deal can be done in a yard or garden.

Here are some simple exercises.

Walking to Heel. Pup should already do this on the lead but practise having the puppy really close up. Walk briskly making sharp turns to left or right; the dog has to concentrate the whole time to keep with you. If necessary, give a quick jerk to the lead and say "Heel". From heelwork on the lead you progress to free heelwork. It is well worth spending time now on this exercise. Praise good work.

Sit and Stay. Firmly sit your dog, saying "Stay" with a raised hand. Then walk away backwards for a short distance, always watching the dog. To begin with, as long as the dog has stayed put, walk back to the dog and give lots of praise. Some will do this exercise straightaway, but if you have any doubts, put on the long lead, do the "Sit and Stay", then, still holding a very slack lead, walk away as above. You can also vary this by walking round the dog quite close up but making sure the dog does not get up. The circle can be gradually increased in diameter.

When the dog appears to understand, then progress to doing the exercise off the lead. The circling is helpful otherwise the dog will tend to get up as soon as the handler is not in front. The dog, when 'steady', can be recalled to you from the 'stay' position.

The "Retrieve". Still only occasional. For a straight forward retrieve, if possible have someone else throw the dummy. If you have to be dummy-thrower and handler, which happens to most of us at times, the dog tends to look at the handler. When there is a dummy thrower, the dog still tends to watch the handler instead of looking ahead for the object that is being thrown, which the dog needs to "mark". Then of course, the dog must be attentive to the handler and await the command of 'Hi lost', or whatever command to retrieve is used. At first, just a short out-and-in retrieve. If the youngster doesn't come straight back, call, then run away for a few yards. Usually the dog will follow. Turn round, sit the dog, hold your hands at chest level, say "Hold", then "Dead" (or whatever word you use) taking the dummy. Then praise, quietly, just "good dog".

When sending, it is important that the dog, after seeing the dummy fall, stays at your side. Either say "stay", or this is where I use "wait", then blow your nose, adjust your hat, whatever, but always concentrating on the dog. Make a hand signal clearly and again say "Wait" before giving the command "Hi lost".

Direction is something that can be practised at home. In fact a tiny puppy can get used to watching your hands by having you point things out. There are two easy exercises to learn basics on "direction". Incidentally, throughout all these exercises, have your dummy bag dropped just behind you and the dog must not touch it.

Sit the dog. Place three dummies – they need only be 10 or 11 yards out – one directly in front, one absolutely to your right and one to the left. Indicate clearly the direction in which the dog is to go. At this stage I don't think there is any harm in using your body to block off the unwanted dummies. Vary the order in which you have them collected, also always have a wait before getting the next dummy. Sometimes pick up one yourself.

Round the clock. Sit your dog and place dummies round in a circle, 4 to start with, then put in another three or four. The dog is sent for a specific dummy. It is useful also as a progression from this to sit the dog up and then chuck dummies around and over the dog, who must remain motionless.

All of these exercises must be done in stages, reinforcing each one before going on to the next. Change the area in which you do exercises so that the dog is adaptable and does not become bored. Always end on a good note. If there has been a hiccup, give a very easy retrieve and then praise. Always finish with praise and never at cross-purposes. Time spent on basic training is never time wasted.

INTRODUCTION TO GUNSHOT

A word of warning on the need for care when introducing a young dog to the gun. Obviously it helps enormously if the puppy has already heard gunshot from varying distances. However, this is not always possible. If the puppy is totally unused to gunfire, then at first have the puppy by your side, a distance from the gun. Gradually reduce the distance. Never, ever, have a gun fired unexpectedly at the puppy's side, or a dummy launcher. The noise is different but many dogs who are steady to gunfire are apprehensive about dummy launchers until they associate them with the retrieve. Dogs are made gun-shy by thoughtless handlers. It is helpful for a pup to be taken to tests and classes as an onlooker.

Gwen Knight is a very skilled puppy trainer whose excellent booklet "Training your Flatcoat" is available from the FCRS (UK). Gwen has kindly allowed me to give her list of "Do's and Dont's".

Do delay training if your dog is slow to mature (bitches usually develop before dogs).

Do use the tone of your voice intelligently in encouraging or scolding.

Do go forward and help if your dog is confused or failing to find.

Do go out to your dog if the stop whistle is ignored. Take the dog back by the scruff of the neck to the spot where you were disobeyed. Blow the stop whistle in the dog's ear; leave the dog staying and return to your original position before handling again.

Do make sure your dog understands and has perfected an exercise fully before starting a new one.

Do end a session on a good note. If necessary finish with a relatively simple exercise and return a happy dog to home to contemplate this work experience.

Do always take the direction of wind into consideration in relation to success in finding the dummy.

Do consult text books.

Don't ever lose your temper. Be unhurried and deliberate in your actions in handling.

Don't bore your dog. Use your imagination in devising different exercises and vary the training grounds if possible.

Don't train on fur or game-scented ground until basic obedience has been firmly established.

Brenda Phillips with Exclyst Timemaster SDC A, pictured after winning a heat of the Pup of the Year contest: A beautifully reared youngster, fed on a top-quality diet.

Photo: Mike Alsford.

Chapter Five

CARING FOR YOUR FLAT-COAT

The dictionary describes 'care' as: "To be concerned with; have regard for. Serious attention; protection and supervision". Another definition is "object causing anxiety; charge; responsibility". All of these statements are true when we take a dog, or any other animal, into our home. We are, in effect, the caretaker. Care covers feeding, cleanliness, exercise, maintaining health but giving attention should the dog become ill, and providing appropriate housing.

INGREDIENTS FOR A PROPER DIET

Everyone has his or her own views on the best way to feed, and, frankly, if it works, stick with it. There are two methods of feeding; the old-established one of mixing up a feed of meat and biscuit meal plus any additives that seem necessary, or the widely popular "complete" feeds.

Whatever the type of feeding, the dog has certain essential requirements which the feed needs to contain. In the wild, the dog would eat raw flesh (protein) but would also eat herbage and other roughage as needed. Bones would supply calcium. In other words, diet would consist partly of what the dog could get, but also of things eaten when the dog felt the need for them, thus making up a balance. As a matter of interest, with the current insistence on scissor bites, in the wild most of the wolf family originally had teeth which met, that is they had a level bite, which is the most effective for tearing flesh, particularly when near to the bone.

Protein is a highly complex compound of amino acids in varying amounts, found in meat, fish and milk but also in certain vegetables such as peas and beans; for that matter cereals also contain protein but the vegetable proteins have a different composition from animal-derived ones. Some vegetable proteins contain a very high proportion of amino acids which should preferably be used as a mixture, so that the excess of amino acids in the protein of one ingredient may balance the deficiencies of the same amino acids in the protein of others. Animal proteins are preferable because, on digestion, they yield all the amino acids in about the proportion the animal requires. In simple terms, proteins are essential for normal growth and for tissue repair. The type, that is the origin, of the protein needs to be known.

Carbohydrates provide balance to proteins by giving bulk to aid digestion and also providing a source of energy and warmth, hence biscuit, meal, oatmeal and so on – the "starchy" foods in fact. Fat is an essential as part of a balanced diet, providing a degree of internal "lubrication", it has a part to play in the general body "repairs" that go on constantly, and, of course, is absolutely essential for skin and coat condition. Calcium/phosphorus and other minerals are all essential but, if given as additives, must be in correctly balanced amounts and not in excess. Vitamins are necessary, but preferably as they occur naturally in the diet, not as additives. Having said which, Cod Liver Oil with Vitamin E can be helpful over the winter months and I know there have been very good results with high Vitamin C doses for arthritis. Stainless-steel dog bowls are the most hygienic and satisfactory. Take up bowls immediately after feeding. Never leave bowls down, even with reluctant eaters – in fact, particularly with reluctant feeders. The bowls should be washed immediately in hot sudsy water and then washed with a solution of sodium hypochlorite, the well-known kitchen bleach in fact.

COMPLETE FOODS

An enormous range of these is available and they are very popular for ease of feeding. They are excellent and, literally, there is a feed for every age and every eventuality. I think it is worth remembering that these feeds are carefully balanced. Adding a bit of this and a bit of that merely upsets that balance and is not a good idea. It is important to buy a reputable brand, not one where the analysis states the percentage of ingredients but not the type. For example, you need to know the type of protein. It has to be available protein. Ground up old shoe leather has a high protein content! Most feed firms also have excellent advisory services.

HOMEMADE FOODS

Biscuit meal can vary. If using a baked broken-biscuit type meal it is worth searching to get a milled wheatmeal that still has the wheatgerm and bran. In other words, just the whole grain, milled to flour and then made into biscuits. Boiled brown rice is a useful alternative, especially for occasional use. Meat can be cooked fresh meat. There is a wide range of canned and frozen meats. The biscuit meal and meat are mixed, the biscuit usually damped with broth or hot water. The plain biscuit meals do not swell but "mixer" meals do, so allow them to swell before feeding. If there are only a few dogs then chopped cooked greens, carrots, onion etc. can be added to the feed. A little chopped parsley or alfalfa is good also. Obviously these additions are beneficial for any number of dogs, but I am thinking of the time required when larger numbers of dogs are involved.

Bones are the best way of keeping teeth and gums sound, the proviso being that they are sawn-off sections of shin (marrow) bones. Cooked ones are sold but I find these dangerously brittle. The bones must be hard and non-splinterable. No poultry, rabbit or chop bones. The odd thing is, a dog could eat a whole fresh rabbit (most likely mangy if it is a Flat-Coat eating it!), and come to no harm because, providing the dog eats skin, fur and all, the skin seems to wrap round the bones. There is some truth in this. I've always managed not to have one of the dogs eat a fresh rabbit but we have a demon rabbit-catching cat! Last year Daisy caught, to our knowledge, some eighty half-grown rabbits over the space of three weeks. They were more than half her own size, but she would carry them across the fields some quarter of a mile to the house. As you know, cats always have to show their catch and be praised accordingly. Occasionally, the other cats would share in the booty, but never until Daisy had first go, which was always the head, obviously a great delicacy. Every bit except the tail would be eaten. Bones, skin, fur, the lot and never has there been a problem from pierced guts or some such.

MANHATTAN MIX

You may have realised that I am of the "home cooking" school. We use a very good health-maintaining mix which is sprinkled on the feed once daily. All ingredients are available from any health food shop, except steamed sterilised bone flour which comes from the pet shop.

1.5	cups of yeast powder (Yeastamin or similar)
0.5	cup powdered kelp
1	cup Lecithin granules

1   cup toasted wheatgerm (keep balance in fridge)
1   cup of bran
0.5   cup powdered steamed sterilised bone flour
Mix all together and keep in cool place in tightly lidded jar or tin.
1 dessert spoon sprinkled over one feed daily.
Three times weekly give dessertspoon of Cod Liver Oil with Vitamin E.
Twice weekly, chopped parsley or alfalfa sprouts or other fresh veg as already mentioned.

I have a friend whose husband refuses to take vitamins and she sprinkles this mix on his curries! Healthy skin and gleaming coat come from within, rather than from outward application. Whatever your preference in type of feeding, it must be balanced and nutritious. The Flat-Coated Retriever body is a power house designed for a specific purpose. Food is the fuel.

SPECIAL NEEDS
We mentioned puppy care earlier. The young adult also has different feeding needs from the adult. It is well to continue with smaller but more feeds, that is, two or three rather than one large feed.

A slightly higher protein content is needed than for the adult dog, but this can be overdone, resulting in a hyperactive tendency. My personal feeling is that some of the complete feeds are tending to over-do the protein content. Excessively speedy growth is no benefit to a breed like the Flat-Coated Retriever. Steady growth is much better, rather than a race to produce an over-mature puppy for the show ring.

EXERCISE
As already said, puppies need consistent exercise, building up gradually. The long bones grow so rapidly that care must be taken. Jumping, and scaling fences, should be restricted until growth is finished and the bone hardened. Moderation in all ways while the dog is still growing. I am convinced that problems with hips and patellas are more frequently caused by management and environment than heredity in Flat-Coats. The mature dog can take an enormous amount of exercise, which is not to say that this amount is necessarily needed. In fact a reasonable walk, which includes some free running, of a mile or so, and a short training session where the dog has to indulge in some mental exercise, will do more good than a ten mile walk.

Exercise can be a vicious circle. I know an elderly lady who has a young and very active male Flat-Coat. The dog's need for exercise had been so impressed upon her that when she could no longer take him behind her horse when exercising, she started taking him to a quiet lane in the car, then had him running behind the car. The result was that the dog got fitter and fitter and she could not meet his demands. He was not only excessively fit but he became unmanageable because he was using only physical, not mental energy. Working and exercising, even just playing up and down banks, is marvellous for strengthening and muscling-up hindquarters. But, as I say, all in moderation.

GROOMING
The Flat-Coat is an "easy maintenance" breed to keep tidy and comfortable, but little and often is better than leaving it for weeks and then needing an onslaught. Very little equipment is needed.
Stainless steel combs: One with coarse and fine ends or two separate combs if preferred.
One very fine (nit) comb: This is useful for the very soft hair that grows behind and below the
                        ears. Also, if needs be, to search for lice should disaster strike.
A good brush: The type with a back strap is easy to use. The choice of
                        brushes and combs is really individual.

A hound glove:	This is useful for strapping down as it stimulates the skin.
Curved blunt-ended scissors:	These are useful for trimming hair from between toes and pads.
Pointed hairdresser's scissors:	These scissors can be used in conjunction to thinning scissors to tidy and shape (unobtrusively!) the tail.
Thinning scissors:	
A stripping blade or comb:	If you are unable to tidy off the ears with finger and thumb, you may need to resort to dubious means – the stripping blade, used judiciously, or even thinning scissors. The only warning is, that once you resort to scissors on the ears you have to continue. There is no looking back.
A square of velvet or silk:	This is essential for the final polish.

Ears. Check about once a week, resisting any temptation to poke. Any cleaning must be very carefully done with a twist of cotton wool dipped in warm olive oil. If the ear is definitely waxy, there are some good oils available in the form of drops. Obviously, should there be a strong smell or discharge, then professional advice should be sought. Other than the weekly check, meddle with ears as little as possible.

Nails. Where dogs are mainly on grass, the nails may need regular attention. The type of nail clipper to use is a matter of personal preference. Great care has to be taken with black nails as the "quick" cannot be seen.

Bathing. Need only be very occasional unless for a specific reason. Always use a canine shampoo not a human one. The coat can be rubbed dry or, preferably, blow-dried, combing the hair flat at the same time. If the bath is pre-show, it may need to be a day or two in advance to avoid the coat being "on the blow", but this depends on the type of coat. Ears need to be dried inside, very gently.

BEDS AND BEDDING

These need regular cleaning or washing, depending on type and material. The plastic shell type bed can be very easily cleaned and then wiped over with one of the good disinfectants formulated specifically for canine use. For effective use of the disinfectant the bed must be cleaned first. Duvets, bean-bags and such, can all be dropped in the washing machine.

HOUSING

This can take a variety of forms: to many Flat-Coats it means a bed in the kitchen or the sofa if no-one is looking, but it can also mean outside kennelling, or even a loose box, where dogs can be dried off and have the mud brushed out before returning indoors after a day in the shooting field.

Many Flat-Coat owners have just one or two dogs who live in the house, so the question of alternative housing does not arise. Indeed in the UK there are very few large Flat-Coated Retriever kennels. Even owners and breeders actively involved in the Breed frequently only have four or five dogs. These dogs can live in the house, but it makes life easier if there is alternative accommodation available if needed. At times it may be necessary to separate dogs and bitches, for example. Flat-Coats do not make the best "kennel" dogs. You may remember I mentioned earlier the need for puppies to be gradually introduced to being confined in one way or another. Someone will immediately say: "What about gamekeeper's dogs? They are usually kennelled." True, but the daily routine is different. The dog or dogs are out for periods in the day on paths through woodland, checking on birds, "dogging back" and so on. In other words the dogs are using both physical and mental energy and thus return to the kennel happy to settle down for a snooze.

A Flat-Coat that is kennelled with little outlet for using up energy, frequently becomes noisy, takes to chewing, and is really rather a tiresome dog when let out of the kennel. And who can blame the dog, especial one kennelled alone? Never good practice. I would never have a dog left alone and isolated in a kennel. It is very unkind to leave the dog without companionship, particularly with such a people-oriented breed as the Flat-Coated Retriever.

Having said this, Flat-Coats can be kennelled happily and successfully, especially if the daily routine is of being partly kennelled and partly in the house; and this, in fact, is a very usual pattern in the UK, combined with adequate exercise and mental interest.

With a large kennel of dogs we are on to a different ball game. Presumably there is someone about most of the day, and a definite routine of cleaning out, exercising, training, feeding and so on is carried out The dogs no doubt become used to the routine, but I still feel this is not the best way to enjoy your Flat-Coat. If you don't want their companionship, why have them?

ALTERNATIVE HOUSING

Let's take it that the one or two Flat-Coats have become four or five and some type of extra accommodation is needed. If the kennelling is to be on the part-time or occasional basis we have mentioned, then the needs are different from the requirements of a large kennel complex which usually is self-contained.

Points to consider are:

      Site. Much depends on space available.

      Proximity of neighbours.

      Easy approach from house.

      Drainage.

      Proximity to tap water.

      Electricity supply.

If possible face away from prevalent winds and also avoid direct sun over the hottest part of the day. Make use of trees for shade. If the house is to be permanent, it can be breeze block or brick. A moveable kennel is more likely to be of timber construction: both should preferably have a run. Always have a larger, rather than smaller size, than you think you need. Height should be human standing height for ease of working. Cost should probably come first as this may be the decider on choice! It can vary enormously; obviously brick is excellent but it is the most expensive option.

With timber kennels there is a wide range, and these wooden houses are the most popular with owners who need somewhere comfortable and convenient for occasional or part-time use. Also, providing the house is carefully assembled, it can be taken apart and can be moved if necessary. The styles range from single kennels, which we have decided to ignore, to double kennels, with a run which may be open-topped or covered. I have to say that Flat-Coats love to be outside. I think they get claustrophobic when confined, so that a large run is essential, not just a 6' by 4' area. There are also corridor kennels which are very good, again with a run either at one or at both ends.

Concrete is frequently used for flooring runs, but paving slabs with a drainage outlet are infinitely preferable. They are just as easily cleaned and they dry far quicker. With timber and mesh runs it is as well to have timber cladding to a height of about 2 feet.

Pre-cast material such as breeze block is frequently used in the construction of kennel ranges. A usual size is a 4ft. x 4ft. sleeping compartment with a 4ft. x 6ft. run. The runs could of course be extended to greater length if required and certainly I feel a 4ft. x 6ft. run to be inadequate for Flat-Coated Retrievers. I know there is a theory about dogs having a long narrow run but I feel they are better with a feeling of space all round. Of course if you are going for custom-built, you can choose exactly to your own requirements, with everything close to hand for convenience. It is worth remembering that there may be a local carpenter who will make a dog house to your own

The Riversflight kennels, owned by Peter and Jean Griffiths. This is a custom-built brick and tile kennel range, with kitchen and feed store.

A timber 'corridor' house and paved run.

requirements. In this case do write down clearly and exactly where you need doors, windows, shutters and so on. A further point on timber houses: it is essential that all wood is treated with a reputable and suitable wood preservative (ask for advice in the appropriate shop). Any posts should be treated to below ground level and preferably put in metal sockets. Interior and exterior walls must have regular treatment. This is not as arduous as it sounds – it is very satisfying, because you can get through an impressive amount in a few hours. Given this attention, timber housing can last a remarkably long time. We have a timber corridor house which must be nearly 40 years old and has survived being moved here from our previous farm. It is still fine, although I did have a new set of doors made a few years ago. We took out two of the interior solid dividers so there are two compartments, each 8ft. x 6ft., and two 4ft. x 6ft. that can be used for storage. The centre compartment can be divided either into half or into quarters by low divisions – very useful when being used for puppies. Admittedly the outer slide door is usually open so if the dogs are having an hour or two in there, they are free to run in and out. The run is about 12ft. x 8ft. with a paved base. There used to be a pebble run of the same size at the other end for puppies to run onto, but to my horror I found the pups would eat the pebbles, so we abandoned that – the pebbles anyhow. I thought they would be good for feet!

Pine shavings are very effective to sprinkle on the inside floor (particularly a timber floor). I just have a strip down one side of the compartment, mainly if, for example, in-season bitches need to stay in overnight. House/kennel dogs are usually very clean, but there can be an occasional "accident". The shavings are soft, smell pleasant and are very easy to sweep up. I feel this type of soft shavings is safer than dry, rather harsh sawdust which can get into eyes. Admittedly, with our very few dogs we can go for months without using the dog house. When we do, the dogs are very happy, so although it is a very simple lay-out, it works. The beds can be wooden platforms or separate beds or boxes. The rigid oval plastic beds are good as they are easily cleaned and dogs like them. The washable synthetic fleece type or washable bean bags are excellent inside, but not really practical in an outside house. The dogs tend to pull them outside and they get wet.

There are various other materials, though straw tends to be rather coarse and can have mites. Shredded paper is clean and easy; for years we have used wood wool and find it very good. It has good insulating properties and is very easy to lift out and burn in an ordinary garden incinerator.

Preferably you need a supply of water close at hand, although, with only two or three dogs, a watering can does the job easily enough. Water bowls need to be removable for cleaning but held firm in a ring, or something similar, about 18 inches off the floor. With a kennel complex – by the time you need to make such an investment you will know exactly what your requirements are! No watering-can here, but water with automatic drinking bowls, a kitchen, bathing facilities and so on.

Talking of bathing facilities: if I was setting up bathing arrangements, I would have a shower. The base could be raised to avoid back bending and it is far easier than an orthodox bath.

OLD DOGS

Old friends are very special and need cosseting. The older dog will appreciate two or three small meals a day of nourishing food. If digestion is a bit upset, offer boiled brown rice and a little boiled, boneless fish or chicken. Old dogs occasionally have difficulty with constipation. A little bran sprinkled on the food may help. Older dogs will require gentle exercise and will also need to be let out to relieve themselves more frequently than younger dogs. Recently we had an elderly dog who had always had a wonderful coat. However, with age, the skin became uncomfortably dry and the coat sparse. We put him on high potency (1000mg) Evening Primrose capsules, one daily. There was no immediate reaction, but in just over two months, there was a definite improvement which continued. The skin and coat improved enormously and he was a comfortable dog.

When the time for parting comes and the difficult decision has to be made and faced, then do be there with your friend. It's tough and not easy to accept; but it is the least we can do to ease the last journey.

From Major W.G. Eley's book " Retrievers and Retrieving" (1905)

"I like to think of the work you have done,
 And the shoots we've had together;
The good and bad, the big and small,
 The scent, the fur, the feather.
Sad shall I be when Death steps in –
 That monster grim and cold;
For nothing else shall part us, Jack –
 No, not your weight in gold."

The venerable elder statesman: Can. Am. Eng. Ch. Parkburn Deextenzing of Casuarina Can. Am. CD – the only triple Champion in the breed. Bred by Moira Jewell, owned by Cyraine Dugdale.

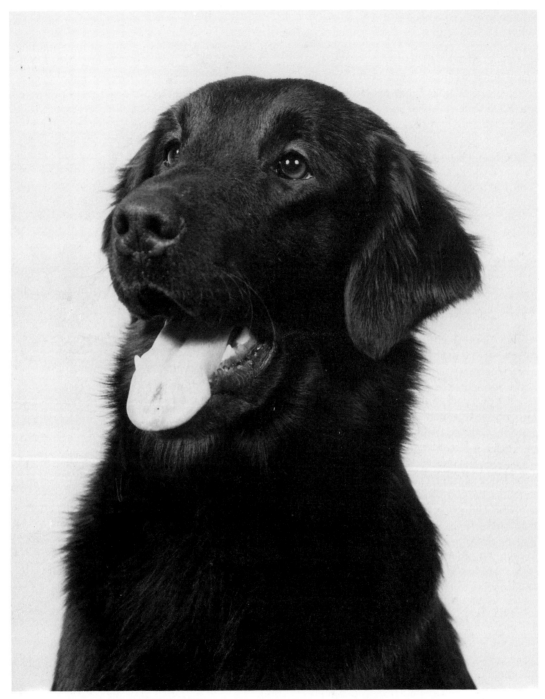

The picture of health: Eskmill Intrigue, owned by Jenny Donnelly.

Photo: Martin Leigh.

Chapter Six

HEALTH MATTERS

The Flat-Coated Retriever is a healthy, resilient breed with the will to live and one which has very few problems with hereditary or congenital defects. Of course, as with any living thing, abnormalities can on occasion occur. I do wonder at times if, because we have this good health record, we tend to overreact when some defect occurs. Of course we should hold a "watching brief" for possible problems but it is important to keep a sense of perspective.

For some years the Flat-Coated Retriever Society in the UK has been working in conjunction with Dr Jane Dobson and the Oncology Unit at the Cambridge School of Veterinary Medicine on a tumour survey. Which means, of course, that we hear of incidences that otherwise would remain unknown. In the same way, recently the breed has taken part in a survey on eye abnormalities. The Flat-Coat was chosen, not because the breed is prone to eye problems, but the reverse. The breed has a good record, so was regarded as being suitable, as there would not be a multiplicity of variations to cloud the issue. Obviously, because we take part in these surveys, we hear results. It is important that these findings are considered in proportion to the size of the breed. It is also important to resist the temptation to make mountains out of molehills.

IMMUNISING INOCULATIONS
These were mentioned earlier when talking about puppies. It is as well to ask the advice of your own vet as to the best age for the puppy's first inoculation. Much depends on local conditions. I prefer to leave the first one till ten weeks, but we live in a fairly isolated position. For example, in a high parvovirus risk area the first inoculation may need to be at six weeks – before the puppy leaves for a new home, in fact. The inoculations provide immunity from distemper (hard pad), infectious canine hepatitis, leptospirosis and parvovirus. Normally the dog has "booster" jabs yearly, although of late there seems to be a feeling that the immunisation lasts longer than was previously thought. In any case, boarding kennels usually insist on a current certificate. In some countries protection also has to be provided against heartworm and hookworms.

INHERITED CONDITIONS

HIP DYSPLASIA
The hip joint is a ball and socket which should fit closely. The socket is the acetabulum into which should fit the "ball", i.e. the rounded head of the femur, the femoral head. The examination is by X-ray usually under general anaesthetic. Placement is all-important so the vet needs to be experienced in this field. In the UK, the dog must be over 12 months of age before having hips radiographed. There is no upper age limit. The plates are sent to the KC for scoring by a panel.

The minimum score for each hip is '0', the maximum is '53', giving a total range of 0 to 106. The lower the score the better. The hip joint is divided into nine parts for assessment, the "marks" given to each section are added up for the total of each hip. The Flat-Coated Retriever Society comes within Dr Malcolm Willis's breed scoring scheme, a way of trying to ascertain the "norm" in a breed. Dr Willis says that the Breed has "good hip status". The "mean score" is 9-10. In the US, hip X-rays are certified when taken after 24 months of age and are submitted to the Orthopaedic Foundation for Animals (OFA), based in Columbia, Missouri. A permanent OFA number is then assigned.

PROGRESSIVE RETINAL ATROPHY

There are two forms of this inherited condition: central PRA and generalised PRA. An early indication of central PRA is night blindness, and the prognosis is total blindness. In generalised PRA, night blindness does not occur. The vision is severely affected, but may not result in total blindness. Eye examinations are usually carried out every one or two years, to ensure a dog is "clear", and therefore suitable to use for breeding.

FIRST AID KIT
Bottle of antiseptic
Tube of antiseptic cream
Wound powder
Small bottle of gentian violet (if available)
Small bottle of benzyl enzoate
Bottle of kaolin and morphine
Ear drops
Cotton wool
Bandages
Adhesive bandage
Blunt-end scissors
Tweezers
Eye dropper
Plastic syringe (5cc useful size) for giving liquid medicine
Thermometer, stubby bulb type
Worming tablets or suspension, according to preference.

    The big snag with a medicine chest is that the contents can remain unused for so long that something like, say, gentian violet tends to have dried out by the time you need it. On the other hand it is essential to have an emergency kit available for unexpected cuts in particular.

TEMPERATURE
Normal temperature is 38 to 39 degrees. To take a dog's temperature, shake down thermometer and apply a little Vaseline to bulb. Have a helper to hold dog firmly. Raise the dog's tail with one hand, and with the other insert the thermometer about 2.5 cms into rectum and hold it angled so that the bulb is against the rectal wall. Wait 30 seconds, remove thermometer and read. Shake down, clean and put the thermometer away. Care must be taken on insertion, so if in doubt, leave it for the vet to do.

COMMON AILMENTS
The following is emphatically not intended to be taken as veterinary advice; the comments are

from practical experience. The first essential is for the owner to be aware of the dog's normal behaviour and to recognise any deviation from this. It is quite possible for a Flat-Coated Retriever to live out life's span with no need for veterinary attention other than boosters.

But even the healthiest dog can have an accident or become unexpectedly ill. My main objective in mentioning some of the following conditions is to highlight the importance of seeking professional advice immediately, should the dog's behaviour and outlook show variation from the norm.

ANAL GLANDS

I have never had an anal gland problem with a Flat-Coat, but have with smaller breeds. The anal glands are situated in the rectum and should be squeezed out by pressure as faeces are passed. If the faeces are insufficiently bulky the glands do not receive enough pressure to do this. Signs are that the dog "toboggans" across the floor, to relieve the irritation; there may also be a smell. It is quite simple to squeeze out the glands but you need to be shown how, so have some tuition from your vet. Providing there is sufficient roughage in the dog's diet, the problem is unlikely to arise.

CUTS

Much depends on severity. Wire cuts can be treated with antiseptic, then either wound-powder or antiseptic cream. If deep and sharp, try to bind them immediately. If even more severe and in need of stitches, then get to the vet immediately. Never overlook the value of plain salt water as a healing agent for cuts.

DIGESTIVE PROBLEMS

In the dog, the stomach is relatively large and the bowels short, which means much of the digestive process is carried out in the stomach. In consequence it is quite easy for a dog to have an "upset" stomach. This is a valid reason for having regular feed times.

Diarrhoea may be from a sudden change in diet or may be of bacterial origin. If it is a matter simply of "loose" motions then a dose of kaolin and morphine should be effective. If motions are blood-stained or frothy, then seek advice at once.

Bloat, gastric dilation and torsion are conditions frequently, but not necessarily, related. Essentially, bloat is the production and retention of gases in the stomach. Puppies are likely to have mild bloat through over-eating, particularly when tired or excited. They may vomit. This degree of distension can usually be dealt with. It does indicate the need to change feeding patterns. Torsion is commonly called "twisted gut". The stomach twists on its axis. If torsion follows distension, gases are unable to escape. This condition is often fatal *so treatment is a matter of the utmost urgency.* If, after feeding, the dog is restless, appears distended, tries to vomit – but will be unable to do so because of the twist in the gut – appears to be an ill dog in fact, immediate action must be taken and the vet called.

CONSTIPATION

Usually connected with the type of feeding giving insufficient bulk. A sprinkle of bran on the food plus some green stuff should remedy this. If necessary a small dose of liquid paraffin should help. Do not let the condition continue as the rectum may become impacted.

EARS

The need for a weekly check was mentioned earlier, in the section on grooming. This should avoid any severe problems developing. However if, in spite of this precaution, the ear feels hot or the dog shakes its head or holds it to one side, then check at once. Some dogs get a heavyish brown wax in the ear. This can be controlled by cleaning the ear with a twist of cotton wool dipped in warm olive oil, or by using preparatory oil drops and then cleaning out with cotton wool. Some ears are very dry and can become closed up. An occasional wipe round with warm oil helps this condition. Never poke. If the ears are red, inflamed and/or smell, then get advice.

Ear mites: Where cats and dogs live together there is an added possibility of ear mites, which cause irritation and may need some specific treatment. With mites, the dog usually shakes its head. This should not be ignored, as at times, it can involve the dog banging the ear flap against a wall or something else solid, which can cause a haemotoma, burst blood vessels in the ear flap. In fact even vigorous head shaking alone can cause this.

EYES

For slight discharge, wiping with gauze and eye lotion or cold tea can help. Any excessive discharge or change in the appearance of the eye needs instant expert advice.

Entropion is an eye condition caused by in-growing eye-lashes: this causes irritation.

Ectropion is when the eye-lid turns outwards, which causes tears to form in the pouch formed by the lid, so the cornea dries out. Not common in Flat-Coats, although very occasionally entropion may occur. Again, get professional advice.

FEET

Nails. Mention was made of the need to keep nails cut in the section on grooming. This may not be necessary where the dog is on hard concrete or paving surfaces. It mainly applies to the dog largely on grass. Great care must be taken with black nails as it is not possible to see the "quick". Angle the cut backwards, then the dog wears down the underside when walking.

Pads. Cracked pads can be painful in winter. Salt and water washing can help, also putting on a thick ointment, although this is difficult with carpets. You can try putting a small sock over the foot until the ointment has been absorbed but Flat-Coats are very good at removing dressings.

Another cause of sore feet may be an allergy to certain types of carpet deodorisers in powder form or too high a concentration of disinfectant on hard floor surfaces.

THE SKIN

Eczema. This is something of a blanket term for skin problems. Usually, when the term 'eczema' is used, the person implies a breaking out of the skin, not necessarily of parasitic origin. It can be that the dog has had some irritation and has scratched, breaking the skin, or sometimes it seems to have dietary origin – what our grandmothers would have described as the blood "overheating". Attention must be immediate. The spread is incredibly rapid, the sore place will double its size overnight.

In the very early stages, benzyl benzoate can help, applied on cotton wool; or tetracycline spray or gentian violet if available. Diet should be very simple – rice and chicken or fish, green stuff, and give additional yeast tablets. If you are not containing the condition quite quickly by this treatment, get other advice.

Fleas and lice: These are another cause of skin problems. Fleas are harder to get rid of than lice. Fleas are reddish, hard-shelled and jump. Lice are somewhat inert, greyish and can be combed out. The flea is an intermediary host to tapeworm. Fleas and lice are in fact parasites.

To get rid of fleas, beds, bedding, indeed carpets and so on, all need treatment, as well as the dog, with one of the proprietary sprays or powders. There are now liquid drops which are specifically designed to be applied to one spot behind the neck, from where they are absorbed into the skin. Repeat monthly. Once the infestation is controlled, the use of a flea collar is said to act as a deterrent. Combing with a flea comb helps, even if only by its disturbing effect on the fleas. Once under control, there is a preparation which can be given in tablet form once monthly. The action is to break the fleas' life cycle by preventing the flea from laying fertile eggs.

Lice are far easier to control. Combing out with a fine nit-comb helps greatly. Burn combings. Obtain a specific shampoo from the vet and use as specified. Usually about three baths are needed at five to seven day intervals to kill adults and hatching larvae. Sprays can be used but seem less effective. It is worth a real onslaught.

Healthy skin comes very largely from within, so nutrition is of enormous importance.

Ticks: These are usually common to certain areas. The ticks feed on the dog's blood and distend. When removing the tick it is essential that the head is removed also. There is no totally foolproof method of removal. The tick can be dabbed with a spirit such as methylated spirits or even gin. It takes two or three minutes for this to have effect. Then with tweezers remove the tick, grasping it near, not on the mouth parts. Dab with antiseptic. More gin might do! Regular use of flea sprays in tick areas has been found to act as a deterrent.

Lyme Disease: Deer ticks can carry Lyme Disease – almost unheard of in the UK but prevalent in certain parts of the USA.

Mange mites: There are three types: Demodex which causes Demodectic mange; Sarcoptic which causes Sarcoptic mange (Scabies); and Otodectes, already mentioned as "ear mites". All these conditions need immediate veterinary treatment. The signs are various: reddened skin, pustules, scaly skin. The dog suffers great irritation.

PATELLA LUXATION
"Slipping kneecaps" in the hind legs. The incidence in Flat-Coats is low.

PERITONITIS
Inflammation of the peritoneum, the membrane lining the abdomen. Can be caused by ingesting some substance which has caused intense aggravation to the peritoneum. High temperature, distress, very likely vomiting. Prompt veterinary action essential.

PYOMETRA
Literally means pus in the womb. Usually develops some 6 to 8 weeks after being in season. The bitch is listless and obviously feels unwell. She may show excessive thirst and sometimes vomits. A smelly, pungent vaginal discharge is likely. There can be a "closed" pyometra, less easy to diagnose, as the discharge is not evident. If the bitch exhibits other symptoms – then better safe than sorry – seek advice from your vet.

TEETH
Sound teeth are important in maintaining a healthy dog. Particular care needs to be taken to keep gums firm and teeth clean, as so many present-day diets are soft, giving no stimulation to the gums. Many vets recommend the use of a canine toothpaste and daily brushing. Fortunately, we are still able to get fresh shin (marrow) bones. These are very hard and can be sawn into two or three sections. Gnawing these keeps the teeth clean and the gums hard. Although with advanced

age the teeth may be slightly worn down, they are quite sound. The cooked bones that are sold tend to be brittle and break up. It is possible to get boiled bones which are still hard and also a manufactured, very hard. bone-shaped "chew".

WORMS
These are internal parasites, the main ones that affect dogs being the round worms Toxocara canis or Toxascaris leonina, both of which live in the small intestine, and the tapeworm Diplidium caninum.

Roundworms live in the dog's intestines feeding on digesting food. They are particularly harmful to puppies as they penetrate the puppy's gut wall and pass via the blood to the liver and then the lungs. From there they crawl up the trachea to be coughed up and swallowed; they are then back in the gut! As the puppy gets older most of the worms travel to the muscles and lie dormant as cysts. When a bitch becomes pregnant, they migrate to the embryo puppies' lungs. Virtually every puppy is born with worms to a lesser or greater degree. You can now see why I stressed the importance of a regular and effective worming programme for all puppies and dogs.

Tapeworms are transmitted by fleas in which the larvae develop. The adult tapeworm can be very long and is segmented. It is the segments that are passed out and can be seen near the dog's anus – little flat white wriggly segments.

While it is possible to treat either roundworms or tapeworms separately there are some very effective broad-spectrum wormers available. Work out a worming programme with your vet. If you have cats, remember they must be included in the programme. Also remember that fleas, sheep, and rabbits act as intermediary hosts to tapeworms. This leads on, automatically, to the removal of faeces.

DISPOSAL OF FAECES
Absolutely essential that all faecal matter is collected and dealt with immediately. If only a few dogs are involved, there is a chemical available which breaks down the faeces. The chemical is put into a covered bucket-type container and the faeces are dropped into this. I think it is an enzyme action. With larger numbers of dogs there are probably incinerator facilities. although it is amazing how long it takes to burn this waste matter.

A follow-on from the question of disposal of faeces, is the disgusting habit some dogs acquire of disposing of faeces themselves. There is a name for it, coprophagia. This eating of faeces is something which has become far more prevalent over the past 15 or so years. Years ago, one never heard of it in normal circumstances. I wonder if it is connected with the high level of nutrition and the amount of flavouring in many present-day foods which comes through in the "droppings". This seems more likely than the widely held view of a deficiency in the diet. The main essential is to remove the temptation. I have heard (but have no proof) that some chopped-up kipper on the food gives an unattractive smell to faeces. Sprinkling pepper on faeces and leaving them is said to act as a deterrent but, again, does not seem foolproof. This habit is common to all breeds, not only Flat-Coated Retrievers. Removal of temptation from puppyhood so that the habit never starts is important and, with an older dog, a scolding if caught in the act.

If you are out with your dog, always have a supply of plastic bags or a "pooper scooper" with you, not only because in many areas there are now enforced fouling laws, but also to avoid offence to others. Sheer hygiene, in fact.

ADMINISTERING MEDICINES
Try to avoid a battle. It is better to hold the dog firmly but gently. Holding very forcibly tends to

make the dog apprehensive. I find it helps to put a smear of butter on a tablet. Insert your left thumb in the mouth across the lower jaw, then draw back slightly, still holding mouth ajar. Speed helps. With your other hand insert the tablet right at the back of the throat and give a gentle shove down the gullet. Hold the mouth closed for a few seconds.

Liquids can be given either in a spoon at the side of the mouth, again closing and holding the mouth, or the syringes, mentioned in the list, are ideal for administering liquids. Far better than a spoon.

Should restraining be necessary, an easy "muzzle" can be made by using a stocking or a tie.

Chapter Seven

THE BREED STANDARDS

Basically any Breed Standard is a written description of the ideal animal of the breed in question. The Kennel Clubs are responsible for compiling Breed Standards, usually in consultation with Breed clubs. A few years ago, the UK Kennel Club decided to standardise all its Standards. Unfortunately this had the effect of losing some of the descriptive passages which helped one visualise the breed in question. Also, with Flat-Coated Retrievers, there has never been a definite size requirement – there is a preferred size but this is very elastic, largely because it had always been recognised that varied terrains and different types of shooting required slightly different physical characteristics, although basically the same dog. In the present Standard, size is mentioned, although it must be emphasised, still only as "preferred" height. The FCI Standard is the same as the one for the UK.

The American Breed Standard is longer and more descriptive than the British one, and I always use it for talks or seminars. Currently the Flat-Coated Retriever Society of America is working on an illustrated standard which will surely prove helpful, especially as it is in the capable and experienced hands of Sally Terroux and her knowledgeable team. I actually feel that the American standard is so comprehensive that there is not a great deal further that needs saying, other than personal observations and comments.

The Swedish Retriever Club recently brought out an illustrated Standard, an extension of a previous one that the long-standing devotee of the breed, Ingemar Borelius, set out. It is extremely well-produced with some good photographs. I believe it was compiled by a panel which included Ingemar and other experienced Flat-Coated Retriever breeders.

Before reading any Standard, it is helpful to study the anatomy of the dog, as it is essential to understand this, as well as the points of the dog.

BRITISH BREED STANDARD

GENERAL APPEARANCE: A bright active dog of medium size with an intelligent expression, showing power without lumber, and raciness without weediness.

CHARACTERISTICS: Generously endowed with natural gun dog ability, optimism and friendliness demonstrated by enthusiastic tail action.

TEMPERAMENT: Confident and kindly.

HEAD AND SKULL: Head, long and nicely moulded. Skull, flat and moderately broad with

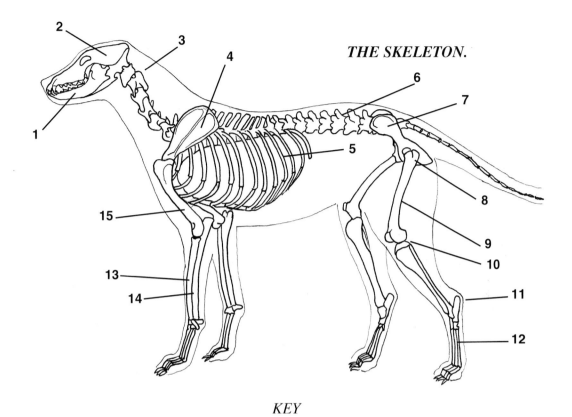

THE SKELETON.

KEY

1. Jaw bone
2. Cranium
3. Neck vertebrae
4. Shoulder blade (Scapula)
5. Rib cage
6. Lumbar vertebrae
7. Pelvic girdle
8. Hip joint (Pelvic girdle fits into acetabulum)

9. Femur
10. Knee joint (Stifle)
11. Hock joint
12. Pastern
13. Radius
14. Ulna
15. Humerus

a slight stop between eyes, in no way accentuated, avoiding a down or dish-faced appearance. Nose of good size, with open nostrils. Jaws long and strong, capable of carrying a hare or pheasant.

EYES: Medium size, dark brown or hazel, with a very intelligent expression (a round prominent eye highly undesirable). Not obliquely placed.

EARS: Small and well set on, close to side of head.

KEY

1. Muzzle
2. Stop
3. Skull
4. Withers
5. Back
6. Loin
7. Croup
8. Tail set
9. Point of hock
10. Pastern

11. Second thigh
12. Stifle
13. Thigh
14. Elbow
15. Forearm
16. Brisket (sternum)
17. Shoulder
18. Neck
19. Rib cage

MOUTH: Jaws strong with a perfect, regular and complete scissor bite, i.e. upper teeth closely overlapping the lower teeth and set square to the jaws. Teeth sound and strong.

NECK: Head well set in neck, the latter reasonably long and free from throatiness, symmetrically set and obliquely placed in shoulders, running well into the back to allow for easy seeking of trail.

FOREQUARTERS: Chest, deep and fairly broad, with well defined brisket, on which elbows should move cleanly and evenly. Forelegs straight, with bone of good quality throughout.

BODY: Fore ribs fairly flat. Body, well ribbed-up showing a gradual spring and well arched in centre but rather lighter towards quarters. Loin short and square. Open couplings highly undesirable.

HINDQUARTERS: Muscular. Moderate bend of stifle and hock, latter well let down. Should stand true all round. Cowhocks highly undesirable.

FEET: Round and strong with toes close and well arched. Soles thick and strong.

TAIL: Short, straight and well set on, gaily carried, but never much above level of back.

GAIT/MOVEMENT: Free and flowing, straight and true as seen from front and rear.

COAT: Dense, of fine to medium texture and good quality, as flat as possible. Legs and tail well feathered. Full furnishings on maturity complete the elegance of a good dog.

COLOUR: Black or Liver only.

SIZE: Preferred weight in hard conditions: Dogs 25-35 kgs (60-80 lbs); Bitches 25-34 kgs (55-70 lbs). Preferred height: Dogs 58-61 cms (23-24 ins); Bitches 56-59 cms (22-23 ins).

FAULTS: Any departure from the foregoing points should be considered a fault and the seriousness with which the fault should be regarded should be in exact proportion to its degree.

NOTE: Male animals should have two apparently normal testicles fully descended into the scrotum.

(Reproduced by kind permission of the Kennel Club)

AMERICAN BREED STANDARD

GENERAL APPEARANCE: The Flat-Coated Retriever is a versatile family companion hunting retriever with a happy and active demeanour, intelligent expression, and clean lines. The Flat-Coat has been traditionally described as showing "power without lumber and raciness without weediness".

The distinctive and most important features of the Flat-Coat are the silhouette (both moving and standing), smooth effortless movement, head type, coat and character. In silhouette the Flat-Coat has a long, strong, clean, "one-piece" head, which is unique to the breed. Free from exaggeration of stop or cheek, the head is set well into a moderately long neck which flows smoothly into well laid back shoulders. A level topline combined with a deep, long rib cage tapering to a moderate tuck-up create the impression of a blunted triangle. The brisket is well developed and the forechest forms a prominent prow. This utilitarian retriever is well balanced, strong, but elegant; never cobby, short legged or rangy. The coat is thick and flat lying, and the legs and tail are well feathered. A proud carriage, responsive attitude, waving tail and overall look of functional strength, quality, style and symmetry complete the picture of the typical Flat-Coat.

Judging the Flat-Coat moving freely on a loose lead and standing naturally is more important that judging him posed. Honourable scars should not count against the dog.

SIZE, PROPORTION, SUBSTANCE: Size – Individuals varying more than an inch either way from the preferred height should be considered not practical for the types of work for which the Flat-Coat was developed. Preferred height is 23 to 24.5 inches at the withers for dogs, 22 to 23.5 inches for bitches. Since the Flat-Coat is a working hunting retriever he should be shown in lean, hard condition, free of excess weight. Proportion – The Flat-Coat is not cobby in build. The length of the body from the point of the shoulder to the rearmost projection of the upper thigh is slightly more than the height at the withers. The female may be slightly longer to better accommodate the carrying of puppies. Substance – Moderate. Medium bone is flat or oval rather than round; strong but never massive, coarse, weedy or fine. This applies throughout the dog.

HEAD: The long, clean, well moulded head is adequate in size and strength to retrieve a large pheasant, duck or hare with ease.

SKULL AND MUZZLE: The impression of the skull and muzzle being "cast in one piece" is created by the fairly flat skull of moderate breadth and flat, clean cheeks, combined with the long, strong, deep muzzle which is well filled in before, between and beneath the eyes. Viewed from above, the muzzle is nearly equal in length and breadth to the skull.

STOP: There is a gradual, slight, barely perceptible stop, avoiding a down or dish-faced appearance. Brows are slightly raised and mobile, giving life to the expression. Stop must be evaluated in profile so that it will not be confused with the raised brow. Occiput not accentuated, the skull forming a gentle curve where it fits well into the neck.

EXPRESSION: alert, intelligent and kind.

EYES: are set widely apart. Medium sized, almond shaped, dark brown or hazel; not large, round or yellow. Eye rims are self-coloured and tight.

EARS: relatively small, well set on, lying close to the side of the head and thickly feathered. Not low set (houndlike or setterish).

NOSE: Large open nostrils. Black on black dogs, brown on liver dogs. Lips fairly tight, firm, clean and dry to minimize the retention of feathers.

JAWS: long and strong, capable of carrying a hare or a pheasant.

BITE: Scissor bite preferred, level bite acceptable. Broken teeth should not count against the dog.

SEVERE FAULTS: Wry and undershot or overshot bites with a noticeable gap must be severely penalized.

NECK, TOPLINE, BODY: Neck strong and slightly arched for retrieving strength.

Moderately long to allow for easy seeking of the trail. Free from throatiness. Coat on neck is untrimmed.

Topline strong and level. Body – Chest (Brisket) – Deep, reaching to the elbow and only moderately broad. Forechest: Prow prominent and well developed. Rib cage deep, showing good length from forechest to last rib (to allow ample space for all body organs), and only moderately broad. The foreribs fairly flat showing a gradual spring, well arched in the centre of the body but rather lighter towards the loin. Underline: Deep chest tapering to a moderate tuck-up. Loin strong, well muscled and long enough to allow for agility, freedom of movement and length of stride, but never weak or loosely coupled. Croup slopes very slightly; rump moderately broad and well muscled. Tail fairly straight, well set on, with bone reaching approximately to the hock joint. When the dog is in motion, the tail is carried happily but without curl as a smooth extension of the topline, never much above the level of the back.

FOREQUARTERS: Shoulders long, well laid back shoulder blade with upper arm of approximately equal length to allow for efficient reach. Musculature wiry rather than bulky. Elbows clean, close to the body and set well back under the withers. Forelegs straight and strong with medium bone of good quality. Pasterns slightly sloping and strong. Dewclaws – Removal of dewclaws is optional. Feet oval or round. Medium sized and tight with well arched toes and thick pads.

HINDQUARTERS: Powerful with angulation in balance with the front assembly. Upper thighs powerful and well muscled. Stifle – Good turn of stifle with sound, strong joint. Second thighs (Stifle to hock joint) -–Second or lower thigh as long as or only slightly longer than upper thigh. Hock – Hock joint strong, well let down. Dewclaws – There are no hind dewclaws. Feet oval or round. Medium sized and tight with well arched toes and thick pads.

COAT: Coat is of moderate length, density and fullness, with a high lustre. The ideal coat is straight and flat lying. A slight waviness is permissible but the coat is not curly, woolly, short, silky or fluffy. The Flat-Coat is a working retriever and the coat must provide protection from all types of weather, water and ground cover. This requires a coat of sufficient texture, length and fullness to allow for adequate insulation. When the dog is in full coat the ears, front, chest, back of forelegs, thighs and underside of tail are thickly feathered without being bushy, stringy or silky. Mane of longer heavier coat on the neck extending over the withers and shoulders is considered typical, especially in the male dog, and can cause the neck to appear thicker and the withers higher, sometimes causing the appearance of a dip behind the withers. Since the Flat-Coat is a hunting retriever, the feathering is not excessively long. Trimming: The Flat-Coat is shown with as natural a coat as possible and must not be penalized for lack of trimming, as long as the coat is clean and well brushed. Tidying of ears, feet, underline and tip of tail is acceptable. Whiskers serve a specific function and it is preferred that they not be trimmed. Shaving or barbering of the head, neck or body coat must be severely penalized.

COLOR: Solid black or solid liver. Disqualification – Yellow, cream or any color other than black or liver.

GAIT: Sound, efficient movement is of critical importance to a hunting retriever. The Flat-

Coat viewed from the side covers ground efficiently and movement appears balanced, free flowing and well co-ordinated, never choppy, mincing or ponderous. Front and rear legs reach well forward and extend well back, achieving long clean strides. Topline appears level, strong and supple while dog is in motion.

SUMMARY: The Flat-Coat is a strong but elegant, cheerful hunting retriever. Quality of structure, balance and harmony of all parts both standing and in motion are essential. As a breed whose purpose is of a utilitarian nature – structure, condition and attitude should give every indication of being suited for hard work.

Temperament: Character is a primary and outstanding asset of the Flat-Coat. He is a responsive, loving member of the family, a versatile working dog, multi-talented, sensible, bright and tractable. In competition the Flat-Coat demonstrates stability and a desire to please with a confident, happy and outgoing attitude characterised by a wagging tail. Nervous, hyperactive, apathetic, shy or obstinate behaviour is undesirable. Severe Fault – Unprovoked aggressive behaviour toward people or animals is totally unacceptable. Character is as important to the evaluation of stock by a potential breeder as any other aspect of the breed standard. The Flat-Coat is primarily a family companion hunting retriever. He is keen and birdy, flushing within gun range, as well as a determined, resourceful retriever on land and water. He has a great desire to hunt with self-reliance and an uncanny ability to adapt to changing circumstances on a variety of upland game and waterfowl.

As a family companion he is sensible, alert and highly intelligent; a lighthearted, affectionate and adaptable friend. He retains these qualities as well as his youthfully good-humored outlook on life into old age. The adult Flat-Coat is usually an adequate alarm dog to give warning, but is a good-natured, optimistic dog, basically inclined to be friendly to all.

The Flat-Coat is a cheerful, devoted companion who requires and appreciates living with and interacting as a member of his family. To reach full potential in any endeavor he absolutely must have a strong personal bond and affectionate individual attention.

DISQUALIFICATION: Yellow, cream or any color other than black or liver.

(Reproduced by kind permission of The American Kennel Club)

CLARIFICATION
GENERAL APPEARANCE
The first impression is important: it is that which, particularly in silhouette, makes you say "a Flat-Coated Retriever". The silhouette is so distinctive: there should be a gentle, flowing effect from head through to wagging tail, no square corners or a match box effect with a leg at each corner. Proportions are all-important, giving a well-balanced dog, with each part of the body merging easily and almost unnoticeably into the next. An essential part of the overall impression should also be of a dog that is full of life and energy. No couch potatoes, these. What the appearance should _not_ be, is that of a longhaired Labrador, a black Golden Retriever or a black Irish Setter.

TEMPERAMENT AND CHARACTER
These I would regard in parallel. Both all important, neither should ever be overlooked in favour of purely physical attributes. The Flat-Coated Retriever should have a confident, outgoing temperament combined with responsiveness and biddability. At times, admittedly, the Flat-Coat

Int. Swiss, Monaco, Austrian, German, Ger. VDH Ch. Swallowsflight Black Oberon: Three times top Swiss Flat-Coated Retriever, twice top male. Bred by Leonie Galderman (Holland), owned by Joseph Joller. The Flat-Coat's outline should be gentle and flowing with no square corners.

sense of fun can emerge, usually at the least appropriate moment. Unless a person is prepared to accept the occasional juvenile behaviour, then that person is better without a Flat-Coat. It is perhaps not so much juvenile as joyous. Every day is a good day and needs living to the full.

Extremes of temperament, either nervousness, hyperactivity or unprovoked aggression are not typical and should be regarded as faults, i.e. unacceptable. The Flat-Coat is one of the most people-oriented of dogs, totally devoted to owner and family, kindly in outlook and amazingly adaptable to changes in circumstances, particularly when still with the dog's own "person". As we have seen earlier, the Flat-Coat also has inherent abilities for work in the shooting field. Even tiny puppies will be found carrying any stick or toy they come across.

Owning a Flat-Coat is a very real commitment of time and energy; the dog's character is such that this is needed. If you cannot give this, as a small return for the devotion you will receive, then again, don't have a Flat-Coated Retriever.

HEAD AND SKULL
Stanley O'Neill despaired until the day he died over the lack of understanding of what constituted a "good head". This was largely because, for many years, there were so few "specialist" judges, and "all-rounders" had no clear guidelines. To some extent the problem still exists. I think it is the degree of "stop" that causes confusion. The Flat-Coat head is so totally individual with its characteristic moulding, almost as if in one piece.

ABOVE: Heronsflight Herald To Torwood, bred by Joan Mason and Rosemary Talbot, owned by Denise Jury.
The stop should be visible, but not accentuated.

LEFT: Ger. Lux. Ned. VDH Int. Ch. Branchalwood Goil, owned by Nicola Bscher in Germany: The distinctive Flat-Coat head.

THE SKULL

The skull, we are told, should be flat and moderately broad, so one has to ask "What is moderately broad?" Well, not the width of say, a Golden Retriever skull, nor with the rounding. The flatness can best be assessed by holding the ears down; it makes an enormous difference. The skull runs into the muzzle with a slight stop, in other words there is a "stop", not a straight line. The "stop" is visible but not accentuated, which would give the impression of skull and muzzle being in two parts that are joined. One also has to allow for the expressive use of eyebrows and ears. When attention is alerted, ears and eyebrows are lifted and the whole profile is changed.

EGG HEADS

Quite incorrect is the head with no stop at all. In fact, between the eyes is convex, giving an egg shape akin to an English Bull Terrier. A slack throat often goes with this type of head. Clever handlers place a hand under the throat, pulling the skin tight. Clever judges know what they are doing!

THE MUZZLE

The muzzle should be about equal in length to the skull, the lips having no slackness but closing tightly, top jaw over bottom. No "floppy flews", as I call them. My personal reference is for a blunt-ended muzzle rather than the "pencil" muzzle.

NOSE

This needs to be of good size, with widely opening nostrils for scenting. The colour is black or brown depending on colour of dog.

EYES

Eyes should be medium-sized and almost almond-shaped but not narrowed or slanting; neither should they be round and/or prominent. Lower lids need to fit tightly to avoid seeds, grit etc. gaining access. Colour should be dark brown or hazel, which is defined as being reddish-brown. Note, there is nothing here to say that an excessively dark i.e. practically black eye is desirable. The almost black eye is frequently oblique also, giving an uncharacteristically hard expression. A yellow or distinctly yellowish/greeny/brown eye is a fault: it is the so called "gooseberry" eye. The expression is very important and should be kindly and intelligent.

EARS

As stated, they are relatively small, and set close to head. The ears should be set about level with a line from the outer corner of the eyes. They are used very expressively.

MOUTH

Strong jaws are essential; the upper teeth should fit tightly just over the lower. Until recently the standard stated that a level bite is acceptable in an otherwise good representative of the Breed. Level bite means when the top and lower teeth meet exactly. In a good dog I will still go along with that, but no deviation beyond that. Overshot – the upper teeth not only over the lower, but with a gap between; undershot – the bottom teeth protruding in front of the upper teeth, or wry mouths (in fact this is more a deformed jaw than actual dentition) are unacceptable and are faults.

Int. Dutch, Belg. Lux. Fr. Ger. VDH Ch. No Other Way Eurohof. Owned and trained by Ellen Hageman-Leoff.
The Flat-Coat must have a muscular neck and a strong muzzle in order to retrieve.

NECK

The head, neck and shoulders should all run into one another smoothly. Obviously the neck must be long enough to allow for reaching down when scenting (although many Flat-Coats air-scent more than other Retrievers). Also the neck must be muscular to allow for carrying game. This muscling often gives the impression of a slight curve on the top. The neck runs obliquely into the shoulder. The throat itself should be tight-skinned (clean throated) with no slackness.

SHOULDERS

These are so important that I am surprised that so little is said. The neck runs into the shoulder; the angle of the actual shoulder blade is of extreme importance, as this, combined with the upper arm, largely controls the forward extension (reach) of the front legs. A shoulder blade that is verging toward upright limits the length of stride. This is the meaning behind the phrase "well-laid shoulder"; the scapula (shoulder blade) is angled at about 45 degrees, obliquely back to allow a wider angle of movement. Short necks and upright shoulders invariably go together.

FOREQUARTERS

The chest needs to have depth and width to accommodate heart and, more particularly, lungs. The heart will go on pumping away in its incredible way. The lungs need room to expand and deflate. The well-defined brisket is very significant to the Breed. In fact, when the term "good brisket" is used in critiques, what is usually meant is that the sternum is well developed. This gives the shape to the front of the Flat-Coat. By running a hand down the chest, the "hook" of the sternum can be felt, and also seen, in profile. The hand does not (or should not!) disappear in a hollow between the front legs. The term "prow" is highly descriptive and apt. Elbows should fit tightly against the body. A "barrel" chest tends to push the elbows out. Forelegs should be straight, with hard oval bone running into well-knuckled and padded feet.

Claverdon Gaff clearing a fence at a British Field Sports Society Test. This demonstrates correct shoulder placement for front extension, a strong back, and muscular hindquarters.

BODY
Again proportions and balance are so essential. The present standard does not mention that the body should be relatively long and this leads to misunderstandings. The body should be long over the ribs but the couplings (between last rib and the pelvic girdle) should be short. The ribs need to be fairly flat showing gradual spring. The body tapers off slightly underneath giving a "tuck up". Strong loins are essential, as is the close coupling.

HINDQUARTERS
Again these must be balanced with the rest of the body. The actual hindquarters should be well muscled to complement the structure. A moderate bend of stifle facilitates the ability to give impetus and drive when moving. The upper and lower thighs should be almost equal in length, although the lower may be slightly longer. The hock joint should be strong and well let down to add impetus to the hindquarter assembly. Cow hocks (when the hock joints are angled in toward one another) are to be deprecated.

FEET
Should be round and well knuckled. The pads should be deep and closely together. You know the old saying, "no foot, no horse". Much the same can be said of a Retriever.

TAIL
The last vertebra should reach to the point of the hock. The croup has a slight curve where the vertebrae run into the tail. When the tail is raised to wag, this straightens out the topline. Good feathering helps protect the tail from thorn damage.

GAIT/MOVEMENT
This is so important in a working dog. The dog needs to cover ground economically. The construction that has been discussed is now brought into use. The shoulder and upper arm aid the forward extension, with the hindquarters pushing off strongly, so that the dog covers the ground easily and with economy of effort. Front extension can be seen most clearly from the side. The dog should flow. Hind and front movement can be assessed as the dog moves away and returns. The dog should move straight and "true". In fact, frequently it is the handler who is incapable of moving in a straight line!

COAT
The description in the present UK standard is somewhat inadequate, I feel. Mention is made of density and of texture (fine to medium) and there is comment on the elegance of the full-coated, mature dog (true), but the practical aspect is hardly acknowledged other than by the word "dense". As this is a working dog, the coat must provide protection both from weather and also from thorns, wire and so on. I suppose "dense" does cover these hazards. It should also have waterproof properties. I would prefer the emphasis on medium texture rather than "fine".

   The coat should be gleaming black (or liver) and preferably flat, although a slight degree of flat i.e. not curly, wave is permissible. Adult males in particular often develop a mane of thicker hair over the neck and withers. When mature and in full coat, as stated, the feathering certainly does add to the elegance of the dog. Trimming should be tidying not barbering; on no account should the neck and front be clipped out as is the practice with some other gundog breeds.

COLOUR
Black or Liver only. No other colour is acceptable.

Ch. Pluto and Kaisa, owned by Tone Loken in Norway.
The Flat-Coat can be black or liver-coloured. The coat must be dense and weather-resistant.

SIZE
As mentioned previously, these are preferred, not a hard and fast requirement.
Preferred weight in hard condition: Dogs 28 to 36 kgs (60 to 80 lbs); Bitches 25 to 32 kgs (55 to 70 lbs)
Preferred height: Dogs 58 to 61 cms (23 to 24 ins) to withers; Bitches 56 to 59 cms (22 to 23 ins) to withers
A 1977 clarification of the Standard stated: "Variation in size should be ample to cater for different types of work in the field, but classical conformation must not be sacrificed by extremes."

FAULTS
The statement on this is self-explanatory, the operative phrase perhaps being "the seriousness with which the fault should be regarded should be in exact proportion to its degree". Therein lies the difficulty. It sounds easy, but comes down to individual decision on degrees of importance. You may remember I said that I will accept a level bite in an otherwise good dog. Conversely I feel construction faults e.g. upright shoulders, cow hocks, lack of sufficient angulation in hindquarters, to be of major importance. Also aesthetically displeasing is the very light (gooseberry) eye.

To me the other "fault" which warrants firm and decisive action is that of the dog with an aggressive attitude even though unprovoked. This is not the male who gives a quick warning "lay off" to another male who, for example, sniffs his rear end; this happens particularly when both are on leashes. In fact the owner of the "sniffing" dog should have the dog under closer control. While unprovoked aggression may, of course, be brought about by extreme circumstances, it still is not acceptable. Male animals must have two descended testicles. Full stop!

To sum up: the perfect dog has not yet been born, so everything is relative. Balance and proportion are important. The Standard for the Flat-Coated Retriever is an essentially practical one and the requirements are to suit the purpose for which the dog was originally evolved. There is a telling phrase which is no longer included in the standard and this was to the effect that the dog should have "no exaggeration" of any part. It is essential to remember this.

Chapter Eight

SHOWING YOUR FLAT-COAT

There are various routes to the show ring. The most frequent is the owner who buys a companion puppy who is subsequently much admired so the owner thinks: "Why not go in for a show?" The irony of this is that so often the original request was for "just a companion puppy, not one for showing" – the whole point being that, had the breeder been able to see into the future, the new owner would probably have had a different puppy! The other route is via another breed, in which case the new owner usually states the intention to show very clearly.

Always remember that no breeder can guarantee that a puppy will be a top show prospect – potential, yes, guarantee, no. Certainly, dog showing can open up a whole new world of getting up at ungodly hours, travelling vast distances – just sometimes returning home on a cloud with the return journey apparently half as far as the outward one. Dog showing is frequently a series of "highs" and "lows" and if you can't take the "lows", forget it.

TYPES OF SHOWS
In the UK all shows have to be licensed at the Kennel Club and all dogs entered must have Kennel Club registration. There is, as always, an exception. Exemption shows are not held under KC rules and regulations (except that the type of classes are specified). Both registered and unregistered dogs can be shown. Organisations or persons wishing to hold an Exemption Show must apply to the Kennel Club. The wide range of classes at British shows differs from other countries in that an exhibit can be entered in a number of classes if eligible. Clear definition of classes is given in schedules. Some classes have an age definition, others on wins.

Exemption show
4 Pedigree classes
4 Novelty classes. Waggiest tail/most like owner and so on.
Matches
Entry is limited to members of the Canine Society in question.
Matches are usually run on a knock-out basis, sometimes within the Club or sometimes as in inter-club event.
Primary shows
Very rarely used. Entry limited to members of the Canine Club/Society.
No class higher than a "Maiden".
Sanction shows
Entry again limited to CS members with a different range of classes available, for example, no class higher than post-graduate.

Handling American style: Gillian Impey with Am. Ch. Quillcrest Heaven Sent (co-owner Kathie Newitt).

Ashbey Photography.

Handling British style: Sh. Ch. Braemist Dusky Queen: Best bitch and RBIS at the FCRS Ch. Show 1995. Bred and owned by Val Jones. In the UK the Flat-Coat is shown on a loose lead.

Limited shows

Entry limited to CS members or may be a restricted geographic radius.

All the above shows have the same restriction, which is:

"Dogs which have won a Challenge Certificate or obtained any award that counts toward the title of Champion under the rules of any governing body recognised by the Kennel Club are not eligible for entry at these shows."

Open shows

Open to all exhibitors. No CCs.

Championship shows

Open to all breeds or Breed Clubs.

Challenge certificates are offered to breeds as approved by the Kennel Club. At a Championship show where Challenge certificates are on offer for the Breed there is a Challenge Certificate (CC) for the Best dog in the Breed, on the day, and a CC for the Best bitch in the Breed; there are also Reserve Challenge certificates in each sex (RCCs). Best of Breed (BoB) is decided from the dog CC and bitch CC winners.

To become a Champion (Show Champion in the case of a Gundog), the dog must obtain three challenge certificates under three different judges.

The qualifier

A gundog needs to obtain a Kennel Club Show Gundog Working Certificate to attain full Champion status.

AMERICAN SHOWS

The AKC lists some eight different types of shows, similar in some respects to the UK range, in that at some shows championship show points are awarded and at others they are not. In the same way, a show may be for a restricted entry with a definite specification.

Gillian Impey, **Quillquest** Flat-Coated Retrievers, has kindly sent information on the most usual types of show.

Championship shows

These can be Group/All-Breed or Specialty (the Club show). The Specialty can be held on its own, or as part of another Championship show. The AKC Gazette lists these shows and will send information on request. Premium lists (known as schedules in UK) will be sent on application to the show supervisor. After the closing date for entries, passes, catalogue numbers etc. are sent to exhibitors.

Championship status is gained on a point system: a total of 15 points under three different judges. This must include two "majors" i.e. a 3, 4, or 5 point win under two different judges. The number of points depends on the number of dogs competing. This is explained in the following paragraphs.

USA DOG SHOW PROCEDURES

All-Breed dog shows

All-Breed Dog shows are open to all breeds registered with the American Kennel Club. The ages are from six months on.

Regular classes

1. PUPPY: 6-12 months of age as long as the dog is not a finished Champion.

2. TWELVE-EIGHTEEN MONTHS: The dog must be twelve months or over yet under eighteen months of age.

3. NOVICE: 6 months and over, open for dogs who have not won a 1st place in Bred-by-Exhibitor, American-Bred or Open Classes and who have not won three first places in the Novice Class.

4. BRED-BY-EXHIBITOR: This class is for dogs whelped in the USA and owned and bred by the exhibitor.

5. AMERICAN-BRED: This class is for all dogs 6 months and up that have been bred in the USA.

6. OPEN: Any dog 6 months and up can be entered in this class. Normally this class is for a fairly mature dog.

All the first-place dogs are eligible to compete for Winners, and points are given to the dog who wins this class. He/she then goes on to compete for the Best-of-Breed, Best of Opposite Sex and Best of Winners. Best of Winners can be awarded additional points if there are more dogs in the other winners' classes. Points can also be made by taking Best of Breed or Best of Opposite over Champions. Additional points can be made by winning in the Groups (1st through 4th placing dogs). Flat-Coats would be in the Sporting Group. Placing in the Group would give additional points, to a maximum of 5 at any one show.

Specialty shows

Specialty Shows are given by the National Club (Flat-Coated Retriever Society of America) once a year in Flat-Coats. The same point system as above. There are additional classes offered as non-regular classes. Points are not earned from these classes.

1. Veterans' Classes: These classes are for dogs 7 years and up.

2. Field Trial Classes: Both winners are eligible for Best-of-Breed but no points are given towards a Championship.

3. Brace Classes: These classes are for two dogs owned by the same owner.

4. Stud Dog Classes: Brood Bitch Class: Two progeny are judged to be awarded Best Stud and Best Brood bitch. Progeny only are judged – not the actual stud dog or brood bitch.

Supported entry

A supported entry is "supported" by a Regional Club and the Flat-Coated Retriever Society of America Parent Club. This show takes place at an All-Breed show – with special trophies awarded through the regional Flat-Coated club – to make it a supported entry.

Sweepstakes

This is a non-regular additional competition, which awards no points and is open for puppies divided 6-9 months, 9-12 months, 12-18 months.

Trophies and prizes are awarded to the 1st through 4th placing dogs – and the Best of Breed and Best of Opposite Sex winners. Sweepstakes are held in conjunction with a Specialty and can also be at a Supported Entry.

Veteran Sweepstakes can also be given as additional shows, with the Puppy Sweepstakes. Veteran Sweepstakes are usually divided 7-9 years, 10-11 years and 12 years and over.

Matches

These are held all over the country. Information is given in a Match Show Bulletin and most dog clubs can supply information on forthcoming matches. Matches are in effect, practice shows: they may be for Obedience and/or conformation and they provide a good training ground both for pups and young dogs as well as for Novice exhibitors and handlers. Champions may not be shown at Matches and no points are awarded.

Entries for "point shows" usually have to be in some 3 to 4 weeks before the show (matches can be entered on the ground). Faxes are accepted. Passes etc. are usually received about a week before the show with details of when the class is on, ring number and number of entries. Always check that the dog's name is stated correctly. Gillian Impey also mentioned the need to allow plenty of time for travel to the show and makes the point that the dog's show preparation needs to be done in advance.

Breed Club National Specialties usually attract a large entry; the judge is someone held in respect in the Breed and at times is an overseas breeder of long standing. The Specialty changes location each year. It needs to – no one area would survive the enormous preparation needed for the week's activities. Pretty well every aspect of the breed is covered – Show, Field, Agility, Educational seminars. An incredible task to be undertaken each year, with exhibitors travelling from all directions by car and plane, frequently several thousand miles, to have a wonderful get-together.

RING TRAINING IN THE UK

Puppies may not be shown until they are six months or over. If the show lasts over more than one day, the puppy must be six months on the first day of the show, to be eligible for entry. Many Ringcraft classes will accept puppies from about 4 months providing the puppy is fully immunised. We have already mentioned the value of getting puppies out to socialise and also to become used to being handled by strangers. It is quite a good idea to take puppy to Ringcraft for a couple of times just to watch before actually taking part, it is amazing how much they assimilate.

Unlike many breeds the Flat-Coat should be shown free-standing. If you go to a class where this is not known, then stand your ground and don't be talked into squatting on the ground holding head and tail out-stretched.

The dog should be on a slack lead. With a youngster, keep just enough "feel" that the dog realises you are in control. Let the dog stand naturally, and keep talking quietly to maintain the dog's attention and the tail gently wagging.

When in the ring, keep concentrating, both on the dog and on the judge. Frequently, a judge will have quick looks around the ring comparing the dog under inspection with ones seen previously.

Also, if you are fortunate enough to be in the "line-up", don't stop concentrating until the cards are handed out. There can always be a last-minute change in the placings.

The giving of 'tidbits' to keep the dog alert and attentive has become excessive. Do restrict this practice to having something that appeals to the dog but limit the amount actually given. Also from a judge's view point, I for one strongly object to trying to assess bite and dentition when the teeth are packed with liver or cheese.

PREPARING YOUR DOG

Ann Youens is someone very skilled at preparing dogs either for the show ring or just to look good at home. She gives the following professional advice on how to make the most of your Flat-Coated Retriever.

1. Grooming. Thoroughly brush the coat the way the hair grows, removing all tangles and any undergrowth collected on the tail and feathers.

2. Stand back, pretend this is not your dog, be critical and consider how you can improve the appearance. You want to try and convince the judge this is the best dog there!

3. Trimming should be started several days before the show to ensure a natural look.

4. Feet. Trim the feet by pulling hair up between the toes, trim with thinning scissors or very carefully with ordinary hairdresser's scissors; quite often this is brownish, dead, hair.

To tidy underneath the feet, pull excess hair down and cut off (I find curved blunt-ended scissors good for this).

Trim round the foot to give a neat appearance. Finally, trim away untidy hair down the hock with

TRIMMING AND PREPARATION
Demonstrated by Ann Youens and 'Topsy'.

Before: Topsy pictured prior to the trimming session.

Ann starts by shaping round the foot.

The hair between the pads is cut.

Ann shows the nail, which needs cutting.

The tip of the nail is cut, using guillotine-type cutters.

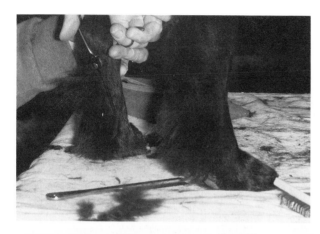

*The hindlegs
are trimmed.*

*Ann uses the finger and thumb method to
remove the dead hair from the ears.*

*ABOVE: Ann shows the hair that will
need to be removed from the neck.*

*RIGHT: Final attention is given to the
ears and the neck.*

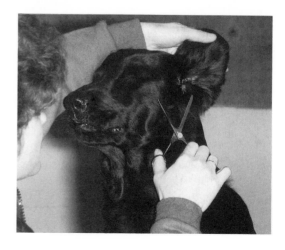

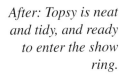

After: Topsy is neat and tidy, and ready to enter the show ring.

thinning scissors; only cut a little at a time to give a smooth finish.

5. Nails. May need the sharp point cutting off if the nails have not worn down.

6. Tail. There are several methods, but I prefer thinning scissors used with care to improve shape and tidiness. The finished effect should not be the "sculpted" Golden Retriever tail. The end of the tail should reach the point of the hock, so trim hair at the end of the tail accordingly and preferably not too sharply tapered.

7. Ears and neck. I usually leave this till the end as it is a tedious job. Comb down the ear with a fairly fine comb. Hold the ear flat in the palm of the hand and pull out small amounts of hair between thumb and first finger. This is hand stripping. If ears are hand-stripped right from the start they will always have a neat smooth appearance and, in fact, will need less attention than if you resort to thinning scissors. (The secret with hand stripping until you get the hair "down", is, in fact, to do a little and often.) There are two types of hair on the ear, a soft, finer, hair and thicker, silkier hair. With hand stripping the soft hair is removed leaving only the glossy silky hair. Obviously thinning scissors remove both types of hair, which is why the hair then tends to grow curly.

The neck. May need a little tidying down from behind and below the ears and again hand stripping gives a more natural appearance.

Keep standing back and looking.

Never, *ever* use clippers on a Flat-Coated Retriever. A clippered neck and front totally ruins the elegant flowing appearance.

8. Bathing. A very important part of show preparation. To show a grubby dog is an insult to the judge.

You will get to know how many days your own dog needs to be bathed before a show to have the best effect. Usually, about three days before is the best time, but then there are Flat-Coat hazards such as muddy ponds, just right for a quick wallow!

Have everything to hand near the bath before starting. A good dog shampoo; conditioner (coconut oil seems good) a brush; and of course a towel. Wet the dog all over except the head. Leave this till last as a dog will shake as soon as the head is in contact with water. (I always put a little plug of cotton wool in each ear.)

Apply shampoo all over, then brush the shampoo in with smooth sweeps, keeping the hair flat.

Rinsing is very important: again keep brushing hair flat, rinse and rinse and when you think all the shampoo is out, rinse again! It is essential that all shampoo is removed.

Conditioner. Whilst I have emphasised that the shampoo must be a dog shampoo (not even a baby shampoo will do), the conditioner can be a mild human one. Apply a little conditioner, gently brush in, do not rub or the hair shafts will be distorted and the shine will disappear. Rinse again thoroughly. Now, let your dog have a good shake.

If drying is with a hair dryer always dry and brush the way the hair lies to keep the coat flat.

Ears need drying very gently, taking care to dry inside, I find cotton wool is good for this. When dry, I wipe round inside with just a smear of warm olive oil on the cotton wool.

A useful tip is, after drying, take your dog a walk on a lead – this sets the coat; otherwise if the dog lies down after bathing, invariably bits of hair stick up.

Whilst skilful tidying and bathing can do much to improve the dog's appearance, remember, a healthy shiny coat comes from within – good feeding and regular exercise are essential.

Rosalie Brady, whose Bordercot Flat-Coats are always immaculately presented and shown to perfection, says that the art of preparing a Flat-Coat is that, however many hours have been spent on preparation, none of it should be apparent. On one occasion, with a dog that was overdue for attention, it took Rosalie eight hours of trimming and tidying before even getting to the bath. Even then, she says, "only a skilled judge will appreciate the hours that have been taken to achieve a totally natural appearance. The dog must never be barbered, noticeably scissored or, horror of horrors, clipped."

THE BIG DAY

As far as possible have everything prepared the night before. Passes safely in your bag. Route written out. Show bag checked and so on. Also allow more time than you think will be needed for the journey.

There should be no need to take a whole range of grooming equipment but it is as well to have a good brush and comb, a pair of scissors (just in case they are needed), and the piece of velvet or silk for polishing. Remember "poop" bags, a water bowl, and I always take a bottle of water, in case the benches are a distance from a tap; feed bowl and some feed, as you may be travelling at the normal feed time. It is better to avoid taking a feed that swells.

At a benched show, a rug will be needed, also a collar and a benching chain; these two latter items are actual KC requirements. Never, ever, fasten a dog to the bench on a check chain. Very dangerous.

A small container with "bait". Small pieces of hard cooked liver is good and not messy, although some dogs go "over the top" at the smell of liver, in which case try just a small biscuit. Often it is sufficient just to have the smell of, say, a bit of liver on one's fingers. The reward then comes at the end of the class. Should it be a very big class then a little something half way through can be given. "Feeding" as opposed to 'baiting' merely encourages the dog to concentrate on food and not on showing. The tidbit should be a reward for good behaviour, not an additional meal!

You need a show lead. There are many types and a wonderful range of tempting colours. Black Flat-Coats look wonderful with a scarlet or emerald lead! RESIST THE TEMPTATION. Black for black dogs and brown for Liver. A coloured slip breaks up the neck line. You want something as unobtrusive as possible. The material can be nylon, leather or a rounded nylon rope type, not as thick as a working rope slip. These are very good.

If you have time, it is worth putting in a flask of coffee and some food for yourself. Some venues have good food, others don't.

In the matter of dress, it is important to be comfortable, but try to be reasonably tidy as well.

Layers help as you can adjust to the temperature; certainly have some wet weather gear in the car. Give some thought to colour, as a dark skirt or trousers do nothing for a black dog, also avoid very full skirts. Shoes should be flat and again comfortable.

HINTS

Make sure your dog has, in the phrase I used before, pooped and peed both before leaving home and, if possible, before arriving at the show. Should an "accident" occur, then use your "pooper scooper" even if it is just a plastic bag. One of the feed firms sells very good dark green deodorised bags.

Once in the ring, keep calm, concentrate on your dog (and the judge) and remember you have paid for that time, so don't waste it. Whatever happens, there is always another day, another show, another judge. The dog you take home is the same one that you took to the show.

ARE JUDGES BORN OR MADE?

A moot point. Certainly, there are people who have an "eye" and others who haven't. For these, sadly, no amount of learning the Breed Standard off by heart and attending breed seminars will ever change the fact, but, if there are shows there have to be judges.

Historically, in the UK, the men who judged dogs from the early days of shows were knowledgeable about other forms of livestock. Gundog judges in particular tended to come from sporting backgrounds with knowledge of horses as well as dogs, so they understood the importance of sound construction. Possibly because of this long association Britain, unlike other countries, has no qualification scheme for would-be judges. Years ago an apprenticeship was served by breeding sound stock that proved its worth in various fields of activities and, eventually, being asked to judge. Judging in itself was never the raison d'etre for involvement with a breed. With the numerical increase in shows, particularly at Open show level, there is a corresponding increase in the need for judges, so the process has speeded up, hence the increase in breed seminars and courses with a judge's diploma at the end.

In Europe and Scandinavia judges need to have been recognised in their particular breed; would-be judges have to take written and practical examinations. They are also watched and assessed by a KC representative.

Would-be judges in the US need to have had some 10 years experience in breeding and exhibiting and to have bred four litters with two Champions resulting from these litters. The applicant must be an experienced steward and be knowledgeable about AKC rules and regulations (with written papers). There is then almost a provisional period, when the new judge is watched and assessed from the ringside by an AKC representative who reports to the AKC. This practice is also carried out with first-time overseas judges. A copy of the assessment is given to the judge.

What are the requirements for judges? They must have a knowledge of anatomy, that is the skeleton beneath the skin and coat: it is the actual construction which governs movement, for example. They must be conversant with the Breed Standard and this is where differences arise. Take four people: each one may know the Breed Standard but each will have a different interpretation. The same problem arises over that indefinable attribute, "type". It is interpretation which causes different judges to choose different dogs – which is just as well otherwise the same dogs would always win.

Judges should be punctual and explain to the stewards their way of controlling the ring and what is expected of them. Good stewards are of enormous value in keeping a ring happy and "rolling", which is essential with large entries. The judge should have worked out the time available per dog according to the entry, should keep an eye on the time, and pace the judging accordingly. Having said that, every exhibitor has paid the same amount to enter and even the least prepossessing exhibit is entitled to time and courtesy. This is of prime importance throughout the judging procedure. Courtesy to stewards and exhibitors, with a kind word to the dogs, costs nothing. Every dog entered is someone's pride and joy.

Never call exhibitors by their name. Always be clear when calling out exhibitors for the line up. I also think it is important to look as if some effort has been made to be neat and presentable. Comfortable shoes are again a must. I take an extra pair to change into halfway through.

The AKC actually states that women must not have swirling skirts, long necklaces or jangly, dangling bracelets. I must say American judges do look very smart – absolutely wonderful in the impressive photographs that are a major part of every big show.

POSITIVE JUDGING

By this I mean looking for and assessing good points rather than picking out the weaknesses. I am always wary of the person who maintains, usually with enormous confidence, "I know a good dog when I see one." Frankly, so do most of us. The problem arises in being able to weigh up pros and cons, particularly in moderate animals.

At times, this is open to question. If the judge finishes with a matching line-up then there is clear indication of the type in mind. Depending on the entry, this is not always possible. If the judge is clearly choosing dogs of his or her own preference, then even if not in agreement, there is no cause for complaint. It is honest opinion.

My personal preference is for a well-constructed dog, balanced, with no exaggerations, who covers the ground well on the move, has a happy, confident demeanour and, for the top winners, that indefinable "touch of class".

Just a word on the difference in judging procedure in Europe and Scandinavia. To start with, each dog is "graded": – Excellent. Very good. Good. Moderate i.e. poor! I often wish with large classes in the UK that we could do this. At least the exhibitor knows, even if unplaced, the quality of the dog. Every single dog has a written critique in triplicate, the owner being handed a copy immediately. The judge is expected to mention faults or weaknesses. Exhibitors are far more robust in accepting criticism than their British counterparts would be. The judge dictates the critique to a clerk who types out the form. Obviously the number of dogs per judge is restricted to allow time for this.

THE FINAL THOUGHT

When dear Patience Locke eventually thought that I was ready for the centre of the ring, she gave me some never-to-be-forgotten advice, which I in turn passed on to my daughter, Rosemary Talbot, when she started judging. "Never, ever, think names of dogs or owners or handlers when judging." Well worth remembering.

My most memorable occasion when judging, was in fact, at the FCRSA Specialty in Denver in 1992. I was standing in that huge hall, with over 100 champions plus the Winners Dog and Bitch for the Best of Breed class. It was an incredible sight, with a marvellous atmosphere, even though the majority of those in the ring would perforce leave empty-handed. It will remain one of the most treasured moments of my life.

Chapter Nine

THE WORKING FLAT-COAT

In this chapter I have been greatly assisted by contributions from several knowledgeable people involved with Flat-Coats who tell of their own experiences.

THE SHOOTING FIELD

Read Flowers is a long-standing member of the Flat-Coated Retriever Society. He has held office as Chairman, then President. On retiring from this position he was made Patron of the Society, an honour previously only bestowed on Dr. Nancy Laughton. Read still serves on the Field Trial sub-committee. He has always bred good working dogs that could more than hold their own in the show ring. "Fenrivers" Flat-Coats have made a major contribution to the breed for many years. Here he writes about his own interest in the shooting field.

I did not exactly choose to become a Flat-Coat fancier. I grew up with Flat-Coats and have never really wanted anything different as a gundog. Our family of unregistered Flat-Coats died out during the '39-45 War years and, as soon as it was possible, I acquired a puppy from Stanley O'Neill. She became Ch. Pewcroft Proper, a very lucky start for me. Using mostly the 'W' dogs of Colin Wells at stud, Proper's line produced some good specimens that could hold their own in the show ring, and do a good day's work on the shoot.

I was a keen showman in those days; it was a way to meet other Flat-Coat fanciers, and to learn what a Flat-Coat should look like. I also attended trials, to learn what could be achieved with a trained dog. I wanted a real all-purpose worker, a dog that would hunt unshot pheasants in our Fen sugar-beet, and retrieve when occasionally I hit one. Also it should be a steady dog on a more formal shoot, and hunt hard and boldly in covert and water when picking-up or wildfowling. I seldom owned such a paragon, but those that didn't quite make that standard were nevertheless good dogs and we had a great deal of enjoyment together.

I started picking-up in 1954 and have just finished my 41st season on the same estate. Including other shoots I managed about 30 days out with my dogs last season. I had to serve a probation period before I was allowed on the estate with a dog on a shooting day. There was driving-in of straying birds, some days with the beaters, with the dog at heel or on a lead, and there was 'cold picking-up' on Sunday mornings after shoots. Eventually my dog and I were deemed acceptable, we were invited to pick-up, and I had discovered an activity that I still enjoy immensely.

Newcomers to the sport, or even old hands on new ground, should always admit their limitations, and try to work with an experienced handler until the dog gains experience, and the handler learns the procedure and the geography of the shoot. Please, don't go picking-up to train your dog. The dog should be under good control before being taken on a shoot. Then experience can be built on to the training, and you will have a Flat-Coat that can do the job for which it was originally bred.

There are several Flat-Coats working on the shoots that I attend, and they can hold their own with any of the other breeds that I see. They mature rather slowly as a rule, but when experienced are hard to beat.

FIELD TRIALS

Peter Johnson is another whose dogs (Downstream) have contributed both on bench and field – aided by wife Shirley. Peter has been Field Trial Secretary since 1986. As a gamekeeper he has an essentially practical approach to both the demands of the shooting field and also of competitive Field Trials. This is his description of what is involved.

The Field Trials are divided into three categories. The Novice trials are confined to dogs which have not gained a first, second or third prize in Open trials, or a first prize or two second prizes in an All-Aged or Novice trial. The All-Aged trial is open to all dogs of a specified breed or breeds without restriction to their age, but which may be restricted by any other conditions which are determined by the organising Society. Lastly there are the Open Trials in which a dog has the opportunity of gaining a qualification towards the title of Field Trial Champion or towards entry in, for retrievers, the Retriever Championship. The trials are either "walked-up" or "driven", or ideally a combination of both. In a walked-up trial there are usually three judges, with six guns and six handlers and their dogs. They form a line and walk through the undergrowth or, if in the east of England, sugarbeet, until a bird is shot.

If a gun in the group with the A judge shot a bird, the judge in that group would instruct one of the handlers in his group to send his dog. If, after what the judge considers a reasonable time, the first dog has not picked the bird he will tell the handler to call his dog up and get the second handler to try his dog. Should this dog succeed he will have achieved an "eye-wipe" over the first dog and be credited with this in the judges' book. Should the bird only be wounded and have run, and the dog follows it and makes a successful retrieve, this must be given more credit than an easy retrieve on a dead bird. This goes on until all the dogs in the trial have had the chance to make two retrieves and it completes the first round.

In the second round the dogs go back into line under a different judge to that of the first round, providing they have not committed a cardinal sin such as damaged game (hard-mouthed), whined or been out of control. In the second round the dogs have one retrieve. At this stage the judges get together and compare notes they have made on the dogs' performances. It is usual in the final stages of the trial to bring the remaining dogs into line together and the distances they are asked to make their retrieves will be increased. In a driven trial the line is formed in the same way as for a walked-up trial, but now the guns and handlers would be stationary and the game be driven towards them and shot. Usually there would be several lying on the ground at the same time. The procedure of sending the dogs would be the same.

From a judging point of view, I find it much easier and more interesting to judge a walked-up trial. There are different types of retrieves, e.g. in front of the line and behind the line. It is usually easier to see the dogs at work, although from the handlers point of view this might not be so good. When judging I like to see a dog go when sent into the area of where the bird has fallen and "stick to its ground" – that is, to hunt the area and not rush about everywhere, as this could disturb game. I like to see a dog "handle" – that is, be directed to an area if necessary, and a quick clean pick-up and retrieve right to hand. Other points must be taken into consideration such as game finding, marking and nose besides the things I have mentioned.

Peter Johnson training his Flat-Coats. Photo: Lars Soderbom.

In over fifty years of being connected with shooting I have seen a vast improvement in the work and training of dogs. I can remember many years ago, when attending a shoot with my employer, the other guns looking on in surprise as I loaded guns for him and my dog sat out in front of us. I must admit that when I moved up to the East of England the standard of trained dogs was much higher, but the sight of most guns trying to handle their dogs over a river onto a dead bird that is lying with the wind blowing the scent away from them, with the dog never having been taught to respond to hand signals, is rather ridiculous. At a Trial a dog that makes a noise is discarded and there is no doubt in my mind that this has helped in breeding everyday shooting dogs: likewise a dog that damages birds is soon detected, as every bird retrieved is examined by the judges. Dogs with these faults should *not* be bred from. It is very unwise to enter a trial until you are sure that your dog will pick up game of any description.

While it is nearly possible to train a retriever for Working Tests in your back garden or on a playing field, one must have some means of getting retrieves of hot, freshly shot game which the dog should pick up and carry with confidence before you even think of entering trials. Over the years as a gamekeeper I have had many requests from prospective triallers who wish to come and give their dogs experience on game, and I like to think that I have been in a position to help. Everybody wants to come and pick-up and it is very rare that I have one that will start at the bottom and come beating, or brushing as it is called locally. It is a wonderful education for the dog to walk through the undergrowth and see the birds exploding all around and, if lucky, the dog might just get a retrieve.

Having trialled my Flat-Coats for many years I do know that the would-be Flat-Coat Trialler should not have a weak heart, as these are not the dog for the faint-hearted but rather the dog for the optimist who has a never-ending supply of determination.

Sue Rogers' talented Wheatmill Dipper.

WORKING TESTS

There could be a difference of opinion as to whether Working Tests count as "field" or "other activities". Rightly or wrongly I tend to the latter view. Working Tests are in effect an extension of one's basic training, using firstly dummies/bumpers and then cold i.e. dead game before introducing the dog to freshly shot fur or feather. The tests were originated by groups of people getting together for training sessions, which led in time to competitions, and thence to official Working Tests. In the UK it was as late as 1966 before the FCRS instituted an annual Working Test.

Originally the tests were regarded as a means of gaining experience for dog and handler as a forerunner to competitive Field Trials. Over the years the emphasis has changed; Working Tests are now enormously popular and attract high entries. While not intending to diminish the pleasure and satisfaction for both handler and dog taking part in Working tests, it must be remembered that a good Working test dog is not necessarily a good shooting dog.

WORKING TRIALS

These are quite different from Working Tests. In the UK Georgina Watts has enjoyed considerable success with her Wanton Warrior CDEx UDEx WDEx, and is currently working on TD. Georgina has written the following:-

Working Trials normally last from two to five days depending on the size of entry, but each dog will only work on one or two of these days. Dogs progress through each stake by a series of qualifications. Companion Dog stake (CD) is an optional stake and does not include tracking. Utility Dog (UD) does include tracking. Working Dog (WD). Tracking Dog (TD). Dogs must qualify through these stakes at Open Trials to enter the equivalent stake at Championship Trials. Winning two TD stakes under different judges, providing the required marks are attained, makes a dog a Working Trial Champion.

Working Trial tests include a control section involving Heel work, Send away, Retrieve, Stays and steadiness to gunshot, all of which a Flat-Coat can do well. The Agility section has a scale, the 3ft clear jump and the 9ft long jump. Again the Flat-Coat enjoys these exercises and shows great scope. The nose-work section is where the Flat-Coat really excels, with an excellent "nose" and keenness to "find". This section involves the search, finding four articles in a 25 yard square, and the track, which is approximately half a mile long. Flat-Coats make first-class tracker dogs, usually taking to it like a duck to water!

Working Trials is a very demanding sport. The most important thing to remember with a Flat-Coat is to make haste SLOWLY. They love to work but have a long adolescence, and patience is needed, giving them time to mature before embarking on advanced training. If you are in a hurry, forget about Flat-Coats. If you like a dog that is fun to train, and you have the required patience, then the Flat-Coat has the all-round ability to make an excellent Working Trial dog.

I have not included the PD stake, as this involves "man work" to which the Flat-Coat is not suited.

Wanton Warrior CDEx, UDEx, WDEx, owned and trained by Georgina Watts.

OBEDIENCE AND AGILITY

Sue Jones has enormous fun with that great extrovert character Ch. Happy Harry, still competing at 12 years of age. Sue writes:

If you are thinking about getting a new dog with the idea of whizzing to the top in either obedience or agility, then don't even consider a Flat-Coat. However, if you like a challenge, have endless patience, enjoy training (of which you will have to do plenty), can be happy with your dog whether or not you go home with a rosette and can still laugh when your dog has made a complete fool of you, then a Flat-Coat may be the dog for you.

Having said that, in Obedience at the moment there is one Flat-Coat working Class "C" (the top class below Championship level) and three or four working the lower classes. Although they seem

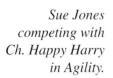

Sue Jones competing with Ch. Happy Harry in Agility.

to do well in Beginner classes it is often difficult to maintain the precision required to win a Novice class. However, if you do want to do competitive obedience with your Flat-Coat, find a trainer who has an empathy with "other breeds", and take things very slowly; don't expect your dog to be winning classes at a year, or even two years old. Generally speaking, a combination of tidbits and toys will provide the motivation you need to teach the individual exercises reliably. By using encouragement, incentive and reward you will eventually have a happy, keen and confident dog who is eager to please you. Teaching good basic obedience – heelwork, recall, presents, stays, retrieve and even distance control and sendaways, will give you the foundation with which to go on to take part in a number of different activities. It will help with your showing, agility and working tests, as your dog will have learnt to enjoy doing things with you but will also understand that you expect complete obedience. With the right training and plenty of determination on your part your Flat-Coat will be stylish and eye-catching in whatever activity you choose.

Remember that, although very much the clown, your Flat-Coat does have a sensitive streak and can easily lose confidence if there is a failure to understand fully what is being asked. Once this understanding is established, however, your dog may try almost too hard and, with the very best of intentions, think independently. When you get that look which says "Leave it to me, it's OK, I know what I'm doing", you must just resign yourself to letting your dog get on with it – for all the shouting and hollering in the world will probably have not the slightest effect! Although generally biddable and eager to please, this independent streak will make training a constant challenge, but it is all part of the lovely mix of characteristics which make up the breed.

There are probably, at the most, a dozen Flat-Coats currently competing in Agility in the UK. Despite being so numerically small, there have been two Senior Flat-Coats over the years. The current Senior dog, Ann Davis's Bothydown Fulmar, finished 14th in the Agility Dog of the Year 1994 league table. Although generally lacking that edge of speed to win, they are often in the placings and can make very good "team" dogs. Teaching the equipment is not usually a problem, although they can sometimes take a while to gain confidence on the see-saw. Weaving through the poles can also take a while to "click" but once this technique has been mastered, the dog's movement through the poles can be stunning! It is controlling the exuberant side of the character which is the most difficult, especially when there is a crowd watching. My own Ch. Happy Harry was well-known for his antics in the ring at Agility Shows; however, eventually, at the age of 7 or 8, he began to do the same course as the judge had set and was getting clear rounds or being placed regularly, so don't despair! Versatile, easy-going and full of fun, a Flat-Coat will fit in with whatever you want to do, provided you can appreciate the dog's sense of humour. A Flat-Coat is a very lively, active dog who needs something to occupy both mind and body even into old age, so is not a dog for the frail or faint-hearted. However, once you have had one you will be totally smitten!

HUNTING WITH THE FLAT-COAT IN THE US

Some two to three years ago I had the pleasure of meeting the Freeman family in Denver. Don had been chairman of that year's National Speciality, ably supported by his wife Toni. Don works his dogs over the awe-inspiring terrain of the Colorado Rockies. Don is not only a good dog man but, like any good hunter, he also knows and respects his prey. Don has written about himself and his Flat-Coats.

I was fourteen when I received my first Flat-Coat, on Christmas Day of 1966. I had lost an older brother in a car accident two months before. He had worked at Sally Terroux's kennels, and had told us many wonderful stories about Ch. Bramcroft Dandy UD. Our Christmas puppy was bought to ease the pain of that first Christmas without my brother. Sally almost never lets a puppy go at Christmas, but this was an exception. We named him Mantayo Duffield Tucker, call-name Duffy. He was out of Ch. Bramcroft Dandy UD and Ch. Claverdon Duchess. Since I have never bred a litter, I don't have a foundation dog. Duffy was where it all started, however.

I do not pretend to speak for all hunting Flat-Coat owners in the US, but I may be as qualified as anyone. The Flat-Coat is quite rare in the States, and I have probably hunted over 15 or so in the 25-plus years I have been hunting with them. As a broad-brush statement, we could safely minimise the discussion of Flat-Coats' use on quail. Bobwhite quail hunting has a huge, devoted following in our country, and represents a vast majority of the bird hunting in several geographic areas, including the Gulf Coast and southern regions. These are gentlemen's birds, in that they generally sit politely in front of a pointer. This fact, combined with the warm climates in which they live, make them the domain of the pointing dogs. To my knowledge, not many Flat-Coats, or many retrievers for that matter, are obtained primarily for hunting quail.

There is also a large contingent of rough-grouse hunters, primarily in the East. I cannot claim any knowledge of Flat-Coat owners hunting or not hunting these woodland birds. Once again, I believe these to be primarily hunted with pointing breeds. Neither do I know of anyone who uses their American Flat-Coat for rabbits. On the contrary, when a rabbit is flushed during a bird hunt, the dogs are typically discouraged from running it. The use of dogs on big game is illegal except for bear and lion in some states, but that of course is a hound sport.

Waterfowl hunting is most commonly done from blinds, although I do not hunt that way myself. The requirements for a waterfowl dog in a blind are pretty straightforward. Manners are quite important, so you either train like crazy, or you start with a dog that is a little calmer. On the other hand, desire can be important if conditions are bad. While you can force a dog into water with good force fetch programme, it is much better if they hit cold water because they want to.

Of course, coat sufficient for freezing conditions is necessary, but I haven't found that length has much to do with protection in water. Full texture seems to be the key, and the hair has to be coarse enough to shed the water when they shake. Fine and wispy (pretty) coat can be a real problem. I have found the Flat-Coat solution to water (that is, get it away from the skin) to be superior to the Golden's undercoat approach. They both seem to work, but I think the quick-dry feature of the Flat-Coat is a real advantage. My dogs have not had a lot of coat, even for Flat-Coats, but they have always done quite well duck-hunting, and never refused water even in really bad conditions. I must point out, however, that I hunt ducks by walking up on ponds and ditches, and flushing the birds with my dogs at heel. The dog doesn't return to a blind where he has to lie down again. If it's really cold, we're back in the truck before long.

Conformation in the waterfowl dog is not as important, in my opinion, as in the upland game dog. We have low waterfowl limits, typically three birds, so a dog in a blind with three people will do nine retrieves on an ideal day, with bed rest in between. While this can be a formidable task if the gunners limit out in a morning flurry, it shouldn't overly tax a dog with a little less angle than we would like for our breed stock, or that slightly sickle-hocked pet dog.

In a day and age where crowded waterfowl hunting from blinds on public lands is becoming increasingly popular, more and more dogs are being trained to handle. The classic hunt test or field trial blind retrieve can and does occur on these types of hunts. In a dog for this type of hunting, biddability may be more of a factor than birdiness. However, a hunter that is going to train enough to do difficult water blinds is probably capable of teaching manners as well. Individual taste dictates the balance here.

Some duck hunting and a lot of goose hunting is done from blinds over fields, not water. Dogs are often used for this, but I don't think many physical demands are placed on these dogs. I have seen some very large dogs used here. The owners claim to prefer these "big boys" for carrying large Canadian Geese. If there is a hunting home for the occasionally oversized or lack-lustre puppy, maybe this would be the place.

Upland bird hunting with Flat-Coats seems to be the sport of a small group of fanatics, whose ranks I joined nearly 30 years ago. There are numerous types of grouse and other species in local areas that are hunted by a devoted few. The terrain and conditions vary from low hot deserts to freezing alpine slopes. I have hunted, or know people who have hunted, all of the following birds with Flat-Coats – sharp-tailed grouse, which are extensively hunted in the bad lands of Nebraska in rolling sand hills; chukkar, which occur in foothills country on very rough mountain hillsides, often in impenetrable cover; and sage grouse, which are as large as a chicken and are hunted in the high sage flats and breaks of Colorado and Wyoming prairie country in early October, when it can be very warm and freezing in the same day. I met one Flat-Coat owner who has hunted ptarmigan with his dog at 12,000 feet above sea level.

I know nothing about the woodcock of the northeast, other than that they are very odd-looking. Those who hunt them are extremely devoted, and consider it a nearly religious experience. I am sure some eastern US Flat-Coats probably spend part of every fall in the bogs and swamps that hold woodcock. I think I am safe in saying that ring-necked pheasants are the most hunted of the upland birds with the Flat-Coat. Pheasants certainly comprise the bulk of the upland game bird-hunting I have done, as is the case with the majority of the people with whom I have discussed the subject. There are numerous reasons for this. First of all, they occur in almost every state, in latitudes from Texas to North Dakota. They are large as game birds go, about the size of a small hen chicken, and two can make a meal for a family. They are also quite delicious. However, the primary reason for the popularity of pheasant hunting with dogs is a deep and abiding love and respect for the quarry itself and a love for the dogs, the dog work and the pursuit of this smarter-than-average bird. At this point it will become obvious that I am a member of a "cult" comprised of terminally addicted dog-owning pheasant hunters.

The essence is that the pheasant can run as fast as a man through extremely tight cover and flush out of range in front of the guns, or can hide in ankle high cover and let you walk by; the pheasant always seems to know which to do. I have seen 20 birds leave a field a mile away when a car door opens, and I have seen a wise old rooster elude an experienced hunter/dog team (me, for instance) in a patch of cover that should not hide a sparrow. This is pheasant hunting. When one gets away, you just smile and hope the bird has lots of chicks next season.

Pheasants are found in farm country. Grain, with a strong preference for corn, is a necessity. They also need heavy cover for shelter. This may be uncut corn or other crop, or it may be weed fields or weed rows along the edge of a field of grain. Blowing weeds (called tumble weeds) will often accumulate along a fence line creating good cover for pheasants. If you find corn with nearby cover, you will find pheasants. Hunting season in my part of the country, the Rocky Mountain west, usually finds most of the corn mowed knee-high or picked with the stalks laid over, usually about waist-high. A few of the fields will still be standing, soon to be harvested for cattle feed.

A very popular method of hunting is by driving the harvested fields in a line with 6 to 10 hunters, or drivers, towards "blockers" at the end of the field. The dogs will run the length of the drive line as flushers, preventing the birds from running back between the drivers. They should work the entire line and stay in range of the gunners. When a bird is dropped, a quick retrieve and delivery will keep the drive going and give remaining birds less chance of escape. The blockers will try and prevent the birds from escaping out of the end of the field, hopefully getting a shot at them if they try. Without dogs, many or all of the birds will escape by running back between drivers and being passed by, or by lying still and letting the drivers pass. In deep cover such as picked corn or deep weeds, they can hold very tightly, nearly having to be stepped on before flushing.

Smaller parties of hunters will choose weed patches near corn, or old wheat stubble. Wheat stubble is less than knee high, but is quite dense. Weed patches are usually knee to waist high tumble weeds, the thicker the better, often in old abandoned farmsteads. For large or small hunting parties, the concerns are the same – prevent birds from flushing too far out, and don't walk by any.

The dog's part is obvious in pushing up the tight birds. However, the running birds are a different story. There are those who believe that a good flushing dog can keep the birds from running, and that a pheasant will not run in front of an experienced dog. I am not convinced, but I am not closed-minded to the possibility. I think that some birds will run in front of any dog, but the presence of a dog may indeed intimidate some into holding. It is a wonderfully complex issue in a wonderfully challenging sport.

A crippled pheasant can present one of the most challenging feats in the retriever world. A bird can appear to be quite dead as it falls, hit the ground hard and still have a lot of run left. In certain cover they will leave almost no scent, and they can cover an astonishing amount of ground in no time, usually unseen. The dog must be at the contact point as soon as possible, and the hunter is usually wise to let the dog take over when he reaches the general area. In a most pronounced departure from field trials or hunt tests, the birds on these "blinds" are seldom where the handler thinks they are. If you spend much time handling the dog to the exact spot, you may lose the bird. This is where I believe the famous Flat-Coat stubborn streak may actually be an asset. The old joke about the Flat-Coat always having a better way is no joke here – the dog usually does have a better way. Its called nose and instinct, and we of the inept olfactory nerve shouldn't argue.

Finally, what do we look for in a pheasant dog? Number-one attribute in my book is desire. Regardless of build or conditioning, eight hours of running miles through picked corn and high weeds will exhaust any dog. The average pheasant dog often ends up hunting long hours on nothing but desire. The limit on pheasants, depending on the state, is from three to six birds, and many days can be birdless, so the replenishing effect of a bird downed and retrieved may not come often. That frothing, quivering, insanely birdy dog that drives you nuts is the one that will still stay in front of the gunners on day two or three, and the one that will drive into the thorny, dense cover on the remote possibility that it might yield something. They can't help you at heel. The other side of this coin is that these birdy dogs can be extremely difficult to steady to the rise. Trailing running birds out of range or chasing close-flushing birds is tough to break, but if you want a hard charging Flat-Coat as your partner, you need to be prepared and able to deal with it.

As the description of the hunt would imply, nose is quite important, both in the flushing and retrieving of pheasants. However, I don't feel that it is as variable or important to breed to as do some people. While I would insist on more nose than the average Lab I have hunted over, I have seen few Flat-Coats or Goldens that seemed to have inadequate scenting abilities. I think that when incidents occur that make it appear so, a little investigating, perhaps with another dog, will usually reveal that perhaps scenting conditions were especially poor in the immediate area, or something else.

God help us when we stop believing that conformation is important for our field dogs. Good angulation and sound movement are a must. I have witnessed more than a few times the advantages of efficient movement in an upland game dog. I have owned Flat-Coats that range from 60 to 90 pounds, and hunted over a wider range than that. I find that the small to mid sized dog, 65 to 75 pounds, will hold up better. I do not subscribe to the "big, cover-busting" dog theory. A small "cover-hopping" dog gets my vote for an extended hunt, even in heavy cover (especially in heavy cover).

Lastly in discussing the pheasant dog, I address the real can of worms – brains? Or is it instinct? Or is it experience? My opinion, for what it's worth, is that, as they gain experience, the hard charging, birdy dogs seem to develop into the thinkers as well. In their early years, these "driven" dogs can appear apparently brainless, seemingly driven without direction, but there's usually hope. On the other hand, I've yet to see a lukewarm young dog mature into a thoughtful, hard-working hunter with purpose on a pheasant hunt. Of the really hot puppies and adolescents I have hunted over, there has been a range of bird sense develop with maturity, but not a broad range. Perhaps it can be said that a dog who really wants birds, will learn and figure out how to get them as experience is gained.

This instinct/brains issue is why I have Flat-Coats. In a part of the country where Labs and Brittanys rule, I have been won over time and time again by "uncanny" bird sense displayed by seasoned, pheasant hunting Flat-Coats. This is the real intangible (or perhaps I should say unexplainable) side of the Flat-Coat that I believe distinguishes them. They will find live birds and downed birds where hunters knew they could not be. When they skip a likely looking patch of cover, you may check it yourself if you like, but it will be empty. Some of the time you can explain it by scent, sometimes not. It is at such times that the instinct, attainable only from their hunting predecessors, is talking.

No hunting dog story written by an American male is complete without a "best-hunt'n-dog-I-ever-saw" story, and that is the best way I know to illustrate this intangible quality of the Flat-Coat. I have owned five hunting Flat-Coats. Notable in any group of hunting dogs was Cindy. She was a little too big, but very sleek and elegant, and had a wonderful ground-eating side gait. She had Scottish preserve dogs in her pedigree, pheasants in her blood, and me in her heart. The story takes place when she was about five. It was just the two of us, and since there were no witnesses, I've never written it down until now. It's a little too perfect, but it is apparently time to tell it.

We had just finished hunting a one mile long wheat stubble patch, walking back along the fence where a weed row had formed. The wind was gentle but consistent from our left, and one inch of new snow was on the ground. To our right was the weed row stacked against the four-strand barbed-wire fence, and to the right of that was a mowed corn field, about mid-calf in depth – pretty bare. To the left, upwind, was the stubble we had just worked. The corn husks were rattling in the wind, we had a bird in the bag, and it was beautiful, even ethereal. As we walked, Cindy flinched up and back like she had been struck by a snake. This was her unmistakable "BIRD REAL CLOSE!" gesture – usually a sudden scent overdose. I turned into the wind toward the stubble, fully expecting a rise. But she was not working the wind. She jumped over the fence and weed row and shot straight into the barren corn stubble, downwind. About 15 yards into the corn, a rooster flushed right off her nose, and in spite of my shock, I shot it. I crossed the fence and looked in the snow for tracks, trying to explain how she had detected a bird 20 yards downwind. The bird had come in on foot from even further downwind. The weed row between Cindy and the bid was way too high for her to see over, and too dense to see through. How did she do it?

I have more stories with no answers, and usually they involve Flat-Coats. We'll sum it up as instinct, and not get overly romantic, hard as that may be when you own a Flat-Coat.

AMERICAN FIELD TRIALS

Bunny Millikin is a true sportswoman. While her main enthusiasm for Flat-Coats has been in the Field, she also takes part in the show ring, usually very creditably. I think it is her enthusiasm for whatever she embarks upon that provides the rapport between her and her dogs. Bunny has written a little about her own introduction to Flat-Coated Retrievers and her continuing involvement.

My first real Flat-Coat was Stolford Black Queen, purchased in 1964 from Peggy Robertson. She was an extraordinary dog especially in the field and led us into field trials, with the ensuing roller-coaster ride of emotions and experiences which we so enjoy to this day. Black Queen's daughter, Wyndham's Wingover Brunhilde, was even better in trials and an awesome shooting dog. Other outstanding dogs I've had include C. Halryn Wingover Mad Mouse, Ch. Hardscrabble Wingover Zip CDX MH, Am/Can. Ch. Wingmaster's Wingover Coot CD MH and Ch. Sunshine's Wingover Janus. All these dogs had American and Canadian field trial wins and other awards and were wonderful shooting dogs.

I used to stay away from the show ring, as much because there just wasn't time, as that I wasn't interested. Then, when Mouse was three years old I went to a show with a friend and was amazed

Bunny Millikin with Ch. Wingmaster's Wingover Coot Am. Can. WCX.

Am. Can. Wingmaster's Wingover Coot CD, MH (winner of three licensed Field Trials), Am. Can. Ch. Twin Oaks Tsar Nicholas CD, MH (National Specialty BOB America and Canada), and Can. Am. Ch. OTCH Hob-B's Knite Ryder MH (High Point Obedience dog in Canada).

at what was winning. The only show Flat-Coats I'd seen had been at the Specialities and they were our best. Mouse immediately experienced a serious primping and was entered in the next show. She became a Show Champion very quickly and I was so proud. Since then all of my dogs have been campaigned in the show ring as well as in the field.

Elizabeth (Biz) Read is a long-standing supporter of the breed, whose interests lie in competent field work, an aspect of the breed which she has worked ceaselessly to promote. Biz has owned many good dogs, not the least being Ch. Claverdon Gamble CD who has been so influential in American pedigrees. Currently, both Biz and Bunny are active members of the "Field" sub-committee of the FCRSA. They have combined to contribute the following account of American Field Trials.

American Retriever Field Trials bear some resemblance to British cold game tests with several live birds added. We do not have keepered estates here, though field trial grounds can be privately owned. More often the grounds are public areas well suited to field events. There is usually no natural game on the ground. We essentially have four stakes offered, Open All-Age, Amateur All-Age, Qualifying and Derby. The first two are self-explanatory, Qualifying is similar to your Novice Stake and Derby is for dogs under 2 years old. The Open, Amateur and Qualifying have multiple retrieves, marks and blinds (seen and unseens) on land and water and an honour (sit steady while another dog works). Derby has marked retrieves only and no honouring.

Our Field Trials start on Friday and go through Sunday. We have no limit on entries, therefore it is not unusual to see 80 or more dogs in the Open Stake which is run over all three days. The level of talent and ability in these dogs is extremely high. As training techniques get more sophisticated it becomes more difficult to create retrieving tests that will clearly separate the dogs. For this reason our tests often include long and complicated retrieves. Sometimes 200 to 300 yards for marked retrieves and possibly longer for blind retrieves. Every effort is made to give each dog the exact same test. No dog is sent for a runner, as that is considered an unequal situation. Most Open

Pictured left to right: Can. FT Ch. Hardscrabble Blac Glory CD, CFC CAFC; Ch. Curlee Hill Black Pacinko CD, MH; and Ch. Sunshine's Wingover Janus. Photo courtesy: Bunny Millikin.

dogs are professionally trained and handled, which is quite expensive but the amount of training needed to be competitive makes it almost a prerequisite.

Field Trials have maintained a steady popularity, but for many people are prohibitive because of the time, effort and money necessary to be successful. The need for a less rigorous field event within the reach of most people brought about the Hunt Test programme. These are non-competitive events where the dog must meet a standard of working ability for the level attempted. There are three levels, Junior Hunter, Senior Hunter and Master Hunter. The **Junior Hunter** requires two single land marked retrieves and two single water retrieves with delivery to hand. Total steadiness is not required. **Senior** requires steadiness, honour, double marks and a blind on both land and water. **Master Hunter** requires more complicated multiple marks and blinds on both land and water, complete steadiness and very crisp whistle response and handling control. No falls are longer than 100 yards in any of the tests. All tests are run under hunting conditions. Four passes are required for a Junior Hunter title, five passes for Senior and six passes for Master. Since these tests are non-competitive, titles earned are suffixes to the dog's name. Titles earned in competition, i.e. field trials, are prefixes. These tests have been enormously popular at all levels, but especially the Junior level. This truly is within the realm of possibilities for everyone and fun to work toward since basic retrieving ability is what is looked for.

To keep the interest high at the Master level, we have an annual Master National for which the dog must qualify by earning five qualifying scores in the year. This has been extraordinarily popular – the 1994 Master National had 226 dogs entered and 35 finalists.

Bunny has added a few personal thoughts on today's Flat-Coated Retrievers.

"Today, 1995 in America, we have fewer Flat-Coats running Field Trials than ten years ago. I can't see any change in the future. This is probably because of the advent of our Hunting Tests and the fact that Field Trial competition is so very stiff. In trials you don't need to fail a test to be eliminated, you just need a few 'fairs' or 'B' retrieves and you are out. Hunt Tests are judged with a more positive outlook – what did the dog do well? Many Flat-Coat owners find this more satisfying than trials. In any case a very large number of Flat-Coat people and dogs participate and are successful. There is less competitive pressure here, aside from the bruised ego when your dog can't find or won't listen.

"A very high percentage of Flat-Coat owners here participate in dog shows. Knowing what dog shows have done to the minds and bodies of so many formerly wonderful breeds I was alarmed but have resolved that, in a breed where an amazing 25% of the registered dogs become champions, showing is essentially a social affair with a special purpose."

Margot Hallet (Hardscrabble) is totally dedicated to Field events, which she describes as being an absolutely wonderful, often frustrating and lonely, pursuit if you like tilting at windmills. There will be many people who understand exactly what she means! She says: "There have been many highs and successes, not the least of which was putting the first field titles ever on a Flat-Coat on the North American continent with the best, most talented dog I've ever had, CFC CAFC Ch. Curlee Hill Blac Pacinko CD, MH, known as Mikan. With proper, modern training and more resources Mikan easily would have become an American AFC, a position filled by Ch. Jon-Lee's Spring Valley Atari.

Margot Hallett with CFC CAFC Ch. Curlee Hill Black Pacinto CD MH.

"American Retriever Field Trials are heartbreakingly difficult, competitive and artificial. While the 'blinds' could conceivably be arguable as genuine hunting situations, however far-fetched, there is nothing realistic about the 'marks'. Not only are the distances and combinations unrealistic, but the level to which these dogs can be trained is breathtaking, combined with most judges' ability these days limited to the technical. They are unable any more to take the given terrain and conditions to set up a fair contest and so rely on 'trained set-ups'.

If your dog has not gone through proper basics taught by a top notch pro, you do not stand a chance of ever completing a trial (and remember American trials are for all that enter on time; they are not limited). All this, whether your dog is talented or not. Of course the thing that would really help the working Flat-Coat would be to find more dedicated owner/handlers."

AGILITY IN THE US
Cheryl Kistner and Barbara DeMascio are both Agility enthusiasts. Cheryl will be remembered, along with her team, for her efficient, cheerful and unflappable chairing of the 1994 Chicago Speciality. Barbara started in Agility back in 1987/8 with her first Flat-Coat, Callie (Ch. Meadowrue Excalibur UD JH VAD). She gives details of Agility titles.

USDAA (United States Dog Agility Association) is the most established agility organisation. The association has used British Agility as its model, and sends a team to the World competition. It offers the following titles:-

Agility Dog (AD): Requires 3 qualifying scores (clear rounds) under 2 different judges.

Advanced Agility Dog (AAD): For dogs with their AD, requires 3 clear rounds under 2 judges – times are faster and rules a bit tougher.

Master Agility Dog (MAD): For dogs with their AAD, requires 3 clear rounds in the standard Masters class under 2 judges, plus a qualifying round in each game: Masters Gamblers, Masters Snooker, Masters Jumpers and Masters Pairs Relay – times are faster still and rules are as in British agility.

Veteran Agility Dog (VAD): For dogs over 7 years regardless of prior titles – the dogs compete at the height 6" lower than their regulation height, also there are no spread jumps, no tire and the A-frame is lower. They are judged under Advanced rules with Starters type courses and time. They need 3 legs under 2 judges.

Games Master: Each game has its own Master title. A dog competing at the Advanced level who earns 2 qualifying scores in a given game can move up to the Masters level of that game. A dog earning 5 qualifying scores in the same Masters level game is awarded the Master game title (Jumpers Master, etc.)

Agility Dog Champion (ADC): Awarded to a dog who earns an MAD plus all 4 Master game titles. This is a new title, and the first title-holder was a Pomeranian!).

As of the latest USDAA newsletter, which contained all title statistics, there are currently four Flat-Coats with the AD title (my Laika was one of the first two). There are no Flat-Coats with higher titles (but we're working on it!). I know of a couple of others preparing to compete, but have not seen any others at competitions here in the Northeast.

As for Flat-Coats in Agility: from my own experience it is a match made in heaven. The dogs love to do things with their owners, and agility requires close teamwork. Flat-Coats love to play, and Agility is a giant playground. They are quite agile on the ramps and most are good jumpers. They also have good speed, which is necessary to do well. They learn the obstacles quickly, control takes a little longer. Food or balls work well as motivators, as does praise. They love the sport enough that I have to watch they don't overheat in the warm weather, as they don't slow down. I think agility is a good sport for Flat-Coats since it develops the dog-owner bond to a high degree, which Flat-Coats crave.

Cheryl has the following to say about Flat-Coats and Agility: "Agility is a fast, fun sport patterned after horse jumping events that involves dogs jumping, scaling, running, and leaping – tailor-made for an active, outgoing breed like the Flat-Coated Retriever. There are five major Agility associations in North America that offer competitive Agility. The five organisations are: United States Dog Agility Association (USDAA), Agility Dog Association of Canada (ADAC), North American Dog Agility Council (NADAC), Trans-National Club for Dog Agility (TNCDA), and the American Kennel Club (AKC). Each club issues its own titles and has different levels of performance, rules, and jump heights.

"Basically USDAA, NADAC, and ADAC are very similar in regard to style and rules, and are all based on the International/English style of Agility. Speed, confidence and control are emphasised, with the major difference between the three organisations being jump heights. The NCDA, soon to be taken over by the United Kennel Club (UKC), emphasises control, precision, and confidence and de-emphasises speed and jump heights. The theme of NCDA is that it is for all handlers and all dogs. The American Kennel Club has blended both the NCDA sytle and USDAA style of Agility – more control and precision than USDAA and more emphasis on speed than NCDA, along with jump heights that are in between the two organisations. In all cases, each organisation has a performance standard for each piece of equipment, with faults assessed for improper performance, and a standard course time. To go over this is to receive time faults. The object is for the dog and handler to run the course that has been set up by the judge without making any mistakes, and to complete the course as quickly as possible.

"Agility is a great confidence builder and muscle conditioner and is a sure bet to become more popular throughout the United States due to its recent sanctioning by the American Kennel Club. Give it a try – Flat-Coats love it!"

FLYBALL

This is another activity which Flat-Coats thoroughly enjoy. As yet there are very few clubs in the UK but there is growing interest. The US is the "home" of Flyball. Chris Chambers of Saginaw, MI has been playing Flyball for 10 years with four Flat-Coats and other breeds and found that Flat-Coats love the game. Their desire to retrieve encourages them to get the ball and their own instinct is to return with the ball, fast. It takes about six months fully to train a dog to play competitively. A new rule by NAFA states that dogs may not compete until at least one year of age.

There are currently 31 Flat-Coats with NAFA numbers. The top point dog belongs to Luann Walraven of Michigan – Wyndhams Wizzard of Essex (Rebel) who has 9,962 points as of March 20th 1995. The next highest dog is "Dazzle" from Illinois who has 3,813 points.

Chris's first two Flat-Coats died before the points system came in; her present one, Essex Grousemoor Twilite Eyes (Ember), has 2,591 points. Chris says Flyball is a great team sport for people as well as dogs. Flat-Coats are particularly good, as often the whole team of 13 dogs are turned loose to play together! She does mention a problem if the tournament is near water; she has known her dog do the jumps, get the ball, run back, and then run straight past the handler into the water! Chris explains about Flyball: "The sport had its beginnings in the 1970s when Californian Herbert Wagner developed the first tennis ball launcher. Using rules developed for his obedience class graduations he eventually gave a demonstration on television's "The Tonight Show". This revolutionary new idea was then introduced in the Toronto-Detroit area by several dog training clubs. After a few small tournaments were held in conjunction with dog shows, the first-ever Flyball tournament was held in 1983.

"To standardise the rules, keep records of tournaments, and guide the development of the sport of Flyball, the North American Flyball Association (NAFA) was formed in 1985 by a group representing 12 teams from Michigan and Ontario and headed by Mike Randall, who remained as Executive Director until 1991. Interest and participation in the sport of Flyball has soared since its beginning and is now enjoyed throughout North America and the United Kingdom. NAFA has over 200 member clubs with more than 4,000 registered dogs.

"Flyball competition consists of races between two teams of four dogs each, racing side-by-side over a 51 foot long course. Each team's racing lane consists of 4 jumps spaced at 10 foot intervals, the first jump being 6 feet after the start/finish line, and a Flyball box placed 15 feet after the 4th jump. The Flyball box tosses a tennis ball at the dog after the dog pushes a pedal on the front of the box. Each dog must run in relay fashion down the jumps, trigger the release of the ball, retrieve the ball, and return over the jumps. The next dog is released to run the course but can't cross the start/finish line until the previous dog has returned over all 4 jumps and reached the start/finish line. Jump heights are set 4 inches shorter than the shoulder height of the smallest dog racing in

Anne Lee's Shadow practising Flyball.

the heat, with a minimum jump height of 8 inches and a maximum jump height of 16 inches. The first team to have all 4 dogs finish the course without error wins the heat. Missed jumps, dropped balls, etc. require the dog to be re-run after the rest of the team has finished.

Competition is fast paced with plenty of excitement for dogs, handlers, and especially spectators. Many teams run all 4 dogs through the course in less than 20 seconds, with a NAFA record time of less than 17.5 seconds. NAFA tournaments are divided into Divisions so that teams compete against other teams of equal abilities. All dogs over the age of 1 year including mixed breeds are eligible to compete and earn titles in NAFA sanctioned tournaments. Titles are earned by a point system based on the speed of the team running with your dog in the heats. All four dogs earn the same points per heat. Possible points per heat are 1 for a time from 28-32 seconds; 5 from 24-28 seconds; or 25 from 0-24 seconds.

It has to be said that, on looking at show entries, the number of Flat-Coats that carry titles of one sort or another is quite impressive. No other breed can show such achievements. This fact was mentioned by a group of "all breed" judges at a meeting of judges in Ottawa.

CANADA

As Margot Hallett said, "field training can be a lonely business" and I imagine never more so than in a vast country such as Canada, where Flat-Coat owners are widely scattered. There are a few areas where Flat-Coat owners can gather together, but for many training tends to be a single-handed task. One has to admire the determination and enthusiasm of those who make a real effort to train their dogs despite difficulties. There must be a characteristic of feeling that difficulties exist to be overcome!

Margaret Hall's name has been synonymous with producing Flat-Coated Retrievers of exceptional ability in competitive field work for many years. One only has to see the "Thornfield" affix to think "that should be a dog worth watching". Margaret has written about competitive field work in Canada and about some of her dogs including FTCh./Ch. Hardscrabble Blac Glory CD (Skoshi) bred by Margot Hallett. She says: "My first FC came from Vernon Vogel in 1979, a pretty black bitch who lived up to all her advance notice. She was a real all-rounder with titles in all the areas of competition. At the time of her death she was Am. Can. Ch. Bolingbroke Moon Shadow

Am CD WC, Can. CDX WCX, and the first Flat-Coat to win a singles championship. She was great to own, and exciting to work with, beautiful, talented, and clever. Since that time I have never been without a Flat-Coat. My kennel name is Thornfield, and I have done limited breeding under that prefix. While my dogs certainly see the show ring and compete in obedience, my first interest is definitely retrieving. Here in Canada we have two possible means of proving the retrieving talent of our dogs. The simpler of these is the Working Certificate programme.

"This is run on three levels, the Working Certificate, the Working Certificate Intermediate and the Working Certificate Excellent, known to participants as the WC, WCI and WCX. These are not competitions between dogs, but measurement against a standard. All Retrievers, Irish Water Spaniels and Standard Poodles are eligible.

"The certificate programme tests dogs according to training stages. The first step, the WC, has back-to-back singles on land followed by back-to-back singles in water. It is intended to test natural abilities such as nose, marking, memory, desire and courage. Training is of less importance. The dog may come to the line on lead and be held there but delivery must be to hand. Cover is expected to be light to moderate on land, and falls to vary from fifty to seventy-five yards in length, according to cover and terrain. Birds

Margaret Hall with Bolingbroke Moon Shadow Can. Ch. CDX, WCX, Am. Ch. CD, WC.

should land in cover. Water retrieves should be in swimming water and the line should be back from the edge of the water. Falls should be twenty-five to forty yards away, not hidden, in the water or at the edge of reeds.

"WCI tests include a land double, a water double and an honour. Distance, cover and falls will be more testing. Training assumes greater importance. Dogs come to the line off lead and must be steady. Decoys are used in water.

"WCX indicates a dog who would be an asset on a hunt. Tests are a walk-up with an honour to a land or land/water double, honouring on a repeat of that walk-up, a water double, land blind and a water blind. The handler carries a gun for the walk-up, and shoots for the water double and the land blind.

"The other choice is competition in Field Trials. This is much more demanding and exciting and is open to all Retrievers and Irish Water Spaniels. It is an elimination contest so you must meet the expectation of the judges in order to return for the next test. Stakes may include Puppy, Junior, Qualifying, and one of several classes of All Aged stakes. Amateurs may compete in any stake but professionals are not eligible for All Aged Amateur. Championship points are won in the All Age stakes, and the level of difficulty in some of the tests is amazing. Without great talent and highly developed skills, success is unlikely.

"To be a Field Trial Champion a dog must win a minimum of ten points in Open, Limited or Special All Aged Stakes of which five must come from a first placing. The dog has won over all-comers, whether trained or handled by an amateur or professional. The Amateur Field Trial Champion must earn at least 15 points while handled by an amateur, of which five were earned from a first placing.

"Our trials are very different from those in GB. The goal is to compare dogs as they each run the same test. While this is never fully achieved, the effort is made. Dogs run individually, and a second dog is on the line only if that dog is to honour. Puppies and Juniors get retrieve-only marks, but from qualifying on, blinds are added. By the time you are competing for points the tests become extremely demanding. Usually land work is done first, marks followed by blinds, the third test is a water blind and the final series will be marks on water. Work on each bird is scored, and the dogs whose work was satisfactory are invited back for the next series. Dogs are eliminated as they fail tests or accumulate enough faults that they are no longer in contention for placings. Should you be so lucky as to be there to the very end, your reward will be a ribbon. First place is a blue ribbon worth five points, second a red worth three points, third a yellow for one point and a fourth white is one half. Should you pass all the tests but not a place you may be awarded a green ribbon for a Certificate of Merit. While blue is my favourite colour I would not refuse any!

"The path through field trials is the one Skoshi followed to become FTCh./Ch. Hardscrabble's Blac Glory CD. After Shadow died it was so lonesome without a working retriever that I started looking for a Flat-Coat with whom to go training. Then the newsletter of the FCRSA arrived with an offer of sale for a three year old bitch who was placing in field trials, was qualified both in the USA and Canada for Open, and was believed by breeder/owner Margot Hallett to be a possible dual champion. She was by Ch. Destiny the London Times out of Can FTCh./AFTCh. Ch.(US) Curlee Hill Blac Pacinko CD. Tempting? Well, at New Year's of 1986 I drove to Margot's, looked once and brought her home. On a month's approval, of course. One must be practical about these things. So Skoshi became mine. Or was I hers? I have been grateful to Margot ever since. Skoshi was trained and usually handled by Dan DeVos. Winter training was in the southern States so water work could be done. In the remainder of the year she was nearer home and spent more time with me. It was a busy time training and trialling, with obedience competition, the show ring and puppies fitted in between. Skoshi gave me the greatest thrills I have known with dogs, and more than once the tears were running down my face while I watched her run. She died last May, aged eleven and a half, a charmer to the last.

"Trialling with a Flat-Coat is very different now. When Skoshi began running in this area, she was a curiosity to the many people who had never seen the breed before and were absolutely certain no such creature needed to be taken seriously. Indeed, her right to compete was questioned by an occasional ignoramus. At one training trial I attended with a Flat-Coat a brash fellow informed me that the trial was limited to registered animals. Fortunately for my equanimity these were greatly outnumbered by the supportive people who have made trials a joy to remember. There are good working Flat-Coats out there following the elusive gleam. Two have achieved the title in Canada, and more will do so in the future.

Chapter Ten

BREEDING AND MATING

TO BREED OR NOT TO BREED?

This is not intended to paraphrase "Hamlet" but is a question that needs a great deal of consideration. Having a bitch does not mean that she either needs to be, or should be, bred from, in the same way that a male animal does not need to be used at stud. At one time vets tended to recommend that a bitch should have one litter, as this was thought to inhibit the chances of her developing pyometra at some stage. In fact, it was always doubtful if the production of large numbers of litters, regardless of quality, was warranted on this premise. Don't forget, we are talking here of all breeds. With the constant improvement in modern drugs, providing the illness is recognised in the very early stages, there is a good chance of controlling it without resource to surgery. Action has to be swift.

The obvious reason why an established breeder breeds is to continue the line and it is carefully thought out, often two or three generations ahead – not necessarily down to the actual males to be used, but deciding on the intended blood lines.

I am talking about breeders, not puppy producers; they are two entirely different concepts. Until very recently puppy producers were virtually unheard of in Flat-Coated Retrievers, particularly while puppy prices were kept low. There was no financial incentive to breed. Sadly, with the increase in popularity, prices have risen and in some countries, the Far East for example, the Flat-Coat is now a "status symbol" and much sought after. The worrying aspect of this is that, like all status symbols, the trend is short-lived and the "symbol" is then discarded in the same way as an outdated TV.

What are the other categories of people who think of taking a litter? There are still the people who trot out the "good for the bitch" reason, usually with pound, krone or dollar symbols floating in their heads; the people who adore their bitch and feel she would have wonderful puppies which other people could then enjoy; and the person who has bought a good bitch, has done something with her, be it in field, show or some other activity, and wants to start a serious breeding programme.

Let us just accept the reasons given above, even if one feels the first to be questionable, understands and sympathises with the second, and finds the third the most positive.

There is more to having a litter than just producing puppies. There are certain very real requirements – knowledge, time, facilities, money and, the most important factor: "Will these puppies have something to offer the breed?" The would-be breeder needs to give thought to other considerations as well. Suppose the litter is large and consists mainly of males. Has the breeder the facilities for running on, say, three or four dog puppies if suitable homes cannot be found? Indeed, is the breeder in a position to find suitable homes for the puppies at all?

Eskmill Gambit with her puppies, Dash, Taryn and Smiley. Bred by Jenny Donnelly. A brood bitch must be a sound representative of the breed with a reliable, responsive temperament. Photo: Julie Condron.

REQUIREMENTS IN A BREEDING BITCH

My own view is that a brood bitch should fulfil certain requirements. She should be a good, sound, healthy representative of the breed. She should have a reliable, sensible and responsive temperament. She should have shown herself capable of undertaking some activity, not only in the show ring, but also Field, Agility, Tracking, Obedience or whatever. Personally, I like a bitch to show aptitude for field training, not necessarily on a competitive basis, although fine if this is so, but with the ability and stamina to do a creditable day's work in the shooting field – hunting, for our USA friends. Or she should at least have been responsive to training and show potential as a working dog.

It is important to take into account hip scores and freedom from other defects (this includes eye checks). Figures and charts would not be among my own first requirements; I started by saying, "good, sound, healthy". However, I do have other requirements which, in my view are generally grossly undervalued and if I was ever in the position of having to buy a potential brood bitch – a situation now unlikely for me – they would rate high in my enquiries.

Does the bitch come from a prolific line?

Do the bitches ovulate regularly; that is, come into season regularly?

Are the bitches in the line easy whelpers?

Are they sensible when whelping?

Are they good milk producers?

Are they good and sensible mothers?

How often do people give consideration to these essential characteristics? If they did, many problems and anxieties would be avoided.

THE STUD DOG

Having considered the brood bitch this may be a good time to consider the stud dog. Because a dog happens to be male this does not automatically mean that he should be used to reproduce himself. There is an old saying "the bull is half the herd" and this is true equally of the stud dog.

As with the brood bitch, there are essential requirements. I consider sound construction to be essential – a dog that looks masculine and not one that could be mistaken for a bitch. Temperament is important; allowances must be made for male characteristics but these must not be confused with a generally aggressive attitude. There is a difference between a male's natural protective attitude when his "family" is threatened and the male who is needlessly and impetuously aggressive in his normal response to meeting other dogs, sometimes regardless of whether they are dogs or bitches.

Like my preferred bitch, the dog should have proved himself in some sphere other than the show ring. Again my preference is for a dog with good natural ability in the field, but I would accept a dog that has shown ability in another direction. The main objective is that the dog is responsive to training and has the inherent ability to use this training. Do you remember the "imponderables" I referred to in an earlier chapter?

CHOOSING A STUD DOG

Having decided to take the step of breeding a litter, one then needs to choose a suitable mate. It is all-important when one starts breeding to use a proven stud dog – not just a dog who has produced puppies, but a dog who has produced puppies of type and worth. In other words, a dog who is prepotent and reproduces himself. Look at progeny from several bitches, of different lines if possible, and always study the grandparents of both the bitch and stud dog. An experienced breeder can afford to follow hunches, but not the beginner.

The bitch needs to be considered without prejudice, acknowledging any weaknesses which need to be compensated; and the use to which the puppies will eventually be put is very important. Unless the bloodlines happen to be compatible, it is not a good idea to use the latest winning male or the newest import. It is also advisable to enquire about the dog's hip scores and the results of eye tests.

COLOUR

When considering the choice of sire, colour preference must be considered. Two colours are acceptable, black or liver. Black is the dominant colour but, if the dog and bitch carry liver, even six or seven generations back, there could be liver puppies in the litter. A liver male mated to a liver bitch will produce only liver puppies.

Over the past few years some lines have been found to produce yellow puppies. If you know that the lines you have come into this category, then extra care must be taken in the choice of a male. Preferably use a male of known all-black breeding, but certainly one that has proved not to be a yellow producer or carrier.

METHODS OF BREEDING

Line breeding: this is my own favoured method. Some of the same animals appear in both sides of the pedigree, even though they may be three generations back. These dogs must be of proven worth in the breed from progeny already produced.

In breeding: this is closer, e.g. father to daughter, half-brother to half-sister for example, preferably no closer than that, so not between siblings. In breeding will stamp type and reinforce characteristics but will also accentuate weaknesses. The Toy Poodle was achieved very largely by

COLOUR TRANSFERENCE
Diagrams by kind permission of Rosemarie Wild (Switzerland).

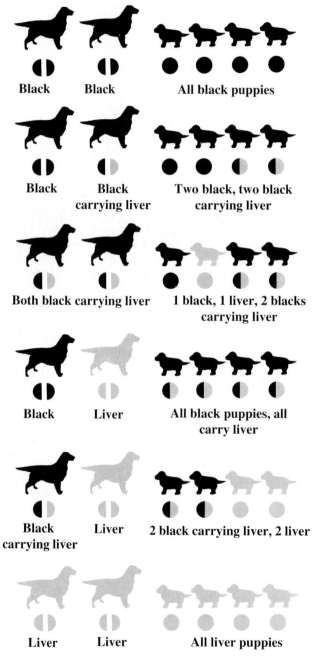

Black is dominant to liver.

Atherbram Ability, a liver-coloured Flat-Coat, bred by Annabel Payne, owned by Sarah Whittaker. Choosing colour is one of the decisions to make when planning a breeding programme.

successive generations of very close breeding. In breeding should be left to the experienced as, for safety, every so often an outcross must be introduced.

Outcross: this is when the two animals to be mated are totally unrelated. The result will be the gamble of how the genes happen to combine. A lack of uniformity within the litter is likely. Even if the litter contains a "flyer", this has happened by chance and there is no certainty that his or her quality will be reproduced.

Whatever the breeding pattern embarked upon, always look at grandparents on both sides; puppies so frequently throw back to them.

MAKING ARRANGEMENTS

Having considered all the relevant factors and studied pedigrees, hopefully you have found a suitable sire.

Approach the owner and ask if you may use the dog. If your bitch is not known, the stud dog owner will want to know more about her; if possible, see her; certainly see her pedigree, and need to know approximately when she is due in season and will later need to be notified as soon as this happens.

It is essential that arrangements on stud fees, or alternative arrangements, are clear to both parties at this stage, to avoid future problems. The stud fee is payable when a mating has taken place. The fee is for the service, not for the ensuing litter. Quite often two matings are given, with a day in between – a sort of belt and braces approach. However if the bitch is at the optimum time, she seems to hold to the first mating.

If no puppies ensue most stud dog owners will give a free repeat mating at a future date. There is no legal obligation to do this, it is purely a matter of goodwill.

If "payment" is by "puppy in lieu of stud fee", the owner of the dog has first choice of puppy unless otherwise stated. It is helpful to know in advance, if possible, if this would be a dog or bitch but one has to be a bit fluid on this, and there must be mutual agreement.

Some stud dog owners insist on all bitches being swabbed by the vet before mating, but no doubt will state this when the arrangements are being made.

BREEDING AGE

The first season can be as early as six months or as late as twelve. The age at which this happens often gives an indication of the interval that can then be expected between seasons and, certainly, ,the interval between first and second season sets the pattern for the future. Relatively few Flat-Coats come in season at six months, nine is far more usual.

One of the most irresponsible and misguided statements is that a bitch can be bred from at her second heat. Flat-Coat bitches are slow to mature physically and, more especially, mentally. Even at two years they are still very "young in the head". Two years is the absolute minimum age at which a litter should be taken and in truth it should be later, as a litter at the age of two will only interrupt the training programme. Rising three is a good age.

THE IN-SEASON BITCH

If a litter is to be bred, remember to keep immunising jabs/shots up to date, so that the bitch has good maternal immunity to pass on to the puppies. The normal worming programme should be kept up, and the bitch wormed before mating.

The season has three stages:-

1. The onset when the vulva swells and looks obviously pinkish with a discharge, slight at first but then definitely red. The bitch becomes very flirtatious, but at this stage repels any advances by the male.
2. The "acceptance" stage; careful watch needs to be kept. Hold a piece of cotton wool against the bitch to check the colour of the discharge. First thing in the morning is the best time. When the discharge becomes pale salmon pink and if the bitch turns her tail when you rub her croup behind the tail, you could be in business. The tail-turning bit is not infallible – some bitches always do this!
3. Post-oestrus: When, although the bitch is still technically on heat, she again repels advances.

One develops a sixth sense about when a bitch is ready; around the 11/12/13th day is very usual, but it can be as early as the ninth day or as late as the 16th, although this is unusual. For example, if you mate on the 11th day then a second mating could be on the 13th, but if she appears to be "going off" you can mate on two consecutive days or, indeed, just once and wait and see!

If you are using an experienced stud dog, and owner, you can leave most of the actual mating arrangements to them and just do as you are asked in the way of any assistance. That way you will learn yourself.

RELUCTANT BITCHES
Providing the timing is right, it is unusual for Flat-Coat bitches to be actually bad-tempered about being mated. A slight tetchiness in the initial stages is not unusual but, should the bitch be adamantly resistant, I would have doubts about pursuing the mating. If the bitch is just a bit snappy a nylon stocking can be criss-crossed round the muzzle, but this is very rarely necessary. With a truly resistant bitch, try her, if possible, with a different dog and see if for some reason she does not like her chosen mate. If she is still reluctant, even on a different day, I would give up. It is a very rare occurrence but strangely, if you persist and actually get a litter, you may well find the bitch is also a reluctant mother – bad mother in fact.

SCIENTIFIC HELP
Nowadays there are certain very common practices to help when embarking on a litter. With the help of your vet, tests can be made when the bitch comes in season and the optimum time for mating given. After mating, at the time suggested by your vet, a scan can be made and you will know if the bitch is in whelp or not.

Many people seem to find this helpful but I must admit to not using either service. I feel very strongly that the less interference there is with the bitch the better. It works for us. A masterly inactivity you could say.

STUD DOG MANAGEMENT
Having discussed the bitch owner's procedure, it is worth giving further thought to the stud dog and owner.

When a young dog is to be used at stud, it helps greatly if there is an experienced bitch on which to prove him. This is not always possible, so in that case, do try and use him for the first time on an older bitch who has been bred. It helps if this can take place when the dog is about 18 months of age, and then, preferably, wait and see how the progeny turn out. Also, the dog himself should be making progress in one sphere or another to give him the credentials to warrant use at stud.

If it is a case of the dog being used once, then never again, I would say, don't. What he has never had, he will never miss. In North America the question of breeding/spaying/castrating is often included in the sales agreement, but it is virtually never mentioned in the UK, unless it is in regard to, say, "a puppy back" or something like that and this is frequently only a verbal agreement.

Actual management is largely a matter of the dog having total confidence in his handler and also, from the start, not being allowed to play about for hours. I well remember, back in the late fifties, taking a Golden bitch to a well-known Golden breeder. After some five hours the Golden owner fetched brandy for the stud dog and I could not help saying that I felt my need was as great as his!

A brief "getting to know" period is fine, although this may be extremely short with a competent, experienced stud, but don't let the dog get into the habit of prolonging this. I have known too many folk who have spent a day in a cold wet field while the dog and bitch raced round and round until both were exhausted. You will have grasped that I don't go along with the "let them loose in a field and do it themselves" school of thought. For one thing a good stud dog could easily be hurt and ruined forever.

PRE-MATING PREPARATION
Before starting the mating it is often helpful to cut away some of the hair round the vulva and apply a tiny smear of Vaseline. If there is an appreciable height difference in the dog and bitch, make use of sloping ground. You have to think out which way round they need to be for the dog to reach.

THE MATING
Once they have met, far better to steady the bitch at the head end and have the stud dog owner at the business end. If the male has confidence in his handler, a little shove up with the knee against the dog's hindquarters, and/or a little guidance at the crucial moment can save a lot of wasted time and effort. Simultaneously, warn the bitch owner to "hold tight" – that is, firmly but without agitation, which will transmit to the bitch. The dog also needs to be steadied until tied. Never ever try to separate a dog and bitch when they are tied. This can be very painful and also injurious.

THE TIE
Most owners feel happier with a long tie – apart from all parties involved growing bored and running out of small talk! In fact the length of the "tie" does not seem to be the criterion. Some dogs swell more than others and take longer to deflate. I've known a quick in/out to have results. Always praise both the dog and the bitch; they can be very self-conscious when owners are present. In fact, at times, particularly with the pet-type owner, it is better to put the owner away with a book – possibly on puppy-rearing – and a cup of coffee, until the deed is accomplished.

Only breed from good, sound stock. If you are new to the breed, ask advice and the opinion of a long-established breeder.

Only breed if you feel the ensuing litter will have something positive to benefit the Breed.

Only breed if you have the facilities and wherewithal to cope with puppies should suitable owners not be immediately available.

My own view is that breeding, to be of benefit, must be on a selective basis. This is how various breeds were evolved in the first place, and it is the only way in which not only type, but character and abilities can be maintained.

Never breed for one aspect only.

Chapter Eleven

PREGNANCY AND WHELPING

THE IN-WHELP BITCH

One almost feels like adding "hopefully", because indeed that is the usual feeling and no doubt why scanning is popular. If you wish to have a scan, contact your vet after the mating for advice on the best time. If, like myself, you are prepared to "wait and see", then just carry on as normal. I think it is advisable to keep the bitch quiet immediately after the mating, but otherwise continue with the usual routine. I find, at about three weeks, I perhaps look out of the kitchen window as the bitch crosses the garden and just have a flash of thought, "that bitch is in whelp". Strangely, there is no further indication. It can easily be five weeks before the body shape changes slightly.

The more normally the bitch is treated, the better, but one must use common-sense. As the weeks progress it is unwise to have her taking part in excessively energetic pastimes such as high wall scaling in Agility. In fact, often the bitch herself will indicate that she is feeling a mite fragile and is taking care of herself. It is worth taking heed. Do not cut down on the normal exercise to which her body is accustomed. It must be regular and not strenuous.

WORMING

Mention was made earlier of keeping up a worming routine appropriate to one's area. Opinions vary on the most effective programme for in-whelp bitches. Certainly the bitch should be wormed before mating; then comes the difference of opinion.

One school of thought is that the bitch be wormed two weeks after mating and not again until the puppies have their first worming. Another suggests worming before mating, nothing at all during pregnancy, but then three days after whelping – but just the bitch.

A different type of programme is suggested by a very reputable drug company which produces a very effective broad-spectrum wormer. This consists of a small daily dose (as prescribed) from day 40 of pregnancy to two days post whelping (approximately 25 days). This is said to reduce the incidence of worms in the pups by reducing pre-natal infection. We have followed this programme very successfully about three times although I have this reluctance to give the bitch any type of drug during pregnancy – yet I know the drug is safe and effective. As with most of these matters, I feel discussion with your vet is the answer.

FEEDING

In the early stages there need be no dramatic change in the feeding routine, always taking it for granted that nutritionally good quality feed is used. With the wide range of complete feeds available there are diets to suit every stage, from puppyhood to old age. Most companies also have excellent advisory services.

If feeding is of the "home-cooking" type – that is basically the broken biscuit type meal with meat – again, continue as usual. If the meat used, be it fresh, frozen or canned, is largely of chicken, lamb or tripe origin, then at least once a week red meat (cooked) should be substituted. Liver is excellent, although it has the reputation for "going through" the dog; actually I find this applies to canned feed with a high liver content more than with freshly cooked liver. Regulate the amount. A few chopped "greens", carrots and onion are all excellent added to this type of feed. Moderation at all times.

Whatever type of feed is used, as pregnancy proceeds, it is advisable to divide the feeds, giving only slightly greater quantity but in, say, three small feeds a day. Late on in pregnancy, I give one of the feeds as a milky one, which is milk and uncooked porridge oats with an occasional beaten egg dropped in. Yes, I know about eggs, but I did say occasional, in this case once or twice a week so that the amount of albumen will not be a problem; also I do mean FRESH eggs.

"Complete" feed means just that, so no additions should be needed, although there is no harm in giving yeast tablets. On "home feed", we sprinkle a mix made up from ingredients that can be obtained at any Health Food Shop. We call it 'Manhattan Mix' and it is a wonderful health maintainer. The recipe is given in Chapter Five. Raspberry leaf tablets are an old-time remedy that has come back in fashion and is said to aid easy whelping. They may do; they won't cause any harm and may help the owner enormously.

WHELPING BEDS/BOXES

A few years ago while at the Club show, I had an emergency call: "Come home at once, Pansy is whelping." The pups were due some ten days later and, before leaving, I had mentioned to Pansy that, according to statistics, her puppies could not be born before the following Wednesday, the earliest date given for parturition in relation to the date of mating. Pansy did not want me to go, but certainly gave no physical sign of being about to produce. How wrong can you be?

Some time after I had left, my husband came back into the house for breakfast and was met at the door by Pansy who handed him a puppy! She more or less said "so there!" Hence the frantic phone call to the show ground. She had two more puppies and then resolutely refused to have any more until I arrived home, just over an hour later. She then settled down and had a further eleven. All big, robust pups. Her body had obviously decided that it could or would no longer carry this load, regardless of records and statistics. They all survived and did well.

Part of the point of this story is that for some eight or nine weeks I had been saying that we needed a new whelping box; my menfolk kept assuring me that there was plenty of time. I arrived home to find husband sitting with Pansy, who was ignoring him, and number one son sawing wood madly in the garage!

Oblong wooden dog beds are good, but there must be enough width for the bitch to stretch out full length. The wood must be smooth and closely joined for hygienic reasons, and it certainly appears warmer than other materials.

There are now a variety of composition beds. Some are of the same design as a wooden bed but constructed from an easy-clean material. Others are more like a plastic shell design with the inner part being curved, so there are no corners. We have used one of this type for about three litters and found it excellent. If so wished, there can be a heated pad underneath the base.

The size and shape makes the bed a bit cumbersome but it is very light-weight, so easy to move and easy to clean. The big bonus I feel is that the curved inner shape means that, when whelping, the bitch can brace herself against it, which seems helpful. Also there is no space behind the bitch's back and the bed for a pup to get into. This type of bed can be fitted with rails but of course that cuts down on the inner dimensions.

A purpose-built whelping box.

THE "SHOPPING LIST"

Let the bitch become accustomed to the bed in advance – Pansy had to use the bed I intended to replace with the new one.

Newspapers or, if available, incontinence pads are good.

'Vet bed' or similar. A synthetic sheepskin type material. When puppies are first born it is better to use some middle-aged vet bed. New vet bed is too "plushy".

Old towels

Kitchen roll (paper towels)

Cotton wool

Iodine

Savlon/Dettol or similar antiseptic

Disposable polythene gloves

Blunt-ended scissors

Eye dropper (blunt-ended type)

Large plastic refuse/garbage bag

Glucose

Casilan (an easily digested invalid food)

Evaporated Milk

ABIDEC high concentrate vitamin syrup

Brandy (can be useful should the bitch need a quick stimulant)

The last three are for emergency use.

Some of the above items may not be used but, if required, need to be immediately available.

Have some light, nutritious food ready for the bitch for her first feed when she has rested after whelping. Chicken or fish with boiled rice, or rice pudding. Natural live yoghurt is also good.

THE LABOUR

Years ago, when I had Griffons, I always notified my vet of the date the puppies were due. Griffons are hell to whelp. Most Flat-Coats are easy whelpers, so hopefully there will not be problems but, if the owner is anxious, then it helps to know that professional back-up is available. It is so essential that the owner does not transmit his or her feelings of concern to the bitch. To her this is a normal function and it should be regarded as such.

Have old newspapers in the bed (not any type of material). The bitch will probably start panting and getting huffy-puffy. Also she may tear up the paper into nicely shredded pieces.

At this stage it is inadvisable to let the bitch out into the garden on her own, particularly if the area is large or has access to hedgerows and fields. She is quite likely to decide to find herself a secluded well-hidden hole in which to have the puppies.

Avoid great comings and goings in the whelping area. Calm and quiet is the message. For some years I have felt that we tend to over-assist when the bitch is whelping: we hover. This made me question "why"? The answer of course is that it is our own anxieties that we are alleviating. So, masterly inactivity and a watching brief is all that is necessary.

Having said this, once labour starts and the bitch is actually straining, a puppy should appear quite soon. I am talking minutes not hours. If the straining continues, then seek professional advice. Between puppies the interval can vary; as long as the bitch appears comfortable, no need to worry. Again the sign to watch for is actual straining to no avail, or if the bitch seems suddenly to lose interest and just give up, yet you feel she hasn't finished. In a large litter, she may in fact, "take a break", but her attitude is different. Never delay in seeking advice if there is doubt. It can be the difference between live or dead puppies. In fact, I have never needed veterinary assistance with a Flat-Coat, so don't be worried unnecessarily, but be prepared.

It doesn't matter if the puppies come front-wards or backwards. This is where we tend to get over-anxious. In most cases the bitch will remove the "bag" herself, will welcome the puppy with licks and will chew the cord to free the puppy. Providing she does this, let her cope. If by any chance she does not, immediately clear the bag from the head, then make sure the mouth and nostrils are clear of mucus. If you need to sever the cord – well, I know the list mentioned scissors, but a thumbnail used in a firm rubbing/fraying action is preferable. Less sudden. Always keep any tension at the bitch end, not the puppy. A pull from the puppy end can result in a hernia. The bitch's licking will stimulate the puppy as well as removing all the gunge.

The bed will get very wet; this is where the kitchen roll comes in. The garbage bag is for wet newspaper or other rubbish.

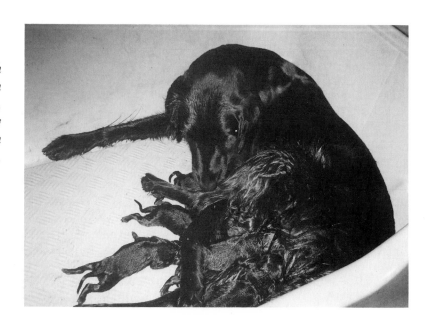

A bitch with her newborn puppies, halfway through whelping.

Should the severed cord bleed too freely, a dab of iodine on cotton wool should be held against pup and the cord. The bitch will eat afterbirths. If possible try and keep count so that you see the same number of afterbirths as there are puppies. Sometimes this is difficult. I let the bitch eat two or three and try to remove any others into the garbage bag. I know some people feel they must remove all afterbirths, but they have a high concentration of minerals etc. which the bitch is losing.

A small drink can be given to the bitch if she seems thirsty.

THE WEAK PUPPY
A floppy or weak puppy can be given vigorous rubbing with an old towel. If this fails, hold the puppy in your hand, with head and neck very firmly held in the palm, (otherwise you will break the pup's neck) hold your arm above your head, then swing down sharply.

Very, very gentle mouth resuscitation can be tried (GENTLE, else baby lungs will be damaged).

Heart areas can be massaged with ball of thumb.

Plunging in and out of very warm and then cold water and more rubbing.

A tiny drop of brandy from the eye dropper.

If all efforts fail, do put puppy away without the bitch seeing, or else she may try to go searching. Bitches can count. Of course there could be valid comment that, by the "law of the jungle", if a pup is a really weakly specimen, not just traumatised, then it is better to let go, early rather than later.

COLOSTRUM
It is better not to give a puppy anything at this stage. The mother's first milk, colostrum, is very high in protein, anti-bodies and vitamin A, so it provides an essential start for the puppies. A weaker puppy should be put to the mother by you, and watched to avoid being pushed out. If it seems essential to give something then, at this stage, boiled water, plain or with the addition of a small amount of glucose, can be given from the eye dropper.

TIDYING UP
The Casilan is good if the bitch is very exhausted after whelping and needs high nourishment that is easily digested. When the bitch has finished, dry around the her and the puppies again, then leave her quietly on clean paper or slide in an oldish piece of 'vet bed' – not new because this is so plushy that new pups can get down into the fleece, and a tired bitch may not feel them and may inadvertently lie on one. A worn piece that still has some substance is best. There are few more satisfying sights than seeing the bitch settle down, warm and comfortable with her brood.

When she has rested, a small palatable feed should be offered and, of course, liquid. The bitches food and liquid requirements will rise enormously over the next few days and weeks. If there are any doubts that there may be a retained afterbirth or an unborn puppy, seek professional advice at once. It is not a bad idea to have a check in any case.

COMPLEMENTARY FEEDINGS
Never rush to complementary feed. I have mentioned putting and holding a weaker pup on the dam. The bitch and puppies will usually adjust. If a puppy seems to be dropping back, then continue to make sure that the puppy has some mother's milk; anything extra must only complement this, not be a substitute. In these very early days, evaporated milk seems to work well. Only slightly dilute it with some hot water to take chill off. Just one small droplet of the Abidec, the high concentrate vitamin syrup used for babies, can be added, once a day. Always regard complementary feeding as a temporary measure. The idea is to boost the weaker puppy to get on a

par with the rest of the litter. Always have newspaper under the 'vet bed'; both paper and bed will need changing daily. The simulated sheepskin is machine-washable. The bitch will need three or four meals a day. One can be a milky feed.

DEWCLAWS
Quite tricky. Vets are now reluctant to remove dewclaws, which is a problem because they can be troublesome in a working dog. They catch in brambles and even wire, sometimes being partially torn out, which is painful and may even need surgery. So in many ways it is simpler to have them removed at four days. A skilled vet can do the job quickly and there seems no after -trauma.

VISITORS
At this stage the bitch needs rest and quiet to adjust to her family. Later she will enjoy showing them to admirers, and visitors in moderation will help socialise the puppies.

INITIAL "NEST" CLEANLINESS
There are excellent products available specifically formulated for animal use. Some even claim to inactivate parvovirus.
    Once the pups start to shuffle round the bed, have the 'vet bed' covering about three quarters of the bed, at the remaining end leave the newspaper uncovered. They will use this as a "poop and pee" area and keep their actual bed clean. On the whole, that is!

PUPPIES' PROGRESS
At first the puppies eat and sleep, with little sprawling expeditions to the milk bar. At ten days their eyes start to open and they will have approximately doubled their birth weight. At two weeks the puppies start to make little barking noises instead of squeaks. At three weeks, or depending on your selected programme, worm the puppies with basic-type wormer such as a piperazine citrate syrup. The bitch can have tablets.

The puppies are now two days old, and the bitch is caring for all their needs, feeding them and cleaning them.

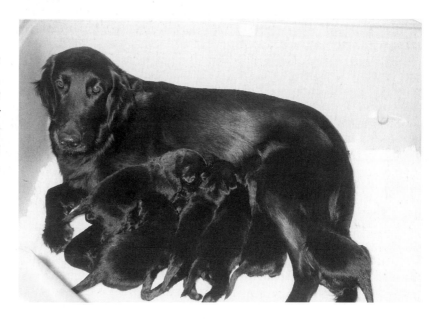

Puppies are born blind and helpless. The eyes generally open at around ten days.

Once weaning is under way, the puppies' development is very rapid.

EARLY FEEDING

At between three and four weeks of age additional feeding can be introduced. Be governed by the puppies' needs.

The first day give just one milky feed: the next day give two, adding some unflavoured baby cereal. Within days minced meat and soaked puppy biscuit meal or boiled brown rice can be given. By the fourth day of commencing feeding, four feeds daily should be given.

If you are feeding a complete feed, then feed as directed.

Never over-feed, whatever the type of feeding followed.

Fresh water must be available at all times.

Worming programme should be continued. I give a broad spectrum wormer at six weeks.

BEDDING

If 'Vet bed' is used, it is important that the under paper is changed daily and that the 'Vet bed' is washed daily. Even if not soiled, it becomes slightly damp and any form of humidity can result in mild skin problems. Occasionally for no apparent reason pups may have lice, particularly when living in rural areas. A specific shampoo from the vet is the answer (also for the dam).

TOYS

No need to be expensive. Strips of old strong linen with two or three knots make good "dollies" to tug and play with. Empty plastic mineral-water bottles, with top and loose bands removed, are great for rolling round the floor. Watching the puppies play also gives good insight into their characters and can give an indication of which puppy will suit which new owner.

HOUSE TRAINING

In good dry weather, if the pups can run out immediately on waking and after food it helps enormously with "house" training. This is less easy in winter. If the pups are in the house then continuing with the newspaper area helps. In a dog house there can be an area with soft pine shavings – but not sawdust. Shavings are very easy to clean up and smell good.

A beautifully reared puppy, ready to go to its new home.

REGISTRATION

To be eligible to enter shows, Field trials or other competitive events, dogs need to be registered with the Kennel Club of the country concerned. The registration also gives validity to the pedigree. Most breeders have their own kennel name (affix) which is for their sole use and makes naming the dogs easier, and also from the name one can tell who has bred the dog.

The form has to be countersigned by the owner of the stud dog, so this is frequently done at the time of mating.

As soon as the puppies are settled and thriving, it is as well to send in the application, as processing can take a few weeks and it helps to have the papers to hand when the puppies are ready to leave.

NEW HOMES

By now, hopefully, the puppies will be sturdy, confident little characters of around eight weeks old, ready for the big, wide world. Every puppy must be checked carefully before going to a new owner. Skin, ears, eyes and teeth must be examined. The change needs to be made with as little trauma as possible; to this end the new owner needs information – an "Owner's package" in fact.

OWNER'S PACKAGE

Pedigree.

Kennel Club registration papers with the transfer slip signed. Any endorsement such as "not for export", or "progeny not to be bred from", must have been discussed previously with the new owner.

Insurance certificate, as agreed upon.

Diet sheet. Very important. Details of number of feeds the puppy has been having, the type of feed and the maker (brand name).

It helps to give the new owner a little bag of "goodies", small bags or tins of appropriate food to start the puppy off in his new home.

There should also be details of worming programme and date of last treatment.

Date when first immunising injections will be needed – although I prefer the owner to consult with their own vet. Local conditions vary.

Give some advice on early management and behaviour.

Give guidelines on amount of exercise required – not excessive or erratic.

Give details of Breed clubs and other organisations involved in appropriate activities. Have a clear written statement if the puppy is not to be exported (even if the registration form is endorsed). Recently the KC (UK) has stated that any endorsement, for example "not to be exported" or "progeny not to be bred from", needs to have been discussed with the prospective purchaser. Verbal agreement on the part of the buyer is not sufficient. The Kennel Club will only implement the endorsement providing a written and signed agreement is made at the time of the sale. A copy should be kept by the breeder as well as the buyer.

It is also as well to state clearly that if, for any reason, the puppy needs re-homing at any stage in life, you, the breeder, must be contacted first. It is not always possible to have the dog back, but at least help can be given to find a suitable new home. The breeder's responsibility does not end when the cheque is banked!

Chapter Twelve

CONTEMPORARY BRITISH KENNELS

Many breeds are dominated by a number of large Kennels but this is not the case with Flat-Coats. The few larger kennels could be counted on one hand, and even the largest would be regarded as small in many other breeds. The fact that many dedicated Flat-Coat owners and skilled breeders only have 2, 3, 4 or 5 Flat-Coats has made it extremely difficult to decide on a few "significant" kennels to write about, so there are omissions which sadly are unavoidable, even though I have tried to write less on more! The famous ATHERBRAM, dating from the early part of this century, originally PHIZAKLEA and now HILARY HUGHES has already been mentioned.

BELSUD (1962): MARY GRIMES
Mary Grimes had her first Flat-Coat, Bella of Whiterails in 1959. She has always had an interest in Livers but has also bred many good blacks which have done well here and overseas. Mary is a Championship show judge and in fact awarded Ch. IrCh. Shargleam Blackcap the CC and BoB at Crufts in 1980 when he went on to win the Gundog group and then Best in Show. The Belsud dogs are well known in the show ring but in the winter also form part of a working picking-up team.

Mary has had so many good dogs over the years but her choice of "special" Flat-Coat goes to Ch. Belsud Brown Guillemot, "perfect to live with, work and show". That is certainly true. I remember seeing her partner a junior handler, and the bitch was so skilful in the ring, the young handler had no chance to show her expertise.

BORDERCOT (1955): ROSALIE BRADY
When Rosalie Brady was 10 years old, her parents bought her a well-bred and much longed for Papillon puppy. From this came Rosalie's life-long involvement with the world of dogs. When she married Gerald in 1967, he needed a shooting dog. As Rosalie still enjoyed showing, they decided on a Flat-Coated Retriever and bought the puppy from Peggy Robertson that became Ch. Bordercot Stolford Doonigan. Later Rosalie took over Stolford Missis Mopp from Peggy and gained her elusive third CC, followed by a further three, and two Field Trial Awards. Doonigan was the Breed record holder for a considerable time, gaining 22 CCs under different judges.

Rosalie continued this record-breaking ability with Doonigan's grandson, Bordercot Guy (Ch.), purchased in 1979. In 1990, due to Tom and Caroline Gates' ill-health, Rosalie took over a son of Guy's Lacetrom Cardow, who became "of Bordercot" and a show champion, winning the Gundog group at WKC in 1992.

CANNIMORE: MICHAEL AND LESLEY ANDERSON
Truly dual-purpose, the present dogs include the FT winner Riversflight Genil, Ch. Heronsflight Magic, Heronsflight Go Softly and Cannimore Vagabond.

ABOVE: Ch. Bordercot Guy, bred and owned by Rosalie Brady. Photo: Sally Anne Thompson.

LEFT: Tarncourt Cavalier of Casuarina SDC. Bred by Joan Marsden, owned by Cyraine Dugdale.

CASUARINA (1970s): PETER AND CYRAINE DUGDALE

In 1971, Peter and Cyraine Dugdale were looking for a family pet as a scholarship present for their son, Mark. Next door lived the Downings, from whom they purchased a Flat-Coat puppy of largely Halstock/Collyers breeding, Creekside Bubbles of Casuarina, called Sherpa.

The Dugdales went to Canada for three years, taking Sherpa with them. Having gained her CD, she became the first Canadian Flat-Coated Retriever Champion in 40 years. She was joined by a puppy, Parkburn Deextenzing of Casuarina, bred by Moira Jewel who, with Bobby, had recently arrived in British Columbia from Scotland with their dogs, Sh. Ch. Parkburn Brandy Boy (later

Am. Can. Ch.) and The Parc Dawn (later Can. Ch.). Moira mated these two and Tenzing was one of the litter. Tenzing became Can. Am. Ch. with Can. Am. CD before the Dugdales returned to England, where he became a full Champion – the only triple champion in the breed. While in Canada the Dugdales played a leading part in setting up the Canadian Flat-Coated Retriever Society. While waiting for Tenzing to come out of quarantine, Cyraine bought a bitch, Heronsflight Toss of Casuarina (Heronsflight Tercel x Fenrivers Lily), in 1976. Having participated in various activities in Canda, Cyraine felt the time had come to set about Field training in earnest. Toss, called Deva, picked up regularly, ran in working tests and gained a couple of Field Trial Awards. Cyraine is a staunch upholder of the Society's Shooting dog certificate scheme and has endeavoured, very successfully, to qualify her dogs since the scheme's inception.

Tarncourt Cavalier of Casuarina (Lingwood Medlar/Tarncourt Bronte) was a useful addition in 1980 and has produced good, sound working stock. Agra of Newbury, a grandson of Tenzing and Sherpa, also proved of value at stud.

CLAVERDON (1944): DR NANCY LAUGHTON

One of the most prestigious kennels in the breed, founded by Dr Nancy Laughton in 1944 with the purchase from Will Phizaklea of Claverdon Jet, sired by Atherbram Gunner from a Welsh bitch Cemlyn. Jet was the foundation upon which the Claverdon line was founded. The ability to work competently in the shooting field has always been of prime importance; the fact that the Claverdon dogs could also hold their own in the show ring was merely a bonus.

The Claverdon influence has been significant not only in Britain but wherever there are Flat-Coated Retriever enthusiasts. Over the years Dr Laughton has bred so many good litters and produced so many top-class Flat-Coats that it is hardly possible to single out one dog or one litter. Claverdon Jorracks Junior and Claverdon Gaff were both influential sires transmitting different qualities to their progeny. Today, over 50 years on, the Claverdon dogs still epitomize the best in the Breed. During this long association with the Breed, Dr Laughton has held office in the Society as Secretary, Field Trial secretary, Chairman, President and finally in 1985 was awarded the distinction of being made Patron to the Society.

Dr Nancy Laughton with three of her Claverdon Flat-Coats.

CLEOVINE: JUDY AND DAVID SHOWELL

This affix was originally taken out in 1980 for Irish Setters, but in 1982 the first Flat-Coat arrived, Pendlewych Plover from Marion Ayre (Tonggreen Storm Petrel/Ch. Larg Linnet of Pendlewych). Plover gained 2 CCs, 1 RCC and also attained the Kennel Club Show Gundog Qualifier and Shooting Dog A Certificate.

Judy says that while all dogs have their special qualities, Branchalwood Skye at Cleovine is her most loyal and devoted companion, he sleeps next to her pillow and grieves if they have to be separated. Skye hated the show ring so Judy respected his wishes; nonetheless he is the sire of three full champions. Judy and David are interested in both show and field work; David is currently having a successful run in Field events with the liver dog, Fossdyke Bronze Justin.

Judy is fascinated by pedigrees; also she is the Editor of the Society Year Book and News Letter, a member of the general committee and a championship show judge.

COLLYERS: AMELIA JESSEL

The Hon. Amelia Jessel is President of the Flat-Coated Retriever Society, Chair of the Field Trial sub-committee and previously served as Hon. Secretary to the Society for 23 years; she is a Field Trial "A" judge, represents all Retriever breeds on the KC Field Trial Committee and is a Championship show judge. She says: "After being left in charge of my Father's Flat-Coat while he was away at sea during the Second World War, I was bitten by the Flat-Coat bug, so to speak. Later, when married and dogless in 1955 I returned to my first choice and bought Asperula (Ch. Waterman x Ch. Pewcroft Proper) from Read Flowers. By the time she was three years old I had made her up to full Champion. Mated to Mrs Izzard's Rungles Trademark she produced, among others, Collyers Chiffchaff.

"My next Flat-Coat was Claverdon Skipper bred by Nancy Laughton (Bob of Riverglade x Claverdon Turtledove). He did much better in the field than Asperula, winning the Flat-Coat Open Stake. Although I showed him extensively, he only managed a reserve CC. Mated to Ch. Chiffchaff he sired Collyers Christina.

"On to the scene now came Collyers Blakeholme Brewster bred by Barbara Hall who had the knack of breeding good-looking workers. By Blakeholme Jem out of Retendon Spoonbill, Brewster put his stamp on the breed in the late 60s. A racy dog with plenty of bone and lovely dark eyes, I mated him to Collyers Christina. A bitch from this litter, Ch. Rose, by a strange chance, was mated by her father and produced Ch. Skeets who was an outstanding bitch both on the bench and in the field. Before the field trial season in 1973 she died from Lymphatic Sarcoma. Luckily I had bred from her to Tonggreen Starling, producing Collyers Juno, an excellent working bitch which I gave to my daughter. She was neither shown nor field trialled, but she turned out one of the best and most hardworking of picking-up dogs. Her daughter, by Ch. Wizardwood Sandpiper, was Werrion Redwing of Collyers, a biggish and very stylish bitch. Like her mother, she worked hard with much stamina and would brave the toughest thorns. Redwing became a Field Trial Champion.

"Sadly, my female line virtually ended with Redwing. I regret not keeping a good daughter of hers. She was mated twice to Lingwood Medlar who carried the genes of the only other post-war FT Ch. bitch, Helen Wilson's Hartshorn Sorrel. This union resulted in the dog Collyers Mannered whose son, Tarncourt Ranger of Collyers, out of Tarncourt Nimbus, mated to Claverdon Dollar produced my present dog, Claverdon Raffles of Collyers. So I have switched from female to male lines, a decision which suits the kind of life I lead.

"Raffles won the Flat-Coated Retriever Society Novice Stake on his first outing. He has been mated several times to approved bitches, including a successful Artificial Insemination in New

Zealand and so far seems to be producing a good stamp of Flat-Coat. My only other Flat-Coat is a young dog by Fenrivers Reedmace x Moonlight Padarn."

COURTBECK (1968): HELEN BECKWITH
Helen Beckwith bought Halstock Joanna (later Sh. Ch.) from Patience Lock in 1964. Joanna was mated to Ch. Claverdon Comet and in 1968 produced the important "Planet" litter which included Percy and Dora Parson's Ch. Courtbeck Mercury, Mary Grimes' Ch. Belsud Courtbeck Taurus and Joan Chester Perks Ch. Tonggreen Courtbeck Venus, each of whom has been influential in the Breed.

With home commitments, Helen only showed and bred on a limited scale, but has continued to breed good stock following a definite pattern. Many of her dogs act as PAT and CARE dogs. Marcus a son of Mercury, regularly attended Brownie meetings and always went to camp with disabled Girl Guides. Helen feels 'Joanna' would be her "special" choice.

DARILLENS (1980): BOB ALLEN
Bob's first Flat-Coat was Torwood Laughing Girl. His main interests are showing and obedience. Bob is a committee member of the FCRS and Chairman of the (proposed) Northern Flat-Coated Retriever Association. His "special" by a very short head is T. Laughing Girl. Bob is a very fine steward in the show ring, and is a championship show judge.

HAZEL WILSON (No affix)
Hazel is included for her length of time supporting the breed. She has shown good dogs, including Sh.Ch. Darillens Super Trouper who, she says, must count as her "special". Hazel enjoys judging and stewarding.

DOWNSTREAM (1963): PETER AND SHIRLEY JOHNSON
Shirley Johnson writes: "Peter and I both owned Flat-Coats in the 1950s and when we married in 1963 we founded the Downstream Kennel. We are mainly a working kennel, but enjoy showing and feel it is very important to keep to the standard of the breed, be it show or work. From one of our early litters we bred two champions, Downstream Hercules and Int. Nat. Ch. D. Hestia, who was owned by Bat Brulin of the famous Puhs Kennels in Sweden. She was the foundation bitch for much of the stock over there. Peter bought Woodway from Colin Wells "W" Kennel. He was an excellent worker and also became a Champion. Sadly he died from Torsion while still in his prime.

"Dogs from our kennels who have been successful at Field Trials are Downstream Manto, D. Charm of Roysia, D. Keepers Girl of Chadwell, D. Fiddler and D. Robina, most of these were show winners as well. We only breed the occasional litter now, but are very much involved with the breed. Peter has achieved his ambition of being a "dual purpose" judge, being on the "A" panel of Field Trial judges and a Championship Show judge – only four other people in Flat-Coats have reached this status – and is at present the society's Field Trial Secretary. I am also a Championship Show judge, and we both judge overseas. For many years I have been the Litter Registrar for the Flat-Coat Society and our daughter Becky looks after the needs of the Junior Members."

EMANON: PEGGY MILLER
Peggy Miller is the daughter of the late "Tinker" Davis, co-owner with Georgina Fletcher ("Fletch") of the noted Rungles Curly Coated and Flat-Coated Retrievers. Their Sh. Ch. Rungles Lady Barbara was one of the most beautiful bitches I have ever seen. Peggy is a Championship show judge. She writes: "My first Flat-Coat was Rungles Whistler, given to me by my father on

Ch. Halstock Bridget: The foundation of Peggy Miller's Emanon kennel, bred by Patience Lock.

Photo: Roger Chambers.

return from HMF duties in Gibraltar in 1959. My second was Rungles Brilla who 'Fletch' gave to me on the death of my Dad in 1969. She had one litter with me which was her only litter; the bitch I kept was Emanon Brills Girl, who was never bred owing to an accident on the way to her very first show: she was 15 years old when she died. Then in 1978 I got Halstock Bridget who was just over one year old. I still think of her as one of the most beautiful of all time. You only have to look at her photos to see the quality. I kept a daughter Emanon Onyx who is still with us at the age of nearly 13 years (Tarncourt Cavalier of Casuarina/Ch. Halstock Bridget). Onyx was only shown on a very limited basis, but was a most fantastic worker. She got her SDC and also a RCC.

"I also kept a dog Emanon Water Starwort, sire Collyers Mannered. He was born in 1985 and I believe would have been a full champion had he lived. He died having a tooth repair, a result of knocking his mouth on the tail gate of the Range Rover. He was just 4 years old and had two CCs, one with BoB at Crufts 1989. The Flat-Coats that I have at Emanon all descend from Ch. Halstock Bridget."

ESKMILL (1980): HUGH AND JENNY DONNELLY

The foundation Flat-Coat was Torwood Jonquil of Eskmill (Ch. Puhfuh Phineas Finn/Heronsflight Twirl of Torwood), who was a fast, stylish bitch in the field with great natural ability. Breeding has been on a limited scale but planned with care. "Special" is Ch. Eskmill Explorer.

EXCLYST WYNDHAMIAN: BRENDA PHILLIPS

jointly with Ed Atkins, USA

In the early sixties Brenda's husband Chris was a member of The Devon Wildfowlers and remembered hearing a talk on gun dogs given by the Rev. Steele, who mentioned Flat-Coated Retrievers. The couple visited Mr. Steele, who suggested getting in touch with either the Hon. Amelia Jessel or Patience Lock. Consequently Collyers Albertine was bought from

Ch. Eskmill Explorer, bred and owned by Hugh and Jenny Donnelly.

Brenda Phillips with Ch. Watchman (current top winning male) and Sh. Ch. Exclyst Viking.

Photo: Liz Phillips.

Amelia Jessel. In the late 1960s Patience Lock was keeping a bitch, Woodlass, for Ed. Atkins. Woodlass was bred by Colin Wells, one of the Ch. Tong-green Sparrowboy/Ch. Woodpoppy litter. Patience felt that Brenda and Chris could provide a suitable home with field training for Lass, as Ed had decided he wanted her to remain in the UK, so she moved to Poltimore, where she spent some 13 years. In time, Lass was mated to Heronsflight Tercel and to Forestholm Rufus, with half of each litter going to the US and half remaining here.

Brenda kept a Tercel son, Wyndhamian Christopher of Exclyst, and a daughter, Exclyst Claudette, who was mated to NU Ch. Halstock Lone Ranger before he went to Norway. The litter included Brenda's first champion and prepotent sire of good working dogs, Exclyst Bernard (Ch.). Christopher also was an outstanding sire. In the 1980s Wizardwood Seabird of Exclyst joined the team. His daughter Sequin was Top Brood bitch 1990 along with a Bernard daughter, Mary Grimes' Ch. Belsud Brown Guillemot. Sequin is the dam of Ch. Exclyst Watchman, Top dog and Top Sire 1994.

Brenda's dogs are used regularly for picking up and, while she is interested in competitive field events, she does not take part herself although, for some years, she was secretary of a working gundog club. She is Health monitor to the FCRS, an International show judge and, with Sue Kearton, produces the Flat-Coated Retriever Directory.

ABOVE: Elmstock Wild Thyme: DCC and BIS at the Flat-coated Retriever Society Ch. Show 1995. Bred and owned by Dennis and Val Orme.

LEFT: Exclyst Bristol Cream of Ravenhall, bred by Brenda Phillips and owned by Sue Kearton: DCC and BIS at the FCRS Ch. Show 1994 and DCC at Crufts 1995.

FENRIVERS: READ FLOWERS
This is such a noted and long-standing kennel which has been referred to earlier in this book, so it is sufficient just to note the name.

FENSTORM (1978): ALDO AND BARBARA HARKIN
The first Flat-Coat was in 1978. The foundation was Fenstorm Morning Mist (Ch. Wizardwood Tawny Pheasant/Bramatha Tic a Teena by Fenstorm). Interests are equally show and field. "Special" is Pendlewych Piper and Ch. Falswift Black Storm. Barbara is co-ordinator of the Society re-homing scheme.

FOSSDYKE: JILL SAVILLE (1980)
First Flat-Coat was Norton Royal and Regal. Has subsequently made up Ch. Rase Iona of Fossdyke and Ch. Paddiswood Burnt Lobelia of Fossdyke. Aims to produce biddable happy dogs that are a pleasure to own and work with. Jill has an incredible computer "bank" of thousands of Flat-Coated Retriever pedigrees.

GAYPLUME (1974): CHRIS MURRAY
Originally, Chris had Golden Retrievers but in 1980 son Adrian said could he have a retriever but not the same as Mum's; this was how Tokeida Midnight Mischief joined the household. Adrian trained, showed and worked her. When she was 3 and Adrian 16, he mated her to Ch. Bordercot Guy: Chris had a bitch from the litter who became Ch. Saucie Susie of Gayplume, a litter brother

*Sh. Ch.
Gayplume Dixie:
Record-holding
Flat-Coat bitch.
Bred and owned
by Chris Murray.*

is Sue Jones' Ch. Happy Harry, who, as we have read, enjoys showing, Agility, Flyball, Obedience (up to a point) and "picking-up". Not bad for a 16 year old breeder's first effort and more was to come.

Susie was then mated to Sh.Ch. Emanon Parkgate Boy and Chris kept Gayplume Pirouette who, in due course, was bred to Ch. Candease A Hard Days Night. From this litter Chris kept the puppy that became Sh.Ch. Gayplume Dixie, the current Breed record-holding bitch, having exceeded the previous record held by the late Pat Chapman's Ch. Yonday Willow Warbler of Shargleam. Dixie has 26 CCs and 13 RCCs at four-and-a-half years old. Top Junior F/C 1991. BoB Crufts and Top F/C 1992. Top F/C 1993 and Top F/C bitch 1994. Litter brother G. Domino does very creditably in the show ring, picks-up, is a PAT dog and a blood donor.

There are three younger Flat-Coats, each already showing promise of things to come. G. Goes Wild, G. Gamesmaster who has his Show Gundog Working Certificate and, in particular, Dixie's daughter Gayplume Fancy Free who has her JW at 15 months and has gone BIS at an Open Gundog All Breeds Show. As Chris says: "all because Adrian said he would like a Flat-Coated Retriever".

*Sh. Ch. Glidesdown Wendy, bred by
Wyn Garrod, owned by Sally Davies.*

GLIDESDOWN (1960): WIN GARROD

This goes back some 35 years when the late Win and Bill Garrod had mainly Cockers and Labradors. Win's father, Alf Butters, had working Cockers. Bill's first Flat-Coat was one he took away from an under-keeper who Bill felt was unsuitable; there were no papers with this bitch. Later Win had a Rungles puppy, followed by the good bitch Glidesdown Fredwell Wishful. Breeding has only been on a limited scale but Glidesdown dogs feature in many pedigrees. Work prevented the Garrods from showing at all extensively. Bill was delighted recently to be given a Flat-Coat pup by his family as an 80th birthday present.

GUNMAKERS: JOAN MAUDE

This was originally Joan and the late Jeremy Maude. The Maudes started with Flat-Coats when Joan had been ill and her GP felt she needed a boost – there is hardly a bigger boost than a Flat-Coat. The Flat-Coat family started with Manorcot Holly Hobby from Sheila Brocklehurst, then a year later Exclyst Nutmeg from Brenda Phillips. In 1984 Withybed Meadow Falcon, bred by Richard and Ann Adams (Kilminster) joined the family; she was made up to champion. The Maudes also had involvement with Warresmere lines of Tim Woodgate Jones and later Mardick Meg from Molly Marquess. Interests lie in both field and show activities. At one time Jeremy trained his dogs from his wheelchair and they responded amazingly. Since Jeremy died, Joan has been restricted in continuing picking-up due to arthritis. Joan became Hon. Secretary to the Society in 1984 and is determined to encourage a forward-looking attitude in the Society.

HALLBENT (1961): "GEORGIE" BUCHANON, (1994) PAMELA STANLEY

From 1961 this was the prefix of Georgie Buchanon, who originally had Cocker Spaniels but a Flat-Coat followed in 1962 – Strathendrick Dawn, sent down by train from Scotland by her breeders, Mr and Mrs Stevens. Dawn was sired by Ch. Strathendrick Shadow from Claverdon Veracity.

From then on Georgie has bred countless very good Flat-Coats including Nu Ch. Hallbent Dawn Patrol who had such enormous influence on the breed in Norway. Small wonder – the breeding was absolutely classical. For some time Georgie held her prefix in partnership with Pamela Stanley. Then in 1994, because of her advancing years, Georgie had the affix made over to Pamela's sole charge. Georgie's interest is still unbounded, but she is happy to feel the affix is in safe and younger hands.

Pamela's first bitch was Hallbent Soft Music, so the line continues from her. Georgie's "special": it had to be Sh.Ch. Hallbent Kim, such a character – he was a feature of the Veteran classes in Essex for years. Main interests are breeding, showing and rough shooting.

HARTSHEAD (1981): GORDON AND KAREN ROBERTS

The first Flat-Coat in 1981. Foundation was Falswift Black Swallow (Tonggreen Storm Petrel/Ch. Halstock Primula at Ravenscrest). Main interest is in shows. "Special" is Hartshead Conquering Hero, for living up to his name! Karen is a Championship show judge.

HERONSFLIGHT (late 1950s): JOAN MASON AND ROSEMARY TALBOT

Previously, I had the prefix "Rytonend", the same as our Dairy herd; this was before we had Flat-Coated Retrievers. I had Goldens and Griffons and also a few 'working', unregistered terriers. In 1964, through Dr Laughton, I was able to have the puppy that became Ch. Heronsflight Black Bell of Yarlaw (Claverdon Jorracks Junior/Ch. Pewcroft Prop of Yarlaw), bred by the late Walter Hutton. In due course I was most fortunate in being allowed to use Brian Farr's very good dog Teal of Hawk's Nest, possibly the most shot-over Flat-Coat in the country at that time. The ensuing litter proved to be significant including as it did, Tercel, Trust, Tell, Try, Tassel and so on.

Later, when Stanley O'Neill was old and ill, I had Pert from him, the last bitch bred and kept by his wife Kathleen. Pert and Bell were related in that their dams were litter sisters. Unlike Bell, Pert was no oil painting, but her progeny were proof that "blood will out". When mated to Rungles Jerome, the litter included H. Puff who features in so many pedigrees.

Some years ago, my daughter Rosemary Talbot became joint holder of the affix. We only ever have four or five dogs at a time so cannot have a constant supply of youngsters to show. The old ones are very special and have earned our love and care. The dogs we have now are in direct

Ch. Heronsflight Pan's Promise; bred and owned by Joan Mason and Rosemary Talbot.

descent from the two original bitches. We tend to line-breed back to Teal, possibly one of the most influential sires of the time. (Captain Farr only allowed him to be used five times.)

Our present dogs are Ch. Heronsflight Pan's Promise 13 CC, 12 BoB, 11 RCCs, Gundog Group SWKA, Reserve Group Midland Counties, Leading F/C 1985; Paddiswood Amber Nutmeg; and their daughter, Ch. Heronsflight Moss, litter sister to Ch. H. Magic and Nu Ch. H. Morris – the coming together of the original two lines. Rosemary has a daughter of Moss and there is a young bitch bought as a matter of interest to keep the "Rase" line going – an interesting bottom line going directly back to Colin Wells' Ch. Woodpoppy.

The aim now, as always, is to produce good sound Flat-Coats, able to do a competent day's work in the shooting field, hold their own in the show ring and then enjoy a long and happy retirement.

KENJO: JOAN AND KEN RUDKIN

Joan and Ken Rudkin had Glidesdown Melinda in 1972, followed by Glidesdown Ripple (both bred by Win and Bill Garrod). Breeding has been deliberately limited, Joan and Ken tend to keep males. Due to business commitments, showing tends to be restricted, but when in the ring the Kenjo dogs are usually a force to be reckoned with. One remembers that great showman Sh.Ch. Emanon Parkgate Boy who, Joan says, has to count as her "special". At present, Sh.Ch. Kenjo Black Mark is carrying the banner. Joan is Breed note correspondent for *Dog World*.

MARLCOT (1970): TREVOR AND KATH PENNINGTON

Trevor and Kath Pennington had their first Flat-Coat, Nicks Badger in 1969 and registered their affix in 1970. Slightly later they had Nicks Jade. Trevor and Kath support both show and field events. Any breeding has been directed toward Colin Wells' lines.

Trevor says Marlcot Nicks Dolphin would be his "special". A winner of Field Trial awards, a super worker in the shooting field and winner of over 300 show awards, Dolphin was sired by Woodland Whipcord from Nicks Jade.

Sh. Ch. Kenjo Black Mark: One of the most successful dogs of the 1990s. Bred and owned by Ken and Jon Rudkin.

OAKMOSS: GEORGE LANCASTER

George was born into a horse-and-dog-minded family. He became interested in Flat-Coats in the 1960s when he had Halstock Juliet from Patience Lock. Juliet, like her sister Joanna, became a champion. George has bred many good Flat-Coats over the years, including the typey dog Sh.Ch. Oakmoss Ambassador. George and wife Mavis also have strong spaniel interests. George is a long-standing member of the FCRS Committee, was chairman for several years and now is an honorary Vice President.

PUHFUH (1968): JOAN SHORE

Originally registered for Tibetan Spaniels, in 1971 Joan had a Flat-Coat bitch, Halstock Exclyst Lucinda, then in 1972 Linda of Puhfuh (Sh.Ch. Oakmoss Ambassador/Attingham Justice). This was the start of a successful and significant involvement with the Breed. Joan has always enjoyed a wide range of activities with her dogs, not just competing, but achieving a high degree of success in the show ring, working tests, Field Trials and Working Trials, also picking-up regularly. Breeding has not been of major interest – ironic when Joan, in fact, bred one of the finest and most talented Flat-Coats of all time, Ch. Puhfuh Phineas Finn CDEx UDEx WD. Finn was the result of the mating between Linda and Wyndhamian Christopher of Exclyst; the litter was born on April 20th 1974.

Finn was BoB at the Breed shows of 1979 and 1981; BoB at Crufts 1978 and 1979; three times runner up in the Gundog group; 27 CCs, 16 BoB, and 22 RCCs. It was in the middle of 'Finn's' show career that Joan decided that being a show dog and competent working dog was fine but perhaps they could tackle something else. Working Trials? A different concept from the previous activities. Finn gained his CDEx UDEx but the WD remained without the Ex. He would do his long stay perfectly, then at the crucial moment would decide he needed to scratch! A typical Flat-Coat – as when, having won the prestigious WAGBI Safari and multi pick-up, he went with Joan to collect the trophy, promptly put both front feet on the table and turned to laugh at the photographers, tongue lolling from the side of his mouth. By Joan's choice, Finn was only used once at stud; this was to Heronsflight Twirl of Torwood. Joan had one of the puppies, Torwood Jovial, then in 1981, Eskmill Boonwood, a grandson of Finn's. Joan is such a talented trainer, she adjusts to the dog's character, hence her success, not just with Finn.

RASE (about 1968): THE LATE PADDY PETCH
Paddy died on March 19th 1992 following a tragic accident. Many Rase dogs appear in present-day pedigrees. Paddy and husband George started with Woodwren from the late Colin Wells' "W" kennel. She was litter sister to Brenda Phillips' Woodlass. George trained the dogs and Paddy showed them, an ebullient figure round the show rings.

Paddy bred carefully, with a definite pattern, and produced many champions both here and overseas. She never really recovered from George's death and worked ever more frenetically – local radio, weekly columns (including the breed notes in *Dog World*), a book on Flat-Coated Retrievers and another on her second love, Bernese. Paddy was a fair and knowledgeable judge.

RAVENHALL (1985): SUE KEARTON
Foundation was Exclyst Samantha of Ravenhall (Wizardwood Seabird of Exclyst/Ch. Midnight Star of Exclyst). Main interests are show and work. Sue is also co-producer with Brenda Phillips of the Flat-Coated Retriever Directory; she also produces Flat-Coat Christmas cards and calendars. Her "special" is Ravenhall Chartreuse, for her sheer grit and determination to live.

RIVERSFLIGHT (1980): PETER AND JEAN GRIFFITHS

Foundation bitch was Torwood Poppet (Heronsflight Tercel/Heronsflight Puff) who gained JW and later became Ch., won awards in Breed and A.V. Working tests, was an outstanding game finder in the shooting field, and a successful dam. Peter also has a very soft spot for Cliffordene Solo of Riversflight (sired by R. Twill) a tremendous working test dog who represented the breed at the Game Fair on three occasions and was a Field Trial winner. A very honest, courageous worker. There is a second "line" headed by Braemist Storm Lady of Riversflight, dam of Sh.Ch. Riversflight Lady Dee.

The kennel also includes Ch. Tom Thumb, R. Leader (top puppy 1993), R.Meig (top puppy 1994). Litter mates, Mella and the Eggintons' Marling each have JWs. (The Eggintons are part of the Colson family.) A newcomer of whom Peter has high hopes is Greatwood Moonraker of Riversflight (Claverdon Raffles of Collyers/Waddicombe Holly of Greatwood). The aims are to have good temperament and to maintain classical

Ch. Riversflight Inny, bred and owned by Jean and Peter Griffiths.

type combined with working ability.
RONDIX: RONA DIXON
Has been associated with, and owned, Flat-Coats for a very long time. Truly dual-purpose, aims to produce sound, competent dogs. Rona has a computer bank of several thousand pedigrees.

SHARGLEAM (1958): THE LATE PAT CHAPMAN, now JENNIFER CHAPMAN
Originally for Golden Retrievers. Mention has already been made of the start of Pat's interest in Flat-Coated Retrievers. The record of the Shargleam Flat-Coated Retrievers is phenomenal: in all they gained over 150 CCs, which includes Ch. Yonday Willow Warbler's achievements as bitch record holder for so many years and, of course, the legendary Ch.IrCh. Shargleam Blackcap, the top winning gundog of all time. "Brett" gained 63 CCs, 50 BoB, 59 Green stars, 18 Groups, 5 Res. Groups and 3 BIS All breeds at Championship shows.

Pat's death on May 24th 1993 was greeted with great sadness, not only by friends but by many people to whom she was just a name. Pat's twin sister, Jennifer, now holds the Shargleam affix.

Sh. Ch. Shiredale Magic Touch: BCC and BOB at Crufts 1995. Bred and owned by Jenny Bird.

SHIREDALE (1972): JENNY BIRD
Affix originally for Irish Setters. First Flat-Coat arrived on October 26th 1979, the day "Scott" was collected (later to become Ch. Shargleam Sparrow Hawk). Foundation bitch was Wizardwood Lark, lent to Jenny by Peter and Audrey Forster. Scott and Lark were mated: Peter and Audrey kept Wizardwood Water Witch (Ch.) and gave W. Black Magic to Jenny; she too gained her champion's crown. Interests: Jenny shows and Mike picks up. "Special" has to be Ch. Shargleam Sparrow Hawk. Jenny also used to show "Brett" (Ch. Shargleam Blackcap) very successfully for Pat, if Pat was unable to show him herself.

STONEMEAD/BRAMATHA:
THE LATE PHILIP WHITTAKER/SARAH WHITTAKER
The late Philip Whittaker had the Stonemeade affix from the 1940s; following his death in 1989 his wife Suzanne took it over. Philip's first Flat-Coat was bought in 1970, Hallbent New Novel (Ch.); later he was able to buy her dam, Hallbent Dusk. These formed the base of the Stonemeade Flat-Coats. As he was a farmer, the dogs were expected to work as well as show.

Bramatha is daughter Sarah's affix. Philip gave her Stonemeade Prince Charming in 1971; all Sarah's stock goes back to that dog.

Over the years Sarah has sent notable stock to Sweden and more recently Australia. Sarah's "special" is the beautiful liver bitch, Atherbram Ability.

TARNCOURT: JOAN MARSDEN
Joan Marsden's interest lies mainly in Field activities. She was largely instrumental in setting up the Working Group mentioned earlier. The aim was to try and find good working stock to improve working ability within the breed. Joan has been very dedicated in these efforts and certainly with her own skills as a trainer has done very creditably with her own dogs in Field Trials.

TONGGREEN (1950): JOAN CHESTER PERKS
Joan Chester Perks is a real dyed-in-the-wool dog person, including it being almost impossible to get her to put pen to paper. The Tonggreen affix dates from 1950 although Joan had started breeding Labradors in 1945, followed by Basenjis (the first breed she actually showed); she also had Cavaliers and Cockers but in 1959 became a Flat-Coat person.

Joan has only bred 14 litters over 36 years but these litters have included many worthy champions – Ch. Tonggreen Courtbeck Venus, Ch. Leahador Dusk of Tonggreen, Ch. Tonggreen Song Linnet, Reed Flowers' male, Ch. Tonggreen Sparrow Boy, who had enormous influence on the Breed, Pat Chapman's Ch. Tonggreen Swift Lark of Shargleam, and the Dutch Champions Spray and Sprig. In males, in addition to Sparrow Boy, were Ch. T. Squall and Ch. T. Soloman Seal. Quite a record. Joan judged at Crufts in 1995, an honour long overdue. Despite being told that "all of them" would not be accepted as "most special", that is her reply!

TOMSTAN (late 1960s): NORMAN AND PHYLL STANLEY
Norman collected Stolford Doxy from Peggy Robertson on the same day that Rosalie Brady collected litter brother Doonigan. The Stanleys have supported the breed over the years, doing a moderate amount of showing and also working their dogs. Breeding has been limited and has been kept largely to Tonggreen/"W" lines. Graham Stanley, the general secretary of the URC, is their son, prefix Taurgo. Norman is a championship show judge.

TORWOOD/LATHKILL (1970): DENISE JURY AND DAVID BELLAMY
The Torwood affix originally belonged to Denise and Neil Jury and dates from about 1970 when they had a bitch called Ebony Reliance who was mated with Pegasus of Luda. A bitch puppy was kept, Nimrod Reliance. Later they had Heronsflight Puff as an adult, and from these three bitches all the Torwood's and many of the Lathkill's stem. The dogs are undisputedly dual-purpose, a team picking up regularly during the shooting season at Belvoir as well as being shown. Many Shooting Dog Certificate holders will be found to have Torwood bloodlines in their pedigrees. Over the years breeding has been largely intermingled with Heronsflight blood lines. David Bellamy is a committee member of the FCRS and Denise a member of the Show committee. They are both championship show judges.

VARINGO: CHRIS AND GLENYS GWILLIAM
In 1984 the Gwilliams bought Black Jackdaw from Mary Grimes (litter brother to her Ch. Belsud Capercaillie). Their sire was Tarncourt Cavalier of Casuarina, dam was Ch. Belsud Brown Guillemot. Jack gained numerous Field Trial awards and was top dual-purpose Flat-Coat in 1998. In 1986, the Gwilliams had Brown Keston of Varingo from Ken Butler, a liver dog, whose sire was Bridport of Musk, dam Bella's Gemma. Kes also gained his "crown" and has done extremely well in Field events. Was top dual-purpose Flat-Coat in 1989.

Hasweth Jack The Lad and Hasweth Inigo Jones, owned by Denise Jury and David Bellamy (Torwood/Lathkill)

Clive Harris' Paddiswood Affection FTA and Ch. Torwood Blue FTW.

Breeding is always carried out with strong emphasis on producing a dog with natural working ability combined with good conformation and breed type.

WAVERTON: DAVID AND BRENDA HUTCHISON

David and Brenda Hutchison had their first Flat-Coat in 1975 but regard Ch. Black Velvet of Candidacasa as their foundation. Velvet was full sister to Ch. Bordercot Guy and a very typey bitch.

Interests lie in both show and field. David and Brenda are both championship show judges in Flat-Coats and Goldens. David is show manager of the Society show and is much in demand as a speaker at seminars. Brenda has served on various committees but is currently fully occupied working for her doctorate in the Philosophy of Education.

"Specials" are Ch. Waverton Madeira and her daughter W. Renaissance and Ch. Black Velvet of Candidacasa.

WESTERING (late 1960s): JANE SMITH

Jane Smith writes: "Coming from a country sports family it was natural to lose my heart to Flat-Coats. After seeing my first one in 1968, enquiries led me to Read Flowers. I met him and Buster, Fenrivers Kalmia aged 11 months; it was the beginning of a life-long friendship. Buster's temperament was superb. In time he became a full British Champion, joined in 1969 by Dr Nancy Laughton's bitch Claverdon Fidelity (Della), aged two-and-a-half years; already having a FTA at 11 months plus a handful of first prizes in the ring, Della was beautiful and became a full Champion. Meanwhile Kalmia went to the USA having sired two litters from Norman Hawthorne's Claverdon Felicity, giving us Magic Sailor and Magic Sally. Fidelity finally had puppies at nine years old. The mating to Dick Fifield's Fenhunter Jack, who carried the old Ponsbourne line, produced Westering St. Pete at home, Westering Why Not to the USA, behind many Field Trial dogs there, and Westering Warcry to Holland, who became a top show winner in Europe.

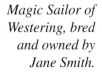

Magic Sailor of Westering, bred and owned by Jane Smith.

"We needed to outcross and I bought Casuarina Ici from Cyraine Dugdale; her line carried Collyers Blakeholme Brewster FTW and some Scottish blood. Mated to Pete she produced Westering Salute and Sandbagger. Salute, trained by Janet Webb, gained three FTAs. Sandbagger accompanied me picking up in Norfolk – my favourite occupation. Salute bred three times: 1. Glenwherry Cinnamon FTW, 2. Fenrivers Plumbago, 3. Magic Prince. The first litter gave me Westering Stormy Waters who I adored, and the second Westering Blues and Royals – 'Missy' – my current bitch, who should have been trialled but I need her for picking up, and until recently work commitments prohibited both activities. Greatly influenced by Colin Wells, working ability is of prime importance to me. Construction is vital in producing a dog that while retaining type will work all day in the field and grace the show ring – the dual-purpose gundog."

WINDYHOLLOWS (1990): THE COLSON FAMILY
Although the Windyhollows affix was only granted in 1990, the Colsons had their first Flat-Coat in 1970. Their actual foundation bitch was Glidesdown Anemone (Ch. Woodway/Glidesdown Rungles Raine). In 1986 Riversflight Ganol joined the family and later had two litters. In 1990 the dog puppy Kulawand Woodnymph (later Ch.) was bought; a litter from this dog and Ganol proved to be very successful. All the dogs are worked as well as shown.

WITHYBED: ANN KILMINSTER
Ann Kilminster writes: "I purchased my first Flat-Coat in 1970, a beautiful lovable pet, who started off my love of Flat-Coats, followed by my show bitch in 1977, Ch. Shargleam Black Abby of Withybed. I was very fortunate to choose Abby, fifth pick from a litter of eight bitches and four dogs – one of the dogs turning out to be Ch. Shargleam Blackcap. Bred by Pat Chapman. Abby did well in the showring: 6 CCs, three with BoB, Gundog Group at Southern Counties Championship Show in 1981. She was also a keen worker, picking up regularly each season, and winning awards in working tests. She had one litter, by Ch. Tonggreen Squall, producing Ch. Withybed Country Lad (7 CCs, 12 RCCs), Ch. Withybed Country Maid of Shargleam (5 CCs, 5 RCCs) and Withybed

Sh. Ch. Withybed Quartermaster of Huntersdale, bred and owned by Ann Kilminster (Adams).

Country Lass (2 CCs, 1 RCC). Abby tragically died in her prime at 5 years old from a cancerous tumour in her shoulder joint.

"W. Country Lad, Bodie by name, was a wonderful character. He was the world's best at running in and would often have disappeared well before the fall of the dummy! On one working test, having been oh-so-good and stayed in line as if he wouldn't dream of running in, he brought back the biggest bone you ever saw from the middle of a wood! He had no marks for it, but was so pleased with himself!

"W. Country Lass had three litters, out of which were produced Ch. Withybed Silent Knight (by Waverton Drambuie of Earlsworth), owned by Heather James, Ch. Withybed Meadow Falcon at Gunmakers (by Ch. Falswift Apparition), owned by Mrs Joan Maude, and my own Sh.Ch. Withybed Quartermaster (by Ch. Hallbent April Storm) who won his first CC at the age of 8 years swiftly followed by 3 more."

WOLFHILL (about 1976): JENNY MORGAN
In 1974, having had two Labrador puppies with severe H/D, Jenny Morgan decided to look for a gundog with a good health record. This led her to Flat-Coats and Patience Lock. Halstock Leonora became the foundation bitch of the Wolfhill Kennel. In 1976 Jenny bought a puppy, Antigone of Wolfhill (Ch. Wizardwood Sandpiper/Andromeda of Kempton). From these two, a small kennel of house dogs was built up. Breeding has been very limited but Ch. Wolfhill Dolly Parton, Sh.Ch. Wolfhill George Eliot and Wolfhill Box Car Willie have been among the produce. Recently Kiri Leighwarrent of Wolfhill has been having some success in Working tests.

"W" later WOODLAND: THE LATE COLIN WELLS
The "W", later, briefly, "Woodland" Flat-Coated Retrievers form the basis of so many breeders' stock both here and overseas. Their achievements both in the ring and at Field trials was remarkable. In 1933, Colin had Salthill Special from Alf Southam but due to the outbreak of war in 1939 had little chance to establish a line before joining the services. After the war, Colin had Claverdon Faith from Dr Laughton and Waterman from Will Phizaklea; from these, his line was established. Colin won Crufts for 10 consecutive years with three dogs. He was headkeeper to his Grace the Duke of Rutland so his dog activities had to fit in around his work commitments.

The "W" dogs were tough, resilient, good-looking dogs, rather like Colin himself. In 1987, the Country Land Owners Association presented Colin with a long-service award for 43 years continuous service as a keeper. As already mentioned, Colin's son Ron is now headkeeper at Belvoir, in succession to his father.

WIZARDWOOD (about 1968): PETER AND AUDREY FORSTER
Peter, who is a vet, had a client with good Flat-Coated Retrievers, Margaret Mothershill. Peter became interested in the breed and in time had Windgather Delia of Wizardwood from Margaret, at that time with no thought of going "into" the breed; Peter had been a Beagling man. However, as happens, interest kindled. In due course, Delia was mated with Fenrivers Ling and 'get' from this litter formed the basis of the noted "owl" litter from which have come such good livers.

Two other bitches added to the base. Halstock Alicia of Wizardwood and Halstock Jemima of Wizardwood. Jemima, mated to Ch. Tonggreen Sparrowboy, produced the litter that included the Field trial winner, W. Whimbrel, and Ch. W. Sandpiper. It was Sandpiper who, mated to Collyers Juno produced Amelia Jessel's FT.Ch. Werrion Redwing of Collyers.

Wizardwood dogs figure in pedigrees here and overseas, both livers and blacks. Peter and Audrey are both Championship show judges.

Sh. Ch. Wizardwood Black Magic of Shiredale, bred by Peter and Audrey Forster, owned by Jenny Bird.

SCOTTISH KENNELS

There have long been Flat-Coat enthusiasts in Scotland. Years ago, in particular, there were "pockets" of Flat-Coats, frequently unregistered. Even today, many of the bloodlines in Scottish pedigrees are very rare. For these reasons it seemed right and proper that the Scots have a section of their own.

BRAIDWYNN (1960): HELEN AND GEORGE WINTON

Originally for Golden Retrievers. In 1967, Helen bought Braidwynn Halstock Titania (Halstock Dragon Fly/Halstock Home Girl) from Patience Lock. In due course she was mated to Moira Jewell's Sh.Ch. Parkburn Brandy Boy; a bitch B. Beau Blue was kept and used for picking up as well as showing. Sadly Blue and the four pups in her last litter all died. Eventually, Helen was given a wonderful Christmas present by some people who had had a puppy from her years earlier. This puppy was Blue Boy of Braidwynn, later Sh.Ch., whose sire was B. Chancellor and dam Vbos Velour – a continuation of Helen's original line in fact. Blue Boy had great success in the ring and Helen says that when he died a little of her died with him.

In 1986, Fossdyke Cascade of Braidwynn joined the family; from these lines the present-day young stock descend and are of course very successful.

BRANCHALWOOD: THE LATE SCOTT & SHEILA DALZIEL AND MAUREEN & JOHN SCOTT

Scott and Sheila originally had spaniels and Golden Retrievers. When Sheila was a nursing sister at the local hospital she came across Kilbucho Honeybee who belonged to Dr Tom and Sally McComb. The Dalziel's were hooked. When Honeybee had a litter, the bitch Glendaruel Catriona went to the Dalziels and virtually started a dynasty.

Maureen (Scott and Sheila's daughter) and her husband John also became enamoured of Catriona (Trina) so when she had a litter sired by Ch. Wizardwood Sandpiper, Maureen and John had B. Maree and became partners in the Branchalwood affix.

It is quite impossible to mention all the noteworthy Branchalwood Flat-Coats both here and overseas. Over the years there have been numerous champions, none being more successful than one of the later litters when Sh.Ch. Palnure Pride of Branchalwood was mated to Ir. Ch. Shargleam Blackcap. There were five champions in the litter – Ch. B. Stroan, whose achievements are listed elsewhere, Sh.Ch. B. Penwhirn, Ger. Ch. B. Goil, Int. Ch. B. Lochdubh and Int. Ch. B. Ailish.

In males, the purchase of Ch. Stantilaine Rory of Branchalwood in 1975 gave an added boost to the breeding programme; his dam was litter sister to Catriona so he was a valuable addition at this time. Later, Ch.B.Frisa and Sh.Ch.Palnure Pride were highly successful brood bitches.

No account of this Kennel, however brief, would be complete without mention of the good bitch Ch.B.Whinyeon – 17 CCs and Best in Show at National Gundog in 1984. The present young stock is maintaining the Kennel's tradition, shown very expertly by Maureen.

Maureen Scott with Ch. Branchalwood Stroan. Bred and owned by Sheila and the late Scott Dalziel, and John and Maureen Scott.   Photo: David J. Lindsay.

COLONA (1960): JOHN AND FIONA MCKINLAY

Originally held by Fiona's father, John, the foundation Flat-Coat (1984) was Shargleam Crowned Plover of Colona. Breeding has been an intermingling of Branchalwood and Shargleam. Interests are Showing, Obedience, stewarding, judging and instructing Ring Craft. Special Flat-Coat is Sh.Ch. Colona Black Satin.

GLENDARUEL (about 1970): TOM McCOMB

A famous old Scottish prefix from pre-World War 1 days until the 1920s. Tom McComb was able to take it over. Glendaruel is always thought of as jointly Tom and Sally; it is she who mentioned that officially Tom is the holder. The prefix is particularly apt as it is the part of Argyllshire where Sally grew up. Sally is Chairperson of the FCRS having been a committee member of many years. She and Tom are both championship show judges.

Tom and Sally had their first registered Flat-Coat from Dorothy Montgomery in 1968, Kilbucho Honeybee (Sh.Ch. Strathendrick Haze/Fenriver Honeysuckle). She was bought as a shooting dog but in fact gained her full title. Honeybee was mated to Jet of Waveman: a daughter Christina went to the local doctor who in turn mated her to Colin Wells' Whipster. From the ensuing litter the McCombs chose the puppy that became Ch. Stantilaine Garnet of Glendaruel (presumably, litter sister to S. Rory of Branchalwood). On Jimmy Boyd's death, Tom and Sally had Ch. Monarch of Leurbost who was mated to Garnet in 1979. The line continues to the present day through G. Gumboots, G. Hilarity and G. Kelpie, Katrina and Kavalier. Breeding is on a very limited basis, the aims being to produce kindly temperament, pleasing looks and decent working ability.

KILBUCHO (1967): DOROTHY MONTGOMERY
Dorothy had her first Flat-Coat in 1958 but the foundation of the Kilbucho's was Claverdon Lucky Lass bred by Dr Laughton. Lass was sired by Ch. Woodlark from Claverdon Cindy.

Dorothy uses her dogs for rough shooting; while she enjoys shows, these visits are restricted as, living away up in the hills, she has no-one to look after her dogs if she is not there.

Livers have figured largely in Kilbucho breeding over the past few years. It is one of these that is named as the "special" Flat-Coat – Kilbucho Beacon Flame, a great character who had a penchant for catching moles. She also planned her own (and only) nuptials at 8 years old with "Pie" a son of Sh.Ch. Blue Boy of Braidwynn and Kilbucho Moonshine. As always with these self-arranged matings, she loved the pups and was a wonderful Mum. She lived to be 13.

LACETROM: TOM AND CAROLINE GATE
Tom and Caroline have bred for many years, restricted latterly through ill health. Caroline was always prepared to travel long distances to use the right stud dog. Rosalie Brady's Sh.Ch. Lacetrom Cardow of Bordercot and the Heide's AmCan Ch. Lacetrom Auchenstoshan AmCan WC were both bred by the Gates.

LONGFORGAN/CASTLE HUNTLEY: ROBERT LACKIE & daughter JEAN LACKIE
Historically, the Lackie family has been involved with Flat-Coated Retrievers for over 100 years. Early in this century, George Lackie was gamekeeper to Sir George Baxter of Castle Huntley: the Longforgan strain came from here combined with Reginald Cooke's Riverside bloodlines. The Longforgan dogs were used solely for working until the 1930s when George's son, Robert, became interested in showing as well. Robert continued with some success.

Jean mentioned in particular Ch. Longforgan Black Shadow who, she says, won at Birmingham in 1967; in fact he also had the DCC there in 1968 when Ch. Heronsflight Black Bell had the BCC and was Reserve in the Gundog Group. Bob had travelled down from Scotland with the late Jimmy Boyd. The judge was Patience Lock who had 35 Flat-Coats entered under her. A good entry for that time.

Another useful dog was Yonday Tonka bred by the late George Snape. Bob trained Flat-Coats for more than 40 years and from him daughter Jean learned the necessary skills. In 1976, Jean had her own first Flat-Coat, L. Merryman, and thus started her Castle Huntley Kennel.

Jean says she has found that whilst Flat-Coats are not necessarily the easiest breed to train, once trained they make excellent gundogs and good companions with their amiable, willing nature. Jean works and trains dogs other than her own but mentions one of her own dogs in particular, Linfern Thumbelina (Jura). Jura was very difficult to train. One step forward, three back. But she was always willing to try anything asked of her. Suddenly it all fell into place and she became renowned in local shooting circles, continuing to work efficiently at 9 when she had lost the sight in one eye.

A few years ago, Jean and a group of other Flat-Coat owners/breeders decided to form the Flat-Coated Retriever Club of Scotland to provide a central point for scattered enthusiasts, with training classes, get-togethers and so on. Various charities benefited from their efforts. The Club now has its own Championship show.

PENDLEWYCH (late 1970s): MARION AYRE

Marion had been doing obedience with a cross-bred collie when she decided she would like a "pure bred". Having met the Dalziels at classes she decided on a Flat-Coated Retriever, partly because she felt there was little need to trim. As she says, she hadn't allowed for the niceties of getting ears and tail just right. From Joan Chester Perks she had the pup that became Ch. Tonggreen Squall (in this one litter there were 4 champions and one dog with 2 CCs). Squall was not easy to show as he lacked enthusiasm in the ring.

The Dalziels asked to use Squall on B. Maree: the litter included Ch. B. Frisa and Can Ch. B. Feochan. The following year B. Linnhe was also mated to Squall: this litter included Sh.Ch. Palnure Pride of Branchalwood and the puppy that went to Marion and became Ch. Larg Linnet of Pendlewych.

In 1992, Linnet was mated to Tonggreen Storm Petrel: the litter included Am. Ch. Pendlewych Peregrine, P. Plover and Ch. P. Puffin. Later Puffin was mated to B. Gruinart, the litter included Ch. P. Puma, top male F/C in 1993, being beaten by one point for Top overall by Sh.Ch. Gayplume Dixie. The line continues with Cleovine Thyme of Pendlewych (a daughter of Plover) and a son and daughter of hers sired by Ch. Exclyst Watchman. Marion always trains her dogs to work so that each champion became a full champion.

As a matter of interest, Pendlewych is derived from the witches of Pendle in Lancashire who were burned at the stake for witchcraft. Marion comes from the area near Pendle Hill.

RAINSCOURT (1979): ROGER AND CHRIS PARISH

First Flat-Coat in 1989 was Tribyn Canna Queen of Rainscourt (Sh.Ch. Vbos Vervine/Tessa Victrix of Tribyn). Main interests are showing and Obedience. "Special" is Tribyn Cann Queen of Rainscourt.

VBOS: THE LATE VILMA OGILVY-SHEPHERD

No account of Scottish Kennels would be complete without mention of Vilma who died in May 1994. Vilma had bred Cocker Spaniels for many years before having her first Flat-Coat, Stolford Inkspot, in the late 1960s. Vilma's previous breeding experience showed in the Flat-Coats she produced for some 25 years. Vbos dogs have contributed much to the Breed, being true to type – always that touch of elegance that makes such a difference.

One remembers the particularly beautiful V. Velma, Sh.Ch. Vbos Vogue, the dam of Ch. Bordercot Guy and his litter sister Black Velvet of Candidacasa at Waverton, and, of course, Jim Irvine's storming pair Sh.Ch. Vbos Video and Sh.Ch. Vbos Vervine.

Chapter Thirteen

THE FLAT-COAT WORLDWIDE

FRANCE AND BELGIUM
MARIE NOELLE TERLINDEN/BERNARD CHAUVEU: GLEN SHEALLAG
Marie first saw a Flat-Coat some 27 years ago at Crufts and decided that at some time she would like to own one. It was several years before this became possible. Eventually Marie had Exclyst Kiss, a useful bitch who produced Multi Ch. TR Fairman of Glen Sheallag and Multi Ch. TR James of Glen Sheallag. Some time later, in 1985, Marie had a puppy from Scott and Sheila Dalziel and Maureen and John Scott, Branchalwood Islay, who became Ch. FTCh. Ch.IB,

Ch.B.Ch.F, TR, S'TR, S 86 (Ch. Stantilaine Rory of Branchalwood/Ch. Branchalwood Frisa). Islay was the mother of five champions sired by Ch. B. Lochdubh: multi Chs. TR Loch Ness of Glen Sheallag, Leah of G/S, Lindsay of G/S, Nancy Black of G/S, Pillow Talk of G/S. In 1986 Marie became the delighted owner of B. Lochdubh and his litter sister B. Alish. These two have been enormously influential in Europe (litter mates to Ch. B. Stroan). Lochdubh became B Ch., F Ch., Belgian Winner 1989 and 1993, he has over 70 CCs, and sired 7 champions. Alish is Ch. IBCh., B, Ch. F, trialler. Marie Noelle says that breeding is deliberately restricted; she feels very fortunate to have started with sound, talented, good-looking dogs. The kennel young hopeful is Belgium Junior Winner 93 Timberlands Arleen. Bred in Holland by Joachim Van Beek, she is sired by Lleccan Guardian of Oakmoss from Lindsay of Glen Sheallag Ch.NL, Ch.B, Ch.IB, one of the Lochdubh/Islay litter.

Marie and Bernard moved from Belgium to France in 1994.

Marie Noelle's Terlinden's Belg. Lux. Fr. Ch. Branchalwood Lochdubh: Ch. Field trialler, Belgian winner 1989 and 1993, winner of over 70 CCs.

DOMINIQUE AND MONIQUE SCHLOUPT: OF FUNDY BAY'S NAIAD
In 1988 Dominique had the young bitch, Kara du Bois de Flandre (Ch. Maximillion the Great/Odilis Caujolie v Spockendom) and a little later the male Maxim du Bois de Tillegham (Ch. Branchalwood Lochdubh/Jessica). He has brought in bloodlines from Denmark, Pearly Coat Danish Pastry, and from the UK, Gayplume Games Master bred by Chris Murray.

GERMANY
Brigitte Schneidermann who has been both Breed "warden" and secretary has kindly supplied details about the Breed in Germany.

The German Retriever Club (DRC) was founded in 1963; in fact only Golden Retrievers and Labradors were represented at that time. The first Flat-Coat was registered in 1976. Currently there are 605 Flat-Coats registered in Germany but there are about the same number imported from elsewhere, so the Breed totals about 1,000 to 1,200. The first litter was bred in 1980. Between then and now only 53 litters have been bred, largely as a result of the stringent regulations. These are too long to include in full, but extracts include: no bitch to be mated until she has reached a minimum of 24 months: only three litters allowed per bitch: at 8 years breeding permission is withdrawn: within any 24 months only two litters may be taken. No male dog to be used until over 15 months; there is no upper age limit. There are also requirements on hips, eyes, temperament. Stock is graded by an "expert" judge. Future breeding stock has to pass a companion dog test with shooting. One of the parents of a litter must have passed a special Retriever test at high level. If one actually gets as far as having a litter, an "authorised" person comes to assess the bitch and the puppies. The first Flat-Coat, registered in 1976, was VDH Ch. World Winner '76, Club winner '77 and '79 Swallowsflight Black Almighty, bred by Leonie Galdermans (Int. Ch. Heronsflight Trust/Ch. Heronsflight Jinx) owned by Sybille Klostzbucher, the first Breed warden. Sybille did not breed a litter until 1991 when she started her "Mavisflight" kennel.

THE LATE GERHARD WERBKE and RENATE WERBKE: WITCHWOOD
The first registered Flat-Coat bitch was Brakernwood Winsome imported by Gerhardt and Renate from David and Lyn Lees (Leahador Wanderer of Tonggreen/Tormik Elm). Brakern was bred to Erling Kyer Pedersen's Tonggreen Stormbird. The litter included the first German International Champion, Didi and Horst Titt's Int. Ch. Ger Ch. Witchwood Azure Tit.

Renate Werbke with her Witchwood Flat-Coats.

During the 1980s progress was made. The Werbkes had their "C" litter, perhaps their most successful. This was from the mating between their bitch Heronsflight Pan's Pearl and the Dutch male, Ch. Ansoncha Lancer. The litter included Int. Ch. Ger. Ch. VDH Ch. Europaieger '88, Bundessieger 'Witchwood Clincher Int. Ch. Ger VDH Ch. W. Chico and the bitch Ch. W. Comtesse, with whom Roswitha Frucht started her "Pride of Rosendal" kennel. The Werbkes worked unceasingly for the Breed until Gerhardt's death in 1985. Renate has continued as Breed warden from then on.

UTTE HOFF now STROH VON RETHWISCHHOH
In 1984 Ute started to breed good working Flat-Coats. The foundation bitch was Bianca vom Bell. (Vbos Veto/Tryggs Rummy). In particular, Ch. Aga's Magnus von Rethwischhoh was outstanding, Club winner 1987 with excellent working test results also.

HORST AND DIDI TITT: of BLACK TIT'S NEST
In 1986, Horst and Didi Titt imported Riversflight Farah (Ch. Torwood Blue/Ch. R. Weaver); she became Int. Ch. Ger. Ch. VDH Ch. and together with the male, Azure Tit formed the base for the "of Black Tit's Nest" kennel.

NICOLA BSCHER: BRIGHTWATERS
Originally, Nicola had a puppy from the Schneidermanns, "Amy of the Happy Den", the first Flat-Coat bitch in Germany to become International Champion. In 1987 Nicola imported Branchalwood Goil (Ivy) from the Dalziels and the Scotts (Ch. Ir. Ch. Shargleam Blackcap/Sh.Ch. Palnure Pride of Branchalwood). Ivy grew up to be the most successful F/C ever in Germany; she became Int. Ch. Ger. Ch. VDH Ch. NLCh. Lux. Ch. Junior winner Amsterdam '87 and Bundessieger 1991.

HERR and FRAU SEIDENFUSS: EVERLASTING
Their stock is entirely from Leonie Galderman's. In 1981 they had Int. Ch. NL Ch. Ger. Ch. VDH Ch. Swallowsflight Black Everace (Ch. Woodland Way/Ch. Swallowsflight Black Bell Bonfire). He is one of the oldest Flat-Coats in Germany and is the sire of two litters. The foundation bitch was Swallowsflight Black of One's Onion.

CHRISTOPH AND BRIGITTE SCHNEIDERMANN OF THE HAPPY DEN
Christoph is head keeper for all the predators at Krefeld Zoo. Wild cats are often difficult with their first litters and a foster mother needs to be found who will clean and care for the cubs after they have been bottle fed. Christoph and Brigitte had a Large Munsterlander, Harra, who took on this task.When she was 15 a replacement was needed. After much thought a Flat-Coat puppy was bought from Hans Trapp, Andra of Camelot (later Ch.). Andra immediately became friends with an injured snow leopard cub. In time she took over Harra's role as the carer of hand-reared cubs. Christoph's work is recognised as being of great importance in aiding endangered species.

When Andra was three she was mated with Ch. Witchwood Azure Tit. One of the litter went to Nicola Bscher and became Germany's first International Champion bitch, Int Ch. Amy of the Happy Den. In 1984 Sally of the Happy Den was imported. (Ch. Heronsflight Pan's Promise/Courtbeck Wishful). 1995 Lacetrom Lagavulin (Monty) bred by Tom and Caroline Gates joined the family (Ch. Heronsflight Pan's Promise/Branchalwood Tanna at Lacetrom). "Monty" became Int. Ch. Ger. Ch. VDH Ch. Club winner 1989.

The youngest dog is "Badger", a son of Monty and Sally. He too would play with the cheetah cubs but now, as "leader of the pack", he leaves grooming to the bitches. Andra, Sally and Monty have all passed difficult working tests and Christoph takes them picking up when work allows. There are shoots for hare, pheasant and duck in the region. The other hunters are impressed with the will to please, their super nose and enthusiasm in water.

HOLLAND
While there are many enthusiastic Flat-Coat owners and breeders in Holland the Breed had a chequered start there. Over thirty years ago it was introduced, but breeding was attempted with insufficient bloodlines and inevitably problems ensued.

In 1967 Carrie Van Crevel (Britannic) imported Black Cindy of Yarlaw from the Huttons. Being an experienced breeder of Golden Retrievers she realised that future breeding must be on carefully considered lines. She discussed this with Dr Nancy Laughton who suggested a puppy from the Teal of Hawk's Nest/Ch. Heronsflight Black Bell litter. Consequently, a young Leonie Galdermans became the proud owner of the male who was to become Multi Ch. Heronsflight Trust. He also gained the "A" certificate of the Royal Dutch Shooting Club and set the pattern for Leonie's life.

Ove the years breeders made further imports – Wizardwood Chough and W. Turnstone, Hallbent Tuppence, Fenrivers Myrtle, Westering Warcry, Heronsflight Jinx and Tonggreen Sprig, which gave a reasonable gene pool. Later, of course, there were many further imports as the breed gained in popularity.

THE FLAT-COATED RETRIEVER CLUB
From its inception, the strict control of the Dutch Club with the interests of the Breed firmly in mind, has proved to be ambivalent. There are as many breeders outside the Club as within. Wim ter Riet says that current membership stands at 1,300. In 1993, 29 litters were born within the Club, a further 38 litters were bred by non-members. The Club promotes various activities during the year, including a Championship Show. British judges are usually invited to officiate at this event.

ELLEN HAGEMAN-LOEFF: YAROWL
Ellen Hageman-Loeff was first introduced to Field trials by Wout Rueb who obtained Yarlaw

Ch. Ansoncha Lancer, bred by Charlie Henderson, owned by H. Kraan.

Black Mask and Wizardwood Snowy Owl for her. Ellen's present dogs, No Other Way Eurohof and Snowman of Wrenelson Eurohof, are Int Champions. They are both grandsons of Ch. Wizardwood Snowy Owl and Int Multi Ch. Paddiswood Amber Sherry FTA. Field Trials are the sole responsibility of the Royal Dutch Retriever Club.

SASKIA RATHENAU BEYERMAN: WAGGING TAILS
With a long-standing interest in the Breed and for many years secretary of the Club, Saskia had the Liver bitch Paddiswood Amber Chocolate and also has the successful bitch Ch. Jinks.

BRIGHTMOOR: WIES HANSEN
This is a newer name but an enthusiastic owner. Foundation was Dutch Ch. VDHCh. (W '89 Bsg '93) Morrie van de Vijf Lijsterbessen. Wies also has Ch. Swallowsflight Black Stardust and Starcaster Black April Morn. Wies is co-editor of the FRC News letter.

FLAT-CASTLE'S: SYKJE DONGSTRA-WINTER
One of the younger breeders, her original stock is based on "Swallowsflight" but by judicious imports she has widened the bloodlines available. At present she has a particularly good Liver male, VDH Ch. Ger. Ch. Shorebound's Tawny Deveron, sired by Chief Flannan van Oldenny from

Leonie Galderman's Int. Ger. Ch. Swallowsflight Mysterious Meteor.

No Surprise Eurohof FTA.
ARLENE DE GOEDE
She has the outstanding dog Int. Ch. Ned. Ger. Swiss Lux. Ch. Swallowsflight Black Justin JWW '86, WW '88, EK '88, BDSG '88 (Britannic Black Warto/Ch. Swallowsflight Everlasting Echo).

MENNINGE: MVR KRAGT
An old-established kennel that has produced many good dual-purpose dogs. Foundation bitches: Woodlands Watchful and Black Brisca v Heytse.

QUESTIONSFLIGHT: MARJO HANNE
The bitch Questionsflight Black Arrival was BIS at the FRC show in 1994 and also BoB at the World Show in Bern (Swallowsflight Black Reboyd/Swallowsflight Black Quickly).

Camwood Flying Dutchman, owned by Syjke Dongstra, bred by Sven Gmur. Photo: Maud Reys.

SOMPESPOEK: MVR DE VIN-NIEUWENHAUT

Another whose dogs appear in many pedigrees. Foundation bitch: Dutch Ch. Tonggreen Sprig. This kennel supported cold game tests as well as shows.

SWALLOWSFLIGHT: LEONIE GALDERMANS

Leonie has built up one of the most outstanding kennels of Flat-Coated Retrievers, not only in Holland, but in Europe as a whole. As Leonie herself says, when she saw Carrie van Crevel's Black Cindy of Yarlaw in 1969 it was "love at first sight". Leonie then had Heronsflight Trust, who was mated in due course to Cindy. In 1973 H. Jinx (Ch. Wizardwood Sandpiper/H. Tassel) went to join Trust. Leonie says, "a very typy bitch with a beautiful classical head, a very stylish worker".

A bitch, Multi Ch. Swallowsflight Black Bonfire was one of the litter that resulted from mating Ch. Britannic Black Bosco with Ch. Heronsflight Jinx. Leonie feels that Bonfire has had outstanding influence in her descendants. She is the dam of Arlene van de Goede's Multi Ch. Swallowsflight Black Justin, who has done an enormous amount of winning. Then, when mated to Multi Ch. Heronsflight Pan's Pledge FTA's she produced Multi Ch. Swallowsflight Outstanding Onyx FTA. You can go on and on. Over the last two or three years Leonie has brought in two males, Torwood Kite and Wizardwood Major Oak, both of which are doing well.

Leonie says that in her 26 years of breeding there have been 26 Dutch Swallowsflight Champions and many others abroad. As she says: "lots of ups and several downs. Almost all these Champions also worked or passed working tests. The aim now, as always, is to maintain a dual-purpose Flat-Coated Retriever."

With the opening up of Europe and Scandinavia, I think the present generation of Flat-Coated Retriever breeders are not only prepared to widen their horizons, but are well able to do so.

SWITZERLAND

From 1956 to 1968, Retrievers in Switzerland were allowed to join the Swiss Springer Spaniel Club. In 1968 the name was changed to Swiss Springer Spaniel and Retriever Club (SSSRC). Finally in 1987 the Springer Spaniels joined the other Spaniels and the Retriever Club of Switzerland (RCS) was formed which has gone from strength to strength in an amazingly short

Gladys v Schauensee, bred and owned by Joseph Joller.

time. Because actual Field work and even training is difficult due to various restrictions, some Flat-Coats have been trained for other work. Hens Dick with Aika v Chigga has qualified for the European Championship in Agility. Some Flat-Coats are being used as sniffer dogs for drugs and explosives and P, as in Peter, is a rescue dog who recently went to Japan to search for trapped people after the earthquake. There is an estimated number of 1,500 Flat-Coated Retrievers in Switzerland in 1995. The Breed has an unusual pattern there. From 1975 until 1984 Franz Steiner-Luthy was the only breeder; five more followed between 1985 and 1988 when the rapid growth started.

FRANZ STEINER-LUTHY: VON FELSBACH

In 1973 Franz Steiner imported a dog and a bitch. In 1975 the first Swiss litter was born from Ryshot Copper Elation sired by Leonie Galderman's Int Ch. Heronsflight Trust. In 1983 Franz imported the male Black Jewel of the Moor from Susan Worner (Mulberry of Heronsflight/Teasel of the Dale (largely Downstream breeding)). Later Belsud Golden Eagle (Ch.) and more recently Shargleam Eagle Owl (Ch.) have been brought in. For several years Franz Steiner was the only breeder in Switzerland.

YVONNE JAUSSI-JUON: NEALA'S

In 1984 Yvonne bought her first Flat-Coat from Franz, Cedar v Felsbach (Ch. Belsud Golden Eagle/Ulla v Felsbach). Cedar was such a joy that two years later Danja v Felsbach joined him (Black Jewel of the Moor/Erla v Felsbach). Danja became possibly the most successful Swiss-bred bitch. Top puppy 1987, Top opposite sex 1990, top F/C 1992 and Top brood bitch 1991 and 1992. Her daughter Ch. Neala's Fireflame is also doing extremely well, and "Flame's" son, sired by Int Ch. Heronsflight Pan's Pledge, is the first Swiss-bred International Champion – Int. Ch. Neala's Handsome Hawk.

JOSEPH AND HANNI JOLLER: VON SCHAUENSEE

Joseph and Hanni had their first Flat-Coat, Dolly v Felsbach, from Franz Steiner. Her sire was Ruff d'Aikoo and her dam Cina v Felsbach. She was the start of an enthusiastic involvement with the Breed which was destined to have considerable influence. Dolly became the first Swiss-bred champion. When mated to Black Jewel of the Moor, the litter contained Daisy v Shauensee who

Three generations of Champions: Swiss Ch. Danja v Felsbach (bred by Franz Steiner), Swiss Ch. Neala's Fireflame, and her son, Int. Ger. Ch. Neala's Handsome Hawk, owned by Yvonne Jaussi.

was retained by Joseph and Hanni. Daisy too became a champion.

In 1986 Joseph bought Swallowsflight Black Oberon – one needs a page for his achievements: Swiss, Monaco, Aust Ger Ger VDH Champion, also twice BIS at French Retriever Club, three times Top Swiss winner, twice Swiss Top Dog and Progeny Cup winner. In 1987 Swallowsflight Promising Pioneer also joined the family, co-owned with Leonie Galdermans. He too is highly successful, and an Int Champion.

Joseph was president of the Swiss Retriever Club for 1990/1. He also produces the excellent Year Book. In 1994 the Joller family was much involved with the World Show at Berne, an enormous event for a small country to stage.

Among the newer Kennels are: K and SCHORI-WIDMER: BLACKBERRY FOREST. The Liver bitch Mona v Felsbach was the first Swiss Liver champion. When mated to Lardo v Felsbach the litter included Amoi Bright Star of Blackberry Forest who is also very successful.

SVEN GMUR and ANDREA MAUTZ: CAMWOOD have already gathered a large Kennel with a range of bloodlines. Woodstar Linnet (Ch.) was purchased from Erling Kaer Pedersen (Denmark) and other imports have been from Lena Hagglund (O'Flanagan), Ragnhild Ulin (Almanza), both Swedish breeders, and Sykje Dongstra-Winter (Holland).

DENMARK

In terms of interchange there has seemed to be closer links between Germany and Denmark than the other Scandinavian countries, partly for geographic reasons but basically because, for many years, the border between Denmark and the rest of Scandinavia was closed due to quarantine restrictions. The Danish Retriever Club has about 6,650 members. About 940 of these are Flat-Coat owners but less than 200 are actively involved. In 1990, 398 puppies were born; the next year there were 501, and in 1994 there were 541.

There are more than 50 Field events a year, half on cold game. There are about 12 Championship shows a year, two being for Flat-Coats: these are weekend events with the show one day and a cold game Field trial the next. About 50 dogs take part each day.

ERLING KJAER PEDERSEN: WOODSTAR

Erling had bred Goldens for several years when he decided to try a Flat-Coat. Foundations were:

ABOVE: Driver, Reserve Best Dog, World Show 1994, owned by Lone Engel and Hans Jakob Hansen (Melody Makers).

RIGHT: Int. Ch. Blackie, bred by Erling Kyjaer Pedersen, owned by Johan Sonderup.

Woodworker (later Ch.) and Woodwind (later Ch.) bred by Colin Wells (Ch. Tonggreen Sparrowboy/Ch. Woodpoppy). One could hardly have a sounder base on which to build. Erling has gained about 50 CCs with Flat-Coated Retrievers. For 18 years until 1993 he represented the Breed on the committee.

JIGGERS: POUL RONNOW KJELDSON
A brilliant trainer and handler who understandably has been highly successful in competitive Field events.

MELODY MAKERS: LONE ENGEL and JAKOB HANSEN
This kennel started in 1984 with a male Columbo; Citiana from the same breeding followed a year later and then a bitch Corastine. All are champions plus CACIB (Ch. Tonggreen Stormbird/Ch. Woodcraft). Breeding has been with Shargleam Cardinal, Falswift Constellation and Gunhills Dancing Dane. The produce have been good dual-purpose Flat-Coats. "Driver" was Reserve Best dog at the World Show 1994, Res CACIB (Melody Makers Laban/Melody Makers Je T'Aime).

PEARLY COAT: MARIANNE AND CHRISTIAN SONDERGAARD
In 1980 Christian started working as Assistant Forester, needed a gundog and decided upon a Flat-Coat. In fact they had two Danish-bred ones. Later he and Marianne decided to buy a bitch puppy from England; this proved to be Oakmoss Sea Pearl from George and Mavis Lancaster (Wizardwood Tawny Owl/Oakmoss Sea Pigeon). Sea Pearl became DK Champion and also had Field Trial awards.

She proved to be a very worthwhile brood bitch: from three litters sired by different males have come several champions both in Denmark and elsewhere. Sadly, Sea Pearl died at 8. The cause was never diagnosed, but it was thought to be poison of some type. Christian needs good working dogs for his work, for he and Marianne use the dogs in a variety of ways. The aim is to try and produce Flat-Coats as beautiful and versatile as Sea Pearl.

SWEDEN

Ingemar Borelius has had a long-standing interest and involvement in Flat-Coated Retrievers. He and his wife, Inga Lill, have always aimed to maintain useful dual-purpose bloodlines. Their foundation bitch was the lovely Int. Nord U Ch. SJCh. Tittie, whom they mated to Woodlands Wanderer, thus reinforcing the "W" lines of Int. Nord U Ch. Downstream Hestia. Some years later, when visiting England, Ingemar heard from Dr Laughton of a dog she had come across with useful bloodlines. The dog was High Ley Scott who then went to the Borelius household. More recently purchases have been made from Joan Marsden's Tarncourt kennel, giving additional stock of proven working ability.

Ingemar has kindly sent information on the Breed in Sweden, from which I use some excerpts.

No Retrievers were registered in Sweden from 1901 until 1914, when Grace, a Flat-Coat bitch, was shown at the Stockholm Kennel Club show. She was owned by Mr Sjogren at Malsaker Castle, near Stockholm, who was married into the Nobel family which inaugurated the famous international prizes, and was a remarkable man, who built up a magnificent shoot at his estate. Flat-Coats were imported from England. Members of the Swedish Royal family were frequent guests at the castle and its magnificent shooting parties. No documentation is kept about these dogs but I happened to find a number of photos showing Flat-Coats of a type no-one would be ashamed of today.

From those days there is no documentation about Flat-Coats before the breed was reintroduced in Sweden in 1962, when Mona Lilliehook, a well-known breeder of Golden Retrievers, bought Black Penny of Yarlaw (Ch. Woodlark and Ch. Pewcroft Prop of Yarlaw) from the Huttons. Mona also imported Blakeholme Jollyon and Blakeholme Jamie from Barbara Hall. Jamie, who was bred from Claverdon Scott out of Blakeholme Jemima, was a worker second to none.

In 1964 Brit-Marie Brulin of the Puhs Labradors imported Downstream Hestia, by Winkswood out of Downstream Pax. Black Penny, as well as Hestia, was mated to Jamie, thus establishing a line that has become the foundation for the Swedish line of Flat-Coats until today. The majority of all successful working Flat-Coats in Sweden are bred back to those dogs.

Puhs Hestia (Bl Jamie ex D Hestia) produced the first Swedish Flat-Coated Field Trial Champion, Puhs Frigga (by Ryshot Copper Fire) and two other Field Trial champions in two litters. Puhs Dam of Fjolner (sister of Frigga) went to Denmark to establish the outstanding Danish line of working Flat-Coats.

In 1977 the Swedish Flat-Coated Retriever Club was established with the great Flat-Coat man Stig Olsson (of the Hovhill Flat-Coats) as the first chairman. At that time new rules were laid out for Swedish Field Trials by the Spaniel and Retriever Club. They were based on Danish rules and an ambition to create a more realistic setting for trials. Trials are still run on cold game with emphasis on steadiness and biddability over long retrieves on land and water. The dogs were also tested for ability to hunt for a quantity of game over a restricted area, as is necessary in Swedish terrain and conditions. Trialling is very popular. In 1994 584 Flat-Coats made 1,431 entries, compared with 834 Labradors making 2,174 entries.

Most Swedish breeders feel that the Flat-Coat should be preserved as a dual-purpose retriever. In fact the Club recommends that only dogs with proved ability be used at stud. Puppies are only accepted on the puppy register if both parents have proven ability. A new law in Sweden states that all "guns" shall have a dog available for tracking ground game or picking up game birds.

By the end of the seventies, Flat-Coats started to reach the heights in the show ring. The eighties saw the emergence of Ragnhild Ulin's Almanza Kennel, the high spot being Ch. Almanza Larry O'Grady's BIS at the Stockholm International Dog Show in 1991. The Almanza dogs continue to be very significant in the show ring.

Ingemar points out that, while the Breed standard remains the same, judges' interpretations vary, which means that the show world can insidiously change dogs, with certain features being bred in that bear no relation to the dog's original purpose. Show dogs appear to be getting bigger, heavier in bone and body and shorter in the leg. There is also a tendency in Swedish Flat-Coats to encourage over-filled forefaces, excessively heavy coats and over-angulated high quarters, which gives a showy trot in the ring but would be impractical in the field. Additionally, the Swedish show Flat-Coat is trimmed down very hard, giving the dog an unnatural and unbalanced

Int. Nord. U Ch. SFU Ch. SV 1990, 1991, 1993, NV 1991 Almanza Emergency Brake: The hugely successful son of Ch. Larry O'Grady. Bred and owned by Ragnhild Ulin.

appearance. This type of trimming is, of course, strongly condemned in the Breed standard.

ALMANZA: RAGNHILD ULIN
Ragnhild is currently enjoying enormous success. Her first Flat-Coat was the good dog Int SU NU Ch. Laddie, sired by Int Nord U Ch. Puhs Herakles from Apports Penicuik. Foundation bitches were Wolfhill Dolly Parton and Scarlet O'Hara: the former had 5 champions in one litter, all with FT awards as well. Ragnhild's livers come from Sara Whittaker's Bramatha lines. Almanza the First Chocolate Delight has 3 CCs and FT awards. In blacks, A Exotic Tequila Sunrise and A Heaven or Hell are both doing well. A bitch, A Better Than Ever, went to Peter Kennon in Australia and has been made up. There is also Hans and Margarete Berin's Ch. Almanza Wet or Dry at Prairielight in Canada. The Kennel has been in the top ten for Breeder of the Year for 6 years and in 1994 was 4th. Ragnhild says her aim is to produce healthy typical Flat-Coats for both show and work.

BJORSCHULTS: MAUD HYELM AND MARIE CARLSSON
Maud had her first Flat-Coat in 1965, Collyers Celicia (Collyers Blakeholme Brewster/Collyers Christina). Then in 1972, Jacana (Jupitor of Chadwell/Downstream Hal on Tow); these founded the Bjorschults kennel. In 1976 Maud imported Heronsflight Tinker (later Ch.) (Heronsflight Tercel/Fenrivers Lily).

Later imports from Jill Saville include, Fossdyke Britannia, Fossdyke Flamboyant, Fossdyke Heather and the liver dog Fossdyke Bronze Jetsetter. Daughter Marie is now taking a very active role with the Kennel. The aims are to produce Flat-Coats that can be shown or worked. Maud's "special" is "Tinker". Marie's is Fossdyke Britannia.

CINNAMON: JEANETTE MORNEN
Jeanette (Lindquist) is a contemporary of Ann Edman; her interests lay mainly with livers, a liking which stemmed from time spent with Margaret Izzard and the Ryshot Flat-Coats where, at one time, livers predominated. After Margaret died Jeanette had Ch. Ryshot Copper Ring O'Fire whose sire was Ch. Ryshot Copper Ablaze, her dam Ch. Ryshot Idyll, a daughter of the top winning black bitch Ch. Ryshot Velvet.

The dam's side must have been very influential as Ring O'Fire was light years away from the loaded-shouldered "buffalo" type of liver Flat-Coat with heavy heads and loose flews. Jeanette improved type enormously and has continued to produce classical Flat-Coated Retrievers by judiciously introducing lines with type firmly established.

GUNHILLS: GUNNEL WAHLSTROM
This is a very old-established Kennel in North Sweden where there have long been "pockets" of Flat-Coats, rather like parts of Scotland. Gunnel and her family have always been involved with events in the area of Umea. The policy mainly has been to stay within the old-established bloodlines. There is a clear pattern to their pedigrees and type has been firmly established.

O'FLANAGAN KENNEL: LENA HAGGLUND
Lena writes: "The prefix was registered in 1972. The name came from one of Pat Smythe's most successful show jumpers, Flanagan, born in Ireland, so I decided upon "O'Flanagan". The first time I saw a Flat-Coat alive and not just in pictures, was in 1968 and I fell totally in love with the breed, first with a lovely head and expression then, when I learned to know this very special first Flat-Coat better, also with a super temperament.

"I bought my first Flat-Coat, Fiona, in 1972; she quickly got her CCs, lots of BoBs and produced many successful offspring who, in their turn, were the foundation Flat-Coats of other kennels. There are O'Flanagan winners and Champions in Scandinavia, Europe and Canada: for example SF Ch. O'Flanagan The Mighty Ribot in Finland, Can Ch. WC O'Flanagan What's Cooking and Can Ch. WC O'Flanagan Wheel of Fortune in Canada.

"Under our prefix, eight rescue dogs have been bred and even if you hope that it will not be necessary for them to prove their capabilities, it is good to know that the dogs can do service to humanity in case of a catastrophe.

Int. Nord. Ch. NV 1983 Flanagan Rule Britannia, bred and owned by Lena Hagglund.

"The breeding and prefix has since 1985 been joined by Mrs Evalis Johansson, the owner of Ch. O'Flanagan Maida's Toblerone and SU Ch. O'Flanagan Futura Display, mother of SU Ch. O'Flanagan Lilla Fjus Pepparkaka. She also owned and trialled SU Ch. O'Flanagan Just Splendid. Our breeding has also been awarded the Hamilton Award, the most honourable award a Swedish breeder could get."

WATERPROOF: ANN EDMAN
Ann started with such achievement that she hardly had anything else to attain; the main problem must have been to maintain the standard she had set herself. The fact that 25 years later she is still producing good dual-purpose Flat-Coats as well as being a busy vet speaks for itself. Ann's foundation F/C was the bitch Puhs Frigga bred in 1969 by the late "Bat" Brulin. Her sire was Ryshot Copper Fire and her dam, Int. SU NU Finnish Ch. Puhs Hestia. Frigga made history by being the first Flat-Coated Retriever to become a Field Trial Champion. Her title became Int. SU NU and Finnish Ch. and Swedish Field Trial Champion Puhs Frigga. Frigga was also an extremely good brood bitch. Ann largely bred into Colin Wells' "W" lines in her early breeding programme. Ann's present Flat-Coat is also proving very competent in the Field as well as the show ring – SU

SU Ch. Waterproof What Is What, bred and owned by Ann Edman.

Ch. Waterproof What is What.

NORWAY
It seems there may have been scattered, single Flat-Coats in Norway between 1910 and 1930. Only one bitch is named, Tar of Glendanel, imported by Lorentz Bruun of Trondheim in 1910, although there is no record at the Kennel Club. No attempt was made to establish the breed until 1970, when Ninni Thurmann Moe imported the bitch Apports Shimmy from Mona Lilliehook in Sweden. Shimmy became the first Norwegian Flat-Coated Retriever champion. (Ryshot Copper Fire/Apports Black Sarah). Later Shimmy was mated to Int. NU Ch. Apports Macfraser. Ninni kept a male NU Ch. C Black Spot.

In 1972 Cambourne Tango and Halstock Michaela were imported, and Per Iversen brought in Woodland Whip. In 1973, Jenny Hamremoen (Sol-Ham-Na) imported Halstock Lone Ranger (Halstock Downstream Daniel/Halstock Jade) from Patience Lock. Lone Ranger had already sired the litter from Wyndhamian Claudette that included Exclyst Bernard (later Ch.). The following year Bjorg Halldis Lie bought Hallbent Dawn Patrol (Yonday Marshal/Hallbent Dark Dawn) from

Georgie Buchanan. Both dogs became Norwegian Champions and had great influence on the Breed. The influence is most clearly demonstrated with the coming together of the two lines in 1975 with the litter sired by NU Ch. Peik (NU Ch. Exclyst Kestrel/Ki-Ro-Ma's Estells) and Fjell-Bjorns D'Bonnie (NU Ch. C Black Spot/Fjell Bjorns Ara). This litter included the brothers NU Ch. Black Bowie and NU Ch. NV '88 TS Garp, the two Norwegian Flat-Coats that have such an impressive record from the late 1980s, holding their own against current imports. The litter was bred by Fred Isachsen, "Bowie" being owned by Helene Soberg Moe and "Garp" by Jostein Skjefstad.

Per Iversen's breeding has been largely based on Colin Wells' "W" stock. In 1972 he brought in the bitch Kenstaff Whip and these bloodlines were reinforced a few years later by Hjordis Espeland having Woodland Wagtail. In 1979 Per imported NU Ch. Torwood Plague from Denise and Neil Jury which brought in Pewcroft lines but also had a line back to Woodlark and Waveman.

Two very useful Exclyst males also came in: NU Ch. Exclyst Iceman to Bjorg Halldis Lie and NU Ch. Exclyst Kestrel to Kirsten Schjorn. Later, in 1984 NU Ch. Exclyst Sea Hawk came to Anne Berith Waskaas. Of interest to Liver enthusiasts was the litter bred by Hjordis Espeland in 1978 when NU Ch. Woodlands Wagtail was mated to SU Ch. Heronsflight Tinker: the litter included Per Iversen's Brennas Bris and Brennas Bunyan who went to Kjersti Haugen.

Bunyan was a very typy male who became Finnish and NU Champion. In 1983 Kjersti imported a Liver bitch from Norma Padley, Paddiswood Amber Spice (litter sister to Paddiswood Amber Nutmeg, the dam of Inger-Johanne Stockinger's NU Ch. Heronsflight Morris). Kyersti says of Spice: "The best looking Flat-Coat I have ever had, very easy to train, obedient and willing to please. I still miss her."

Sadly Spice died by falling down a crevasse in the forest. Because of this, Norma Padley did a repeat mating of Wizardwood Tawny Owl and Heronsflight Burnt Sugar of Paddiswood. Kyersti had two bitches, P Burnt Willow and P Burnt Bracken. The first Liver litter in Norway was born when Bunyan was mated with P Burnt Willow in 1988.

From 1971 until 1983 there were some 41 imports. Obviously the Breed was set to increase rapidly, which it did, although there was no radical alteration in breeding patterns until the mid '80s when the emphasis changed.

Basically the change followed Ir. Ch. Shargleam Blackcap's BIS win at Crufts, a roll-on effect. In 1985 Kari and Kjell Haug of the long-established Cariena's Kennel had a litter from Cariena's Seven-Ten sired by Blackcap (AI), later that year they bought Shargleam Treecreeper. In 1986/7 Arild and Grete Engedal bought NU SU Ch. Shargleam Sandpiper and in 1989 Bjarne Sorensen brought in NU Ch. Shargleam Woodcock. At more or less the same time, three of Jill Saville's Fossdyke bred Flat-Coats went to Sweden; these carried Shargleam lines. It was also over this time and for a further few years that the home-bred NU Ch. Black Bowie (4 BIS 15 BoB 7 BIM 6 CACIB) and NU Ch. NV '88 Garp (6 CACIB 2 BIS) were continuing to have great success.

In 1987, the Skjelbreds brought in Lussac Crusader (later NU Ch.), bred by Sue Wilmington (Ch. Exclyst Imperial Mint ex Exclyst Rebecca of Lussac). Rebecca was a daughter of Lone Ranger, so would tie in with his progeny in Norway. Crusader became an approved "sniffer" dog in 1989.

Knut and Signe Skjelbred and daughter Nina have had Flat-Coats for 15 years but have only bred two litters. Nina however, has applied for the prefix "Covenstead" and has a litter ready to register, grandchildren of Crusader sired by Exclyst Bronski Beat. Despite owning the breed for a number of years, Crusader is regarded as the foundation and has proved to be a worthwhile sire. The family's main interests are varied, showing but also working trials, tracking and rescue work.

The Cariena's kennel of Kari and Kjell Haug continues to be very significant in the ring, as does

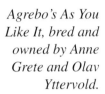

Agrebo's As You Like It, bred and owned by Anne Grete and Olav Yttervold.

the Agrebo Kennel of Anne Grete and Olav Yttervold, who had their first Flat-Coat in 1979, a bitch puppy called Atcha, sired by NU Ch. Brennas Basato from Alvaason's Black Atcha. Atcha became a champion. From a litter sired by NU Ch. Torwood Plague came the dog NU Ch. Agrebo's Bona Lara who became a narcotics search dog. A granddaughter of Atcha's mated to Crusader produced the dog NV '92 NU Ch. Agrebo's Imloth Melui who has had a most successful career. Gunhill Easter Love was bought from Gunnel Wahlstrom (Sweden) in 1988; she had litters sired by Bowie and Garp.

In 1989, by chance, Anne Grete came across a bitch bred by Valerie Bernhardt (USA), Meadowrue Fiance who has done well in the ring and produced some talented offspring. Olav is a Field training instructor and Anne Grete has been a member of the Norwegian Retriever Club Breeders Council for 6 years and was also litter secretary.

Over the past few years there has been continued use of Swedish lines such as Lena Hagglund's O'Flanagan Kennel and of course Ragnhild Ulin's Almanza dogs. Imports seem to have been fewer from the UK. In 1991 the male Exclyst Bronski Beat came to Svein Nesse and the bitch Exclyst Black Magic to Per Iversen (Ch. Exclyst Watchman/Sh.Ch. Exclyst Victoria). In 1992 Inger-Johanne Stockinger bought a bitch puppy from Elaine Whittaker's small dual-purpose Kennel, Falconcliffe Flamenco (Dark Delight Henry Boy from Torwood/Perchance of Heronsflight).

In 1993, Torbjoern Gjemdal imported a promising dog puppy from Ros Maltby, another person whose emphasis is work/show, Coalport Countryman (Heronsflight Go My Way To Lathkill ex Sh.Ch. Coalport Coral Skye). These were followed by Fossdyke Lieutenant from Jill Saville to Mrs A. Mankham and Ebony Saxon Princess from Caroline Young to Merethe Norheim. There is now quite a wide gene pool, so much depends on how it is used.

There is no Flat-Coated Retriever organisation; all retriever breeds come under the aegis of the Norwegian Retriever Club, an enormously powerful and influential body. Over the years sporadic attempts have been made to establish a Flat-Coated Retriever Club but the efforts have always come to nought. At its inception in 1960 the NRC had 20 members. There was an enormous jump from 1970 (650 members) to 1986 where a peak of 6,015 members was reached. Since then, membership appears to have stabilised at around 5,500. There is no individual breed record but it is thought that 25% to 30% of the members are Flat-Coated Retriever owners.

Training is undertaken by groups in different areas who also put on competitive Field Trials. For example, Kjersti Haugen with helpers runs courses of 6 classes taking about 8 dogs. In 1994, 71 Flat-Coats took part in Field Trials/tests. When hunting Elk or Deer, under Norwegian law a competent tracking dog must accompany the hunters. Increasingly Flat-Coats are being used as Narcotic dogs and also as "lavine" (search) dogs, for finding people buried under the snow. Registrations have risen from four in 1972 to 391 in 1982, peaked to 626 in 1991 decreasing to 501 in 1994, with 73 litter registered. Over these past few years the Breed rates as 10th or 11th in the most popular breeds in Norway.

Before leaving Norway, I must mention a memorable visit made by Kjersti Haugen and myself to Barbro Lundstrom of the old-established Caymosa Kennel. Barbro's dogs appear in so many pedigrees. We had such a warm welcome which, combined with the chance to talk (aided by Kjersti) with one so knowledgeable, made this a very special occasion.

FINLAND

In the Spring of 1975, Brit-Marie ("Bat") Brulin entered a recently-acquired British import Flat-Coated Retriever, Downstream Hestia, at the Helsinki International Show. As always when she travelled to Finland from Sweden, she stayed with the Kankkunen family. Son Kenneth says it was "love at first sight" when he saw Hestia (just like Leonie Galdermans with Carrie van Crevel's Black Cindy). I am grateful to Kenneth for the information about Finland.

In 1967, Hestia was mated to Blakeholme Jamie and "Bat" gave Kenneth one of the pups, Puhs Hera, the first Flat-Coat in Finland. Showing was almost non-existent as she had no opposition.

Fin. Ch. Hilwas Pontiac (front) and Fin. Ch. Hilwas Maserati, owned by Christina Helenius.

Photo: M. Hirvonen.

Dual Ch. Roi, bred by Tapio Takala, owned by Jorma Kauppinen.

Retriever tests were in their infancy and for years Kenneth had tried to train his Mother's labs with the help of English books on gundog training. To gain the Labradors titles, permission had to be gained to run them in Spaniel tests.

Despite these difficulties Hera gained her Finnish championship. She had three litters. From the first, sired by Ryshot Copper Fire, came the first Finnish Int Ch. Rolls i Vassen. The second litter, sired by Stolford Sepoy, included Akvavitix i Vassen, the first F/C to go BIS at the Finnish Retriever Club. A litter brother Asterix i Vassen is behind the line that produced the first Finnish Field Trial Champion, FT Ch. Roi.

The third litter, sired by Ch. Woodman, has produced four successive generations of very notable Flat-Coats. These include Ch. Wilhelmina who was BoB and BIS at the All Variety Club show in 1983 under Margot Woolley and myself. Her daughter, Ch. Hilwas Maserati, repeated this win the following year. Maserati's son Hilwas Chevrolet is the 4th Finnish Flat-Coat to gain Field Trial Champion status.

Wilhelmina was the foundation of Christina Helenius' very successful and talented Hilwas Flat-Coated Retrievers. Christina is the key breeder in carrying on the valuable Puhs Hera line.

Kenneth says that, thinking back on Hera, he remembers her overwhelming optimism, a strong will and self-confidence. Snow was her great delight: Kenneth asks is this a legacy of the Canadian forebears on the Eastern coast of Canada 100 years ago? The Breed in Finland is based largely on early Swedish imports which were mainly descended from Downstream Hestia. Fortunately it was possible to line breed to her with no ill effects.

HILWAS: CHRISTINA HELENIUS
As mentioned.

KENNEL FLATTS: BENITA AKERLUND
Benita originally had a puppy from "Bat" Brulin, Puhs Fylgia, then in 1973 Benita bought Gipsy Girl (Ch. Tonggreen Sparrowboy/Downstream Ambleside Jill) from Gunnel Wahlstrom (Sweden). She was the foundation bitch of the Flatts Kennel.

SNIFFENS: KAARINA SUPPANEN
In 1970 a Mrs West imported a bitch from Sweden, Puhs Evoe, who was later sold on and then mated to Jupitor of Chadwell. The litter included Kassuntepun Anina who went to Kaarina as the foundation of the now very well known Sniffens Kennel.

KENNEL MINNIE'S: MINNA LIIRO
Another prominent Swedish import was Sabina (Ch. Stolford Sepoy/Downstream Hal on Tow). Sabina was mated to a Finnish dog, Joakim, producing Kassuntepuntun Cipsi, who formed the base of Minna Liiro's Kennel.

FIELD TRAINING
In the early 1980s The Retriever Club organised an intensive training programme; this was aided and encouraged by the Field Trial successes of Thomas Gottvall's O'Flanagan's Free as Air, bred of course by Lena Hagglund. We have already seen that four F/Cs achieved the status of FT Ch., which is excellent.

THE FINNISH FLAT-COATED RETRIEVER CLUB
Breeding has always been very modest, with just a few litters each year. Most early breeders were

pet owners who only stayed for about five years. One of the most regular and diligent breeders since the early seventies is Benita Akerlund. In 1982 registrations suddenly jumped to 100. During the '90s the number has been over 200 annually, the record year being '93 with 276 registrations with a reduction in '94. Imports are made almost annually from other Scandinavian countries and Britain, in 1994 there were 9 imports, which is about average.

The Club was established in 1982. Many members are pet owners and the membership is geographically very scattered which makes co-ordination difficult. A new generation of more dual-purpose orientated owners seems to be emerging and hopefully bringing some unanimity of purpose. As in many other countries, a certain number of dedicated dual-purpose breeders form a staunch back-bone with some single-purpose breeders creating short-term fashion trends.

NEW ZEALAND

It is a far cry from Ropley in Hampshire to Otaki, North Island, New Zealand and in the early 1960s seemed even further than today. Early in 1962, Doreen Ridley was looking for an intelligent, outgoing dog and happened upon Margaret and Dennis Izzard's Ryshot Kennels. Doreen returned home with a lively 6 month old dog puppy, Ryshot Prospect, little knowing, at that time, that he would be the first Flat-Coat in New Zealand. This did not come about until "Prince" was six, when Doreen and husband Bill, a vet, emigrated to New Zealand and of course "Prince" went too.

Enquiries to the NZ Kennel Club brought the response that there were no other Flat-Coats registered. As far as was known, Prince was the only representative of the Breed in NZ.

When Prince eventually died, at the age of 14, in 1975, Doreen decided that life without a Flat-Coat had a certain emptiness and so in 1976, Heronsflight Tipster (Imp UK) later NZ Ch., arrived in Otaki. Tipster was sired by Heronsflight Tercel from Fenrivers Lily. He was followed by Kenstaff Marigold (Mulberry of Heronsflight ex Heronsflight Joy).

Doreen takes up the tale: "These two dogs had great influence in Australasia, even though only one litter was bred from them. Tipster to my knowledge was the first Flat-Coat to win a Field Trial in Australasia, giving him one challenge point. A male from the Tipster/Marigold litter, Aus Ch. Copsewood Nigra (Imp NZ) went to Gary and Kim Methven; his show record has yet to be broken, including many "In Group" wins and three BIS. He certainly strengthened the Breed in Australia.

"Two of Nigra's sons have become the first Field Trial champions in Australasia for the Breed – the Parkinsons' Aus Ch. Methwinds the Shining and Sovanna Black Stone. Nigra's litter sister Copsewood Plumosa gained two FT challenge points by winning an All Breeds Trial and in turn her daughter, C. Opus, also gained two points for an All Breed win. Another litter sister, Quail, is used for tracking down endangered bird species; she travels the islands by helicopter with her Conservation Officer owner. Two of Plumosa's grandchildren, one sired by Branchalwood Kyle (Imp UK) and the other by NZ Ch. Methwinds Nick the Raider are New Zealand's first Guide Dogs for the Blind.

"Two puppies from the Branchalwood Kyle ex Copsewood Plumosa litter were retained at home, NZ Ch. Copsewood Raven and C Ibis. Raven has been Best Puppy in Group and Best Junior on Parade, besides which he is an excellent gun dog. C.Ibis was served with frozen semen from Aus Ch. Bramatha the Emperor, the first time A.I. had been used. This proved to be successful and one of the puppies was kept. She is shaping very well – NZ Ch. Copsewood Black Velvet.

"I feel it would be advantageous to the breed in New Zealand (or any country that is trying to establish the breed), if there was a rule by the controlling body that a bitch is only allowed two litters – nothing bred afterwards to be registered. It would help the breed to progress slowly.

Pictured left to right: Ch. Copsewood Black Velvet, Copsewood Ibis FTA, and Ch. Copsewood Raven FTA, all bred and owned by Doreen Ridley.

"Our Field Trials are nearly all cold game trials, mainly dead pigeons and a few ducks are used. We have land and water events, each breed having their own specialist trial, i.e. Spaniel, Pointer and Setter, and Retrievers. Also unique to New Zealand is the 'All Breeds' Trial. It is exactly what the title says, for any breed of gundog. It's a find and flush event. The dogs work the ground in a systematic way to find two dead birds hidden in cover and then, still working the ground, they proceed to a live bird hidden in cover in an electronic trap which is activated by the judge on the dog going into flush the bird. The handler fires a blank shot at the bird while in gun range, the dog staying steady to shot until called to heel by the handler on the judges' command. Then the dog has to do a water event, which consists of a double bird retrieve from across the water; two birds having been thrown and a blank shot fired at each bird. Sometimes there is a blind retrieve as well.

"These trials are judged on a points system. For an 'All Breeds' win one gets two challenge points and for a Retriever Trial one challenge point. That is at a Club Championship; at a National or Island Championship more challenge points are awarded. Six challenge points are required for a dog to become a Field Trial Champion. Before a dog enters an Open class it has to win its way through the minor classes.

"New Zealand has just started live game trials, run more or less on the English style of Field Trials. So far, the live game ones are for Spaniels, Pointer and Setter breeds only. Very few birds are bred in captivity for releasing into the wild, so our pheasants are very strong flyers and truly wild and cunning as a fox.

"Currently in New Zealand we have approximately 140 Flat-Coat owners. Most Flat-Coats would be in pet homes, a few in Obedience homes, quite a few go to rough shooters, only two people have Flat-Coats for trialling, at the top level."

RUTH CHAPMAN (originally "Proctors" now "Maplehurst" with Lois Causer)
Ruth Chapman lives in Otago, South Island, New Zealand. In 1975 she was looking for an all-round family dog. Her search led her to Margaret Evans of the Vanrose Golden and Flat-Coated Retrievers. The results was Ch. Vanrose Black Cidy (Gem), sired by Ch. Stolford Kings Ransome (Imp UK) from Blackberry of Vanrose. In due course Gem was mated, perforce to her sire as there was no other male available. The resulting eight puppies proved hard to sell as the breed was unknown.

Gem became a Show Champion, and had a reserve Group under an English judge. Gem was then

Ruth Chapman with Ch. Dunboy Fenian's Pride, winning the Otago Christmas Trial.

trained for trials and won several, although somewhat excitable. Her daughter, Opal, had the same failing, although she was a brilliant rough shooting dog. Opal was mated to Doreen Ridley's NZ Ch. Heronsflight Tipster (Mason), a much calmer character. Their seven pups sold easily – the Flat-Coat was catching on. Another import of the time, Quennington Black Tulip (Ch. Courbeck Mercury/Halstock Primrose) was also mated to Mason. Her daughter and a son of the Mason/Opal mating were bred together, resulting in 4 black and 5 liver puppies. Ruth had a liver dog who became the noted Ch. Dunboy Fenian Pride (Robert).

He has been a great ambassador for the Breed in New Zealand, winning numerous trials at all levels including eleven times placed at Championship Trials. Ruth feels that, had she been more experienced at the time, he could have been an F T Champion.

In 1985 Ruth and Lois Causer became partners under the Maplehurst prefix. Ruth mentioned her young dog. Ch. Maplehurst Brigand (Brig). He has won two Gundog Groups and was BoB at the 1993 National Show. 'Brig' is a tremendous swimmer who has an irresistible urge to "rescue" any human he sees swimming. He dives in, grabs an arm and tows the body to the shore! However, this ability was put to good use on two occasions – once, when an ageing Robert got stuck in shifting sand and Brig tugged him free and, on another occasion, when a six month pup fell into the swiftest, deepest part of the river. She was being tossed like a rag doll when Brig and Tip dived in. They went either side of her and steered her out of the current on to the shore.

Ruth is optimistic about the future, particularly with the possibility of the use of A.I. to widen the gene pool. She and Lois will continue to breed for work, but with an eye to looks. There are now some 200 Flat-Coats registered compared with three some 20 years ago. Also Ruth, after years of handling the only Flat-Coat being trialled on South Island, now has competition, which is satisfying.

AUSTRALIA

There seems no record of the Breed in Australia until 1974 when Robert Pargeter imported Stonemeade Shandygaff and S Fine Lace from Philip Whittaker. In December of the same year two puppies went from Margaret Evans, in New Zealand, to Australia, Vanrose Black Pearl (later NZ and Aus Ch.) and Vanrose Black Jewel who went to the Pargeters. Both were sired by NZ Ch. Stolford King's Ransome from NZ Ch. Blackberry of Vanrose. In fact three more of the same

*Aus. Ch. Copsewood Nigra
(imp. NZ), bred by Doreen
Ridley, owned by Gary and Kim
Methven. 'Nicky's' record in the
show ring is still unbeaten. He
is also the sire of FT Ch.
Methwinds The Shining –
Australia's only Field Trial
Champion to date.*

Photo: Robinson.

*FT Ch. Methwind The
Shining NRD, bred by
Gary and Kim Methven,
owned and trained by
Wayne and Teresa
Parkinson.*

breeding followed in 1976. It does bring home how small was the gene pool.

During 1975, Stonemeade Wild Rose was imported by Dorothy and Albert Sutch (Duffton) with whom she had her first litter, but in 1977 she moved to Peter and Helena Eley; when she died at 10 plus, Helena reckoned that some 126 F/Cs had her in their pedigrees.

On December 1st, 1975 the first litter was born, sired by Aus Ch. Stonemeade Shandygaff from Aus Ch. Stonemeade Fine Lace. The only dog pup, who went to the Rushton family, was the very successful Aus Ch. Tanton Arthur Gaff (Jamie). Jamie was not only Best exhibit at the F/C Association's first three Open shows but also at the first Championship Show, and on top of this had two Best exhibit in Group awards. He also sired 4 litters; the one from S Wild Rose included 5 champions.

Over the succeeding years there was continued interchange between New Zealand and Australia, despite the distance. At that time New Zealand had a slightly wider range of bloodlines available, albeit still very restricted. In 1981 Kim and Gary Methven imported Copsewood Nigra (later Aus Ch.) from Doreen Ridley in New Zealand (NZ Ch. Heronsflight Tipster/Kenstaff Marigold). This dog's record has still not been surpassed: he was the first Flat-Coat able to compete successfully at

Halzephron Sea Hawk, bred by Paul and Jill Lea, owned and trained by Wayne and Teresa Parkinson.

top Group level, plus many "In Group" and Three Best in Show Awards.

By the mid 1980s the Breed seemed to be getting established even though its growth would perforce be slow. Kim Methven was bringing her energy and enthusiasm to work, not only as President of the Association but also helping to produce the lively and informative News Letter.

Over the years there have been further imports including Stonemeade Hamish and later Bramatha the Emperor from Sara Whittaker, a young dog that had already started a promising show career in the UK. Very recently, a comparative newcomer to Flat-Coats has imported stock from the Almanza Kennels – Peter Kennon, who is currently President of the FCRAV. Peter has had and trained other breeds of gundogs so Flat-Coats are something of an afterthought. He has kindly written a few observations:

"The Flat-Coated Retriever Association of Victoria Inc is the Australian breed club. Formed in 1976, there were 16 members in 1977, rising to 58 in 1994. The Flat-Coat remains relatively small in numbers, the show ring being the most popular form of competition. An occasional appearance is seen in Obedience trials and less frequently in Field and Retriever events.

"Having trained and trialled Labrador and Golden Retrievers, Cocker and English Springer Spaniels, I became interested in working Flat-Coats mainly because no-one else appeared to be. In my 25 years experience, which included judging appointments for State and National Field Trial Championships, I had only seen two Flat-Coats in gundog trials.

"It seems there are key reasons for the breed's scarcity. It has never established any credibility with the shooting fraternity probably due to its late introduction to this country and, perhaps more significantly, the Flat-Coat has lacked a 'Champion' – one person committed to breeding, selecting for performance, and training and trialling over the long term. I admit I seriously underestimated the challenge the Flat-Coat would represent. While our early dogs were competent retrievers, their careers were prematurely terminated by HD and Bloat. However, by this time I was President of the Flat-Coat Association, convinced of the breed's potential and determined to persevere. Starting afresh with four pups imported from Ragnhild Ulin's Almanza Kennel in Sweden, we are beginning to see the soundness and natural ability which was common in our Labs and Springers.

"Whether or not the Flat-Coat will achieve any durable distinction in Australia as a Working dog remains to be seen. Trainers such as Wayne Parkinson and Georgina Golle have made worthy contributions but, with declining field access and strict gun laws, the Flat-Coat's future might lie more in other areas of performance including Obedience and agility."

FIELD TRIALS

Two people who really enjoy their dogs, a mix of Flat-Coats and Labs are Wayne and Teresa Parkinson. Teresa has sent some information on Australian Trials. Working (Field) Trials for Retrievers in Australia fall into two categories, having been adapted to suit the unique game and conditions.

1. NON-SLIP RETRIEVER TRIALS

Open to all registered Gundog breeds. These trials are designed primarily to simulate a duck hunt.
Four levels of competition are available: Beginners, Novice, Restricted and All Age.
The number of wins at each level are as follows:-
Beginners, 1. Novice, 2. (Novice Retrieving Dog). Restricted, 3. (RRD) To gain the title
Retrieving Trial Champion the dog must have at least two wins at All Age level (8 championship
points). This involves very difficult retrieves, blind and seen, over difficult terrain. Game is
usually pigeon and rabbit.

2. FIELD TRIALS FOR SPANIELS AND RETRIEVERS

Open to all registered Spaniels and Retriever breeds. These trials test the dog's ability to find,
flush and retrieve live game to the gun. They are usually run on rabbits, quail, duck. There are two
levels of competition – Novice (2 wins permitted to make an NFD – Novice Field Dog) and Open.
To gain the title Field Trial Champion a dog must accumulate 8 championship points, four of
which must come from a win in Open competition. The trials are run on a knock-out basis.

Teresa writes: "Charlie Ball, arguably one of the best Retriever trainers Australia has ever seen
and the first to trial Flat-Coats, once said: 'For a dog to become a good field dog he requires a
good nose, hunting ability, style, eagerness, action and plenty of stamina as he may be required to
cover up to 50 or 60 miles over the day's work. To go with these natural abilities the dog must
have the brains to accept and retain the training that is taught to him. The dog is required to remain
within gun range at all times except when sent on retrieves. He must remain steady to shot and
flushed game, must not steal other dogs' finds, must not run into fallen game and at no time must
he chase however tempting it may be.' "

Teresa's involvement with Flat-Coats started by chance. This is how she describes it: "In 1985
while showing a Springer, I saw my first Flat-Coat, Ch. Copsewood Nigra (Imp NZ), and knew
this was the breed for me. After making enquiries that day, Kim and Gary Methven agreed to let
me have a dog pup from a litter planned for later in the year. The result was the outstanding young
dog, Methwinds the Raven (Ch. Copsewood Nigra (Imp NZ) from Ch. Lavenderpark New Lace).

"At the time, my future husband, Wayne, was a successful Labrador trialler and it was at a
training day that we first met. From then on it was a case of 'love me, love my Flat-Coat'!
Unfortunately we lost Benson at the tender age of 15 months under tragic circumstances, so,
although they had decided not to breed again, Gary and Kim repeated the mating. When we drove
over to collect the pup, Wayne made a commitment to them that, if the dog had it in him, he would
make him up to be a working champion. The end result was the country's first Flat-Coated
Retriever with a Working title – FT Ch. Methwinds the Shining NRD. Unquestionably a great dog.
On Sunday, August 16th, 1992, history was made in the world of Flat-Coats. Woodie became the
first Flat-Coated Retriever in Australia to attain a working championship title, and he was
competing against the cream of the Field Trial World. There were seven Field Trial champions and
three Open winning dogs among the field, including the top Springer Spaniel FT dogs, bred
specifically for Field Trial work."

DOG SHOWS

Basically there are three types of shows. Championship shows are open to all types of dogs
including those with "titles". Points are awarded based on the number of breed exhibits beaten on
the day; e.g. minimum points if you are the only breed representative – 5 points and 1 point for the
dog. Two dogs – 5 points plus one for each dog, and so on (7). 100 points are needed to become a
(Show) Champion. A Best in Group or Best in Show automatically gives 25 points. Open shows

are open to all. No points are awarded. Members competitions are information affairs mainly for experience. No title holders allowed. As yet Kim and Gary Methven's Ch. Copsewood Nigra (Imp NZ) remains the only multiple Group winner with a record yet to be broken.

The number of kennels is really quite few, here are some of the main ones:-

Peter and Helen Eley	Kellick	1975
Gary and Gwen Methven	Methwinds	1977
(Originally Gary and Kim Methven)		
Dorothy Mottram	Torlum	1980
Donna Turner	Hadwin	1980
Tony and Angela Jenkins	Sovanna	1980
Wayne and Teresa Parkinson	Terraway	1983
Chris and Greg Huggett	Lainston	1988
Peter and Carol Kennon)		
Judy Kennon-Wray)	Bushman	1988
Jill and Paul Lea	Halzephron	1990
Margaret Swann and Jill Wake	Heddwyn	1993

Ross and Jean Bryant have a bitch Casuarina Black Pearl (Imp UK) they are Field Trialling but as yet have no prefix and have not bred a litter.

Chapter Fourteen

THE FLAT-COAT IN NORTH AMERICA

With so many good kennels, as with the UK kennels, it is incredibly difficult to know where to begin and end. Obviously only a small proportion can be mentioned, so to the rest of you, my apologies.

ALTAIR 1993: NEAL GOODWIN
Previously co-holder of the Casablanca affix. Recently Neal has chaired the sub-committee responsible for the Code of Ethics proposed by the FCRSA. See CASABLANCA.

AMANI 1986 : ANN MORTENSON
"I got my first Flat-Coat in 1986. Am/Can Ch. Marquin's Hooi UD, MH, WCX, Can CDX, WC FCRSA Hall of Fame (Ch. Wingmaster's Blac Apex CDX, TD, Sh.Ex Ch. Rockledge Marjoran WC). She is my foundation bitch who produced two litters and eleven puppies. I try very hard to produce multi-purpose dogs in my breeding programme, and I personally work my dogs in the field, compete in Field Trials, Hunting Tests, obedience and conformation.

Am. Can. Ch. Marquin's Hooi MH, UD, WCX, Can. CDX, WC, FCRSA Hall of Fame, owned by Ann Mortenson.

"My most special Flat-Coat, although I dearly love them all and hate to show preferences, is Hodi. I currently own five FCs: Hodi (who is 9 years old), two from Hodi's first litter, one from her second litter, and a grandson from a breeding done by Mary Young. Still, Hodi out-hunts all her kids, continues to please me in everything she does and is an absolute joy to live and play with."

Ann is currently Vice-President of the FCRSA.

ATHERCROFT: BONNIE AND GLENN CONNOR

One of the longest established Kennels, the foundation bitch Rolla was from Pauline Jones' very notable "Arr" litter born in May 1967, of which six became champions. She was an excellent brood bitch, producing quality offspring to different stud dogs. Breeding has followed a pattern of using established proven lines going back to Claverdon, Pewcroft and Atherbram. This pattern can still be seen when studying the present day pedigrees; John and Shirley Fippin's Ch. Athercroft Best Intentions born in 1984 is a typical example – not only an achiever himself but produced High in Trial, Best in Show and Field titled offspring.

More recently, Bonnie has had Ch. Athercroft Mo Jo Man CDX SH WCX in partnership with Nancy Schenck and Ch. Athercroft American Gothic in partnership with Cheryl Wych.

BERTSCHIRE 1976: MARK AND NANCY CAVALLO

Foundation Flat-Coat was Ch. Springfield's Black Ibis CDX (Ch. Coulallenby Remus/Ch. Blakeholme Heronsflight Try). First home-bred was Ch. Lady Obsidian Crystal CD from Ibis, sired by Athercroft Char.

Am. Can. Ch. Bertschire's Doc Holliday CD WCX, bred and owned by Mark and Nancy Cavallo.

There have been and are so many good Bertschire Flat-Coats it is indeed difficult to choose which was the most special. On the whole they have that touch of class personified by Michael and Debbie Raho's Ch. Bertschire's Buckingham Butler who was WD and BoB at Farmington in 1987.

Mark and Nancy are interested in show, obedience and Field activities; they also produce the excellent Flat-Coated Retriever Directory.

BLACK GAMIN (1979): WENDY JONES AND ANDY LEINOFF

Foundation bitch was Am Can Ch. Grousemoor Amelia Earhart Am Can CD (Westering Why Not/Ch. Mandingo Fantasy of Wyndham WC). Wendy says:

Amelia was bred twice, firstly to Wyndham Surprisingly Grumpy and later to Ch. Wyndham's Kipper of Meadowrue WC (Jasper). Showing is limited to gaining Ch. title and then restricted to local shows. They have competed in Obedience and also compete at licensed and sanctioned Field events.

Its hard to pick the most special ones, since we have really owned only seven – Amelia, her Grumpy kids Ch. BlackGamin Albert CD WCX (Bert) and BlackGamin Agatha Christie Am CDX Can CD WCX, her Jasper daughter Ch. BlackGamin Brunhilde CD Am and Can WC (Hildy), her granddaughter Am and Can Ch. BlackGamin CT Yankee CD (Doodles) (Mallard x BlackGamin Billie Halliday), and great grandsons BlackGamin El Cid (Monster) (Ch. Rockledge Applause x Doodles) and BlackGamin Faust (Tiger) (Am and Can Ch. Windwhistle Fraser (Storm) x Doodles).

Amelia was special, being our first; she was also extremely talented and had a terrific amount of drive – she almost won several Canadian field trials at the Qualifying level, only to do something ridiculous, deliberately, on the last test. Andy was particularly fond of Bert, who tried very hard to never repeat a mistake and would work until he dropped just for the joy of pleasing you!

BOLINGBROKE (1971): VERNON VOGEL

In the 1971 Fall issue of the FCRSA Newsletter, with Helen Whitmire as temporary Editor, Vernon's name is listed as a new member, his dog being Sassacus Regulus sired by Ch. Sassacus Arr Rufus, the dam being Sassacus Chalice, presumably a black litter brother of the Connors' Ch. Sassacus Romulus CD. Vernon has always had a penchant for Livers, so his next purchase from Sally Terroux was the enormously successful Am Can Bda Ch. Mantayo Bo James Bolingbroke Am Can CDWC (Hall of Fame). Not only was Jamie successful, he was also a prepotent sire; the descendants are quite outstanding. Vernon inclines toward line breeding and looks for type, good heads, correct tailset, sound movement and responsive temperament.

Over the years, Vernon has held office in the FCRSA as secretary, chairman and for many years Archivist.

CASABLANCA 1983: ADRIENNE AYLES & NEAL GOODWIN now STERLING & ALTAIR

First Flat-Coat (1983) Ch. Omega's Fame and Fortune CD JH WCX (Am Can Ch. Bertschire's Doc Holliday CD WCX/Ch. Omega's Bedazzlin' Sunset). Foundation bitch was Ch. Omega's Honeysuckle Rose CDX JH WCX (Am Can Ch. Athercroft's Blac Jac/Ch. Omega's Elusive Dream): "Rosie" is now eleven and retired; she was always a pleasure to train and a great ambassador of the Breed.

Foundation Stud Dog was Ch. Quillquest Express CDX WCX SH (Hall of Fame). (Am Can Ch. Quillquest Eros CD JH WCX Can CD WC/Am Can Ch. Quillquest Artemis Am Can CD).

Representatives of the Casablanca kennel (left to right): Heronsflight Hope, Ch. Casablanca Charisma JH, WC, Ch. Casablanca Amadeus, and Ch. Quillquest Harvest JH, WCX.

"Presto" was co-owned with Gillian Impey and Roger and Peachie Orton and was a fantastic non-stop retriever and a wonderful showman in the ring. The aims of both Adrienne and Neal under their new affixes remains, as with the Casablanca affix, "to balance breed type with working ability and breed Flat-Coated Retrievers that can excel in the Field as well as the show ring".

CURLEE HILL (1973): AL AND CONNIE HOWARD

First Flat-Coat was Hardscrabbles Tory Terror CD (not used in breeding programme) (Wyndham's Cormorant/Mantayo Katrina Gay). Foundation bitches were Ch. Athercroft Blac Circus CD (Ch. Wyndhamian Dash/Ch. Athercroft Blac is Beautiful) and Ch. Curlee Hill Quote JH WC (Ch. Torwood Peerless CDX WCX/Ch. Athercroft Blac Circus CD). The Howards are interested in showing and hunting. Connie is a conformation judge and Al is a judge of Hunt tests. As "specials" Connie eventually chose Ch. Curlee Hill Evo Quote CD WC, Ch. Athercroft Blac Circus CD and Springfields Black Seal.

DESTINY: NANCY SCHENK DVM

Nancy's first Flat-Coat was Ch. Athercroft Study in Black UD WCX, "Katie", born in 1975 (Ch. Wyndhamian Dash/Ch. Athercroft Blac is Beautiful, Hall of Fame). Katie was also Nancy's foundation bitch and the Kennel name of Destiny was taken up when the first litter was born.

Nancy's interests lie in field and show ring, in fact any activity which Flat-Coats enjoy. Destiny-bred dogs have been titled in field, show ring, Obedience and tracking. Agility is being considered as the next challenge!

"Special Dogs" are: BIS Am. Can. Bah. Ch. Destiny Alias Corrigan CDX, TD, WCX, VB, AD (HofF). The first-born of the first litter, Cory was No.1 Flat-Coat in the USA from two years, with multiple group wins and placements. He was a gentleman and a great ambassador for the Breed; a dog full of character. His sire was Am. Can. Bda Ch. Mantayo Bo James of Bolingbroke Am. Can. CDX, Bds, CD.

Am. Can. Bah Ch. Destiny One Gun Salute CDX, WCX, AD (HofF), "Gunner", not only had

A group of Nancy Schenck's versatile Flat-Coats (left to right): Ch. Grousemoor Destiny Take Aim CDX, WCX, JH, Ch. Destiny A Chorus Line CD, WC JH, Ch. Destiny One Gun Salute WCX, Hall of Fame, Ch. Wingmaster Angelic Destiny CD, WCX, Hall of Fame, Ch. Destiny Alias Corrigan CDX, WCX, TD, Hall of Fame.

Photo: Nancy Schenck DVM.

multiple group wins and placements but, Nancy considers, was probably the sweetest dog she ever owned. Ch. Wingmasters Angelic Destiny CD, SH, WCX (HofF) in addition to being a flashy show dog with multiple group placements and B.Opp.Sex at the National Speciality, was a real workman.

DEXMOOR (1981): JUDY AND GEORGE DEXTER
First Flat-Coat was Ch. Omega Discover (1981) (Ch. Wyndham's Javelin/Ch. Mandingo Screamin Demon). Foundation Flat-Coat (1982) was Ch. Omega Flair of Dexmoor JH CD WC (Tootsie). (Am Can Ch. Bertschire's Doc Holliday CD WCX/Ch. Omega's Bedazzlin Sunset). "Tootsie" produced many title winners, champions, obedience, WC and WCX and Hunt test competitors. Main interests, Judy says, have basically been Show and Field but more recently she has been

Ch. Katoc's Arctic Sun Double Scoop CD: BOS at the 1995 American Specialty. Bred by Mary Phelps, owned by Lori Muhm-Kunz and Steven Kunz. Photo: Ludwig.

enjoying Agility and tracking. "Specials" are Ch. Omega Flair at Dexmoor, Ch. Dexmoor Epoch Maker CD WC JH SH CGC and Ch. Dexmoor Happy Hunter. The line breeding to Ch. Athercroft Waylon J appears to have paid off in stamping type whilst maintaining ability.

DUCKACRES: BRENDA GRIFFIN DVM

Brenda's first Flat-Coat was Am Bah Ch. Springvalley Black Bullet. Am Bah CD, TD, TT, CGC bred by Eleanor Bertz in 1981 (Ch. Wyndham's Kipper of Meadowrue/Ch. Wyndham's Nicol Springvalley). Bullet was never used for breeding although he was a healthy, wonderful dog. Ch. Curlee Hill Seas Biscuit Blues CD joined the family in 1983. Brenda says these two dogs and herself were just the best of buddies.

Brenda's actual foundation F/C was the bitch co-owned with Joanie and Rob Sharpe (and bred by the Sharpes and the Cavallos), Am Bah Ch. Twin Oaks Kiss th' Blarney Stone, born in 1984 (Ch. Destiny One Gun Salute CDX/Ch. Grousemoor Miss Bertschire).

Brenda says: "Blair was the all-round best, correct type and temperament Flat-Coat that I ever owned. She was stolen from my locked car outside the Veterinary School in April 1990 and I never saw her again! Blair was a Group Winner, Specialty Open Bitch Winner, all with me, a college student at that time, showing her.

"Blair was bred to Ch. Curlee Hill Star Buck CD and produced the only pup ever sired by Buck – Am Can Ch. Twin Oaks Star of Duckacres (Satchmo) (breeders Brenda Griffin and Joanie and Rob Sharpe). Satchmo is perhaps the most special to me. He was born six weeks before my mother died; he was a focus of life for her in her last few weeks and a life for me to cling to after she passed away.

"Although I have enjoyed many activities with my dogs over the years, showing Satchmo is my passion. He *loves* it and is a show dog like no other I have owned. He was called "Satchmo" as Louis Armstrong was my mother's all-time favourite jazz musician."

FLATFORD: MARV AND MARY FARWELL also TODD (1985)

First Flat-Coat was Ch. Snowdown Canis Major CD (Am Can Ch. Athercroft's Blac Jack/Ch. Grousemoor Evening Jeau). Major was bred by Susan Metzger, a litter born on February 11th 1985. Major was bought primarily because Todd had said he would like a dog and, having looked around very carefully, a Flat-Coat was decided upon – and what a lucky choice Major proved to be!

Marv and Mary Farwell's Am. Can. Ch. Snowdown Canis Major CD: Multiple Group winner, and BOB Westminster 1991 and 1992.

Todd showed him originally, then college intervened, so Mary took over. When Paddy Petch was over she said they should do more with him, so Carlos Puig took over as handler. The rest you could say is history. BoB Westminster 1991 and 1992 then at 10 years an Award of Merit. Won the National Specialty 1994 from the Veteran class having previously won the Veteran Stakes. Numerous BoB and Sporting Group Placements.

Foundation bitch is Ch. Darkside Elegant Velvet CD who is enjoying a successful show career (Ch. Grousemoor Dexmoors Torch/Ch. Cedarlane's After Dark). There has only been one Flatford litter (Major and Velvet) from which the Farwells kept Ch. Flatford Zeus the Major God, who was Reserve Winners dog at the 1994 Specialty. "Special" has to be "Major".

GROUSEMOOR 1974: HELEN AND GERRY SZOSTAK
Helen says: "The actual foundation of the "Grousemoors" was Ch. Torwood Poppy CD WD bred by Neil and Denise Jury, a litter born June 17th 1979 (Torwood Percell/Torwood Dazzler).

"Every present-day dog from my kennel traces to Poppy. She was bred 4 times, producing a total of 30 puppies, of which 20 became American Champions. She was a great lady and lived to be 14 years old. She is still the all-time top-producing dam of Champions in the US. Her pups were versatile also, earning advanced titles in field, Obedience, and tracking.

"My favourite dogs have been Ch. Torwood Poppy CD WC and Ch. Grousemoor Mean Joe Green TDH WC, her son by Ch. Bull Hills Aspen. Joey was a great personality, with a wonderful, perpetually wagging tail and super sense of humour; he loved everyone, and would do his best for you at all times no matter what you asked of him. Another favourite is Ch. Grousemoor Wish Upon a Star. Star has been Best of Opposite Sex at the last two FCRSA National Specialties (1993 and 1994). She is a bitch of excellent movement and type and also a wonderful personality. I enjoy mostly just being with my dogs. I show, track, and do hunting tests. I'm not a good obedience person but am very interested in learning about the relatively new sport of agility."

HARDSCRABBLE: MARGOT HALLET
See Field Trial chapter.

HIHILL (1985): PETER AND MOLLIE HEIDE
Peter and Mollie had Ch. Meadowrue Black Peppercorn in 1984 (Ch. Springold's Jack of Fleetwood/Ch. Meadowrue Dragonfly CD WC). Some two years later they imported the bitch Exclyst Black Vixen (Ch.) from Brenda Phillips, sired by Ch. Ir.Ch. Shargleam Blackcap from the excellent brood bitch Exclyst Sequin.

Lacetrom Auchentoshan, bred by Tom and Caroline Gate, followed in 1987. He achieved his American and Canadian titles and WD; he was, in fact, the first owner-handled Group 1 winner in the Northeast in 10 years.

Following the sad death of Pat Chapman, Ch. Fossdyke Helmsman (Eng Ch. Shargleam Blackcap/Eng Ch. Paddiswood Burnt Lobelia) and Shargleam Winter Shades (Fossdyke Illustrious/Shargleam Terek) crossed the pond to take up their new home with the Heides. These imports have obviously brought in a wider breeding pattern.

Peter is chairman of the 1996 Specialty.

HY-TIMES (1979): PATRICIA LYNN SUTTON
First Flat-Coat was in 1979, a pleasing liver companion dog. The foundation bitch in 1980 was Ch. Bertschire's Orphan Annie (Ch. Wyndham's Fiesty WC/Ch. Lady Obsidian Crystal CD). 'Annie' produced very talented pups in all fields of work. Over 11 bench champions as well as

multiple obedience and field title holders. Foundation stud dog was Ch. Twin Oaks Gone with the Wind CD TD (Ch. Curlee Hill Powerhouse/Ch. Kelly's Gamble CDX WC). Lynn says that Philip produces talented puppies – hardly surprising with his breeding. Main interests started as show and Obedience, but the setting up of hunting tests has given wider scope.

"Specials" are Ch. Twin Oaks Gone with the Wind CD TD, a "once in a lifetime dog"; Ch. Hy-Tymes My Fair Lady Mayfield, a liver daughter of Philip and Annie; and Ch. Hy-Times Echo Sounder CD JH WC, the third generation, sired by Ch. Spring Valley Moonstone UD MH WXC. Lots of talent in all directions.

JO NO RE (1970): JOYCE AND DOROTHY REIN
Started with Goldens. First Flat-Coat was in 1977, called "Cricket". Foundation bitch was virtually by chance, obtained on her 5th birthday, Am and Can Ch. Cracker of Heronsflight Am and Can CD. (Heronsflight Tercel/Heronsflight Rungles Jancy). Cracker had no titles when she went to the Reins, she gained her titles with them. Was only bred once, to Torwood Jetsetter. Main interests: 1970 to 1985 Field, Obedience, tracking etc. 1985 to 1995, due to work commitments, restricted to Obedience and show.

"Specials": Am Can Ch. Cracker of Heronsflight; her daughter Am Can Ch. JoNoRe's Sum Enchanted Evenin' WC Am Can CD; and Am Can Ch. Sunshine JoNoRe Snowy Knight Am CDX WC Can CD WC Group places USA and Canada, who loved to show and enjoyed field work.

Joyce runs Flat-Coated Retriever "rescue".

KISTNER (CHERYL): see ACTIVITY CHAPTER
Currently has the very talented Am Can Ch. U-CDX HR Grousemoor Three's a Crowd CDX TD JH WCX Can UDT WCI (Ch. Grousemoor Dexmoor's Torch WC/Ch. Grousemoor Blue Skies CDX TD MH WCX) and Am Can Ch. Grousemoor Last Starfighter TD JH WC Can TD WC (Ch. Grousemoor Dexmoor's Torch WC/Ch. Grousemoor Abbey Road).

MANTAYO: SALLY TERROUX
Originally, Sally had the prefix "Terrcroft"; I think it must have been around 1966 that she changed it to Mantayo, the Indian name for a wild goose. Sally's name has already been mentioned in connection with early imports: she is one of the diminishing group who know all the problems that arose in the early years of re-establishing the Breed. Consequently her knowledge of the Breed is extensive. She is a true dog person. For some time Sally has chaired a committee to produce an Illustrated Breed Standard, she also writes on various "educational" aspects of dog ownership. A person with loads of common sense – which, as an elderly friend used to say, "is not that common!"

MEADOWRUE (1971): VALERIE BERNHARDT
Valerie writes:

"My love affair with Flat-Coats began some 24 years ago with the purchase of Wyndhamian Constructor (Heronsflight Tercel/Woodlass), 'Darby', from Edward Atkins. I have dedicated my breeding programme to producing Flat-Coats that are good companions as well as workers and showdogs. Over the years I have been lucky to have several noteworthy dogs that have both performed and produced well. The first, Ch. Wyndhamian Constructor, sired two litters prior to his premature death; these included 8 American Champions, multiple group placers and Obedience titlists. I received a puppy from his last litter (out of Ch. Black Jet of Wyndhamian WC), Ch.

Wyndhams Kipper of Meadowrue WC. This dog when bred to my Ch. Wyndhams Hopeful CD WC produced, along with many show champions, a licensed Field placer as well as a Group placer (Ch. Meadowrue Savannah Summer CDX WCX). She in turn produced the 1987 National Specialty Winner Ch. Woodsongs Adamant CD WCX JH. Another bitch from this breeding, Ch. Meadowrue Dragonfly CD WC, when bred to Ch. Springolds Jack of Fleetwood, produced show champions as well as sporting group placers. Among these offspring was Ch. Meadowrue Black Peppercorn who won the Breed at the prestigious Westminster Kennel Club Show. Dragonfly was bred to two other dogs and from these breedings produced 3 Obedience Utility titled offspring as well as an AKC Senior Hunter.

In 1979, I brought over from England perhaps one of the most influential Flat-Coats in the US, Am Can Ch. Torwood Peerless Am Can CDX WCX JH, 'Woody' (Torwood Percell x Torwood Dazzler). Woody was an excellent showdog, winning a sporting group 1 and 4, and consistently in the ribbons at specialties. He was a wonderful dog to live with although a true canine Peter Pan into his old age. Woody's greatest influence was as a stud dog. He was bred to nine different bitches and produced over 25 American champions, two obedience high in trial winners, specialty winners, a Canadian best in show dog, many tracking dogs as well as a licensed field trial Derby list bitch. His offspring in turn have contined to produce. Some of the more notable stud dogs being Ch. Curlee Hill End Quote WC and Am Can Ch. Butterblacs Excalibur CD WC. The most notable brood bitches include Ch. Wingmasters Bella Beauvoir UD MH, and Ch. Woodsong Almost Spring CD WCX JH.

In 1983 I purchased another English dog of mainly working lines, Ch. Jemadar of Casuarina CDX WCX JH. He was bred to 3 different bitches and produced the 1989 Specialty Winner dog, Ch. Grousemoor Dexmoor Torch JH WC. This dog has himself become a successful stud dog producing Multiple Specialty Judges Award of Merit winners, Sweepstakes winners and Best of Opposite Sex in Specialty.

OMEGA (1971): ROGER AND PEACHIE ORTON

First Flat-Coat was in 1971 when Roger bought Athercrofts Gamble on Rolla, a daughter of Ch. Claverdon Gamble and Ch. Sassacus Arr Rufus. She damaged a leg whilst working so was not bred. In the early 80s emphasis was on hunting; the Ortons ran the first Flat-Coats in the California "Picnic Trial". As field access became more restricted, in recent years emphasis has changed to

Ch. Wyndham's Javelin, agd ten, in 1976. Bred by Ed Atkins and owned by Roger and Peachie Orton.

include more showing. Foundation male, and also No.1 "Special": Ch. Wyndham's Javelin (1976) (Ch. Wyndhamian Dash WC/Ch. Claverdon Gossamer WC). He was still being placed in the Sporting group at 11.

Foundation bitch and No.2 "Special": Int. Mex. Am. Can. '78 World Ch. Mandingo's Screamin' Demon (Ch. LaDeja's Black Bart CDX/Ch. Wyndhamian Devil CD WC). A great show girl, she also won the International FT in Mexico City in 1979. Ch. Omega's Final Countdown UD (1982) is No.3 "Special" (Ch. Bertschire's Doc Holliday CDX WCX/Ch. Omega's Bedazzlin' Sunset), who had multiple group placings and multiple high in trial.

Of present dogs mention must be made of Ch. Omega's Quiet Riot, co-owned with the Galvins of Rocky Point. He has many group wins and placings, won Westminster KC (breed) 1995 and was No.2 F/C USA in 1994.

PETERSFIELD (1976): PATRICIA DEBREE
First Flat-Coats: Pat had two, a brother and sister, Sassacus Royal Proxy (Peter) and Pert (Peggy), from a litter bred by Polly Jones (Ch. Sassacus Arr Rufus/Ch. Heronsflight Pertinence). Sadly Peter was killed when two years old, but his memory is kept as he is the "Peter" in Petersfield. Pert was not bred from.

Foundation: Pat feels the male Am. Can. Ch. Gossamer's Black Duck (Ch. Wyndhamian Dare/Ch. Wyndhamian Collector) and the bitch Am. Can. Ch. Jantel's Peggy at Petersfield (Can Am Ch. Branchalwood Feochan/Can. Am. Ch. Casuarina Nootka of Jantel) together form the base of her breeding, as from their union came Ch. Petersfield Maggie Matilda who has been most influential. Her sons include Ch. P Gallant Jacob, and the noted Am. Can. Ch. P Tobias James. Jacob was in the top five F/Cs in the USA for 3 years and is the grandsire of Best in Show, Am Can Ch. Petersfield TJ's Hunter JH WC, and a candidate for the Hall of Fame; he is owned by Jennifer and Jeffrey Andrews. "Toby" is his sire. Am. Can. Ch. P Tobias James won the Canadian Specialty twice.

Pat says that in her breeding she looks for multi-purpose dogs of sound, happy temperament with physical well-being. She also looks for the lovely typey head and expression. "Specials": Maggie Matilda, Jake and his daughter, Ch. Petersfield Karmel Lalique.

QUILLQUEST (1978): GILLIAN IMPEY
Gillian was born in Cheshire, England but moved to North America, firstly working in Canada then moving to California and finally ending up in New Jersey having married Max.

Her first Flat-Coat was Am. Can. Ch. Wyndham's Cracker Am. Can. CD (Melody). Descending from this bitch have come so many multi-talented Flat-Coats that it is difficult to pick out any in particular. The first litter included Am. Can. Ch. Quillquest Euridice CD WCX Can CDX (Pepper) and litter brother Ch. Q Orpheus UD TDX WCX JH, a Hall of Fame inductee owned by Anne Campbell. The litter was sired by Ch. Midnight Star Julius CD WC.

Another Hall of Fame inductee (1995 Specialty) is Ch. Q Express CDX SH WCX, owned by Adrienne Ayles and Neil Goodwin. His litter brother, owned by Mary Scoates, is Can Ch Q Eclipse WC Can WCX CDX. They are sired by Am. Can. Ch. Q Eros JH CD WCX Can CD WC from Am. Can. Ch. Q Artemis Am Can WC (Temmi). Temmi is also the dam of Rosalind Pentecost's good field bitch Am. Can. Ch. Quillquest Gentle Fancy Day CDX JH WCX Can CDX WC1, whose sire is Am Can Ch. Heronsflight Burnet Am. Can. WC.

Gillian had a memorable journey to the Canadian Specialty in 1994. She and five Flat-Coats travelled from New Jersey to Calgary, Alberta. All five Flat-Coats enjoyed the mountains, the rivers and lakes! As it happens the journey was worthwhile, as Am. Can. Ch. Q Falcon went BoB

A group of Gillian Impey's Quillquest Flat-Coats.

from Veteran, sister Fen won the Veteran Sweepstakes, and Am Can Ch. Q Phens Born to Win went BOS for the second year running. Gillian aims to produce versatile Retrievers. Altogether there have been some 30-plus Quillquest bred champions, 3 Hall of Fame inductees, 2 Senior Hunters and 1 Obedience Champion. Ever optimistic, Gillian added "with more to come".

ROCKLEDGE (1977): PATRICIA AND ALEXIS CARLSON
In 1977 Pat had Ch. Gossamer's Top O' the Morgan, a tremendous showman, who helped Alexis in her Junior handling, Alex being around 12 at this time. Over the years Pat has owned and bred many good dogs. Some recent ones include Ch. Rockledge Jubilee and her daughter Am. Can. Ch. Rockledge Treasure at Walden, sired by the noted Rockledge Borago of Birdson WCX.

SASSACUS: PAULINE (POLLY) JONES
Polly's dogs had such influence in the early days. One always remembers the "Arr" litter, Ch. Clavercroft Kite and Ch. Arrogance of Wyndham. The litter included the bitch, Sassacus Arr Rolla, the base on which Bonnie and Glenn Connor founded the Athercroft Kennels, and her litter brother the good sire, Sassacus Arr Rufus.

SPRINGVALLEY (1976): ELEANOR BERTZ
First Flat-Coat was Ch. Springvalley Riparian (Wyndham's Surprise Gunner/Krauth's Bayou Bubble – a daughter of Claverdon Gamble). "Rip" was 1979 National Specialty Winner. Main interest: started with show and Obedience but now almost exclusively Field.

Ch. AFC Jon Lee's Springvalley Atari WCX (Ch. Springvalley Riparian/Ch. Wyndham's Nefertity CD) is the Breed's only Amateur Field Trial Champion. Winner of two Amateur All Age Stakes, the only Flat-Coat ever to qualify and run a National Amateur Championship Stake, he has the most all-age points of any Flat-Coat ever. All this and a Group placing Bench champion too. Eleanor says he was exceptionally intelligent, which, in fact, was a double-edged sword – any knowledgeable trainer will understand exactly what she means.

At present Eleanor is running Ch. Springvalley Kodiak, a grandson of Atari (on the dam's side). Kodi has been highly successful with a Licensed Derby win, two qualifying wins and an Amateur All Age win in 1993. Only surpassed by his grandsire. A powerful dog and spectacular to watch on long retrieves.

Ch. AFC Jon Lee's Spring Valley Atari, owned by Eleanor Bertz.

Then there is the delightful three year old "Fever" – Twin Oaks Spring Fever (Ch. Springvalley Moonstone CD MH WCX/Ch. Spring Hollows Place a Bet). I thought her an absolute joy in Denver in 1992; even as a pup she showed enormous potential and had style. She has already qualified All Aged and has 1st, 4th and Reserve JAMs. She too is a granddaughter of Atari through her sire. Kodi's dam Ch. Karoc Sundance and Springvalley Moonstone are in fact litter mates, but according to Eleanor are totally different.

STERLING: ADRIENNE AYLES. See CASABLANCA

SUMMERHILL (1970): CLAIRE AND MARTIN KOSHAR
Long-time devotees to the Breed, although breeding as such is limited. First Flat-Coat was Mantayo Blackwatch Janie. (Ch. Mantayo Poker Chip CD/Ch. Mantayo Blackwatch Glory). Foundation: Am. Bah. Ch. Destiny Dear Abby Am. Bah. CD (Am. Can. Ch. Mantayo Bo James Bolingbroke CDX BDa Can. CD/Ch. Athercroft Study in Black UD WCX). Work is the major interest, so "trainability" is important and sound temperament a "must". "Specials" are Ch. Mantayo Shoreholme Denver CD and Ch. Casuarina Waikare JH CD. Claire currently has a young male starting to train from Jane Smith's Westering Kennel.

TWIN OAKS: JOANIE AND ROB SHARPE
Joanie's foundation was a bitch, Ch. Kelly's Gamble CDX WC, born in May 1976 (Wyndham's Surprise Gunner/Krauth's Bayou Bubble). Joanie says she has line-bred back to Kelly and her litter brother, Ch. Springvalley Riparian CDX WC (National Specialty Winner 1979). This breeding has consistenly produced excellent working and show stock. Main interests are show, field and Obedience.
"Special" dogs are: Ch. Twin Oaks Sure Bet, a 'Kelly' son by Ch. Athercroft Black Jack. Joanie says: "He really clarified for me what correct head, body and type were all about. A superb example of the breed. And secondly Ch. Twin Oaks Spring Formal; a liver version of Bet. Joanie feels he has proved to judges that liver colour does not mean an inferior specimen of the breed. Beautiful movement and type. He is of course litter brother to Eleanor Bertz' delightful and talented Twin Oaks Spring Fever.
I am going to exercise an author's prerogative and mention a Twin Oaks dog which to me

personifies the Flat-Coated Retriever. Am Can Ch. Twin Oaks Tsar Nicholas CD, MH, WCX (Ch. OT Ch. Twin Oaks Double Exposure UD WC/Ch. Akela's Sure Bet to Win). The youngest Flat-Coat to earn a Master Hunter title, he qualified and competed in two Master Nationals and earned a Field Trial placement. He was BoB at the 1992 National Specialty and the 1993 Canadian Specialty, having previously been unbeaten from classes when under the late Pat Chapman and Paddy Petch. Nick is the "proof of the pudding" that breeding will out. If you study the dogs in his pedigree, Nick is what you would expect and hope to get. Not a one-off chance "flyer", but the result of years of careful and experienced breeding. Many newcomers would do well to give heed to this question of long-term planning in breeding programmes.

WYNDHAM: EDWARD ATKINS
Mention has already been made of Ed's enormous contribution to the establishing of the Breed in the USA and also in the UK by searching out descendants from almost extinct bloodlines and adding them to the gene pool. One only needs to look at present-day pedigrees to appreciate the influence of 'Wyndham' Flat-Coated Retrievers.

CANADA
Early in 1971, I had a 'phone call from Eric Underwood of White Horse, Yukon, saying that he very much wanted to have a Flat-Coat, specifically as a hunting/companion dog. This started a correspondence that was to continue for many years, eventually being taken over by Eric's daughter, Pam. Confidence having been built up on both sides, on July 6th Heronsflight Prospect (Heronsflight Tercel/H Puff) set off on his long journey. Two years later, Heronsflight Jasmine (Ch. Wizardwood Sandpiper/H Tassel) went to Pamela. These were not part of a breeding programme.

It was sometime in the early 1970s that Barbara Hall judged the breed in Scotland and was absolutely delighted with a young Scottish dog, Moira Jewell's Parkburn Brandy Boy, who later became Sh. Ch. In 1973 Bobby and Moira emigrated to British Columbia taking with them Brandy Boy and The Parc Dawn. Our loss was Canada's gain. In 1974, the two dogs were mated, the resulting litter being the first in Canada for over 40 years. These puppies went to widespread homes in Canada and the US and, of course, included Cyraine Dugdale's triple champion, Can Am Ch. Parkburn Deextensing of Casuarina Can Am CD, who returned to the UK with Peter and Cyraine.

Frank and Elaine Bourassa introduced Flat-Coats into Saskatchewan in 1977 when they bought Butterblac's Cruise Control, a Brandy Boy son, who gained his Champion title, WCX and was placed in Trials. He was Canada's first Best in Show Flat-Coat and No.1 Flat-Coat in Canada 1979, 1980 and 1981.

Wayne Sager brought the Breed into Alberta with Butterblac's Total Eclipse also bred by Doug Windsor. Sire this time was Torwood Peerless, the dam, Amberwood's Blac Athercroft (dam of Cruise Control also). From Eclipse, Wayne has bred some very talented stock, earning titles in Show, Obedience, Flyball, Agility and so on.

Moira Jewell says that there are now in excess of 100 Flat-Coats in Western Canada with increasing interest in the breed. Today, Flat-Coats are seen regularly competing in WC tests, Obedience Trials and in the show ring. Particularly gratifying is that more sportsmen are becoming aware of the Flat-Coat as a personal hunting dog.

The FCRSC holds an annual Specialty which the West has hosted three times. Each year the numbers grow. A popular event in BC is an annual picnic held to enable Flat-Coat owners with family companion/hunting dogs to meet and have a get-together. Not easy in view of the distances involved. Moira goes on to say that most of the Flat-Coats seen in competitive events are from the original breeding stock of the seventies; this has now been widened by the Berins' Prairielight stock of which more anon.

PARKBURN (1966) (UK): MOIRA JEWELL

In 1966 Moira purchased a bitch puppy, Leah of Tamara from Tom Campbell. Moira's maternal grandmother had owned Flat-Coats and Moira had always admired Tom's dogs. Brandy was a grandson of Leah. The descendants from the original Canadian mating of Brandy Boy and Parc Dawn have an absolutely impressive record, producing numerous bench champions and title holders in a wide range of other activities. Moira has line-bred to the original stock but, more recently, has very successfully introduced the import, Ch. Windwhistle Fraser (Riversflight Twill/Larksdown Whirlwind).

Gina Luloff's talented Can Ch. OTCH Parkburn Lachlan WCX is sired by Fraser from Parkburn Haida. Lachlan is the first Canadian bred dog to achieve titles in all three areas, Conformation, Obedience and Field.

Moira sums up, saying: "Over the years numerous puppies have gone to homes as personal hunting dogs. As the breed becomes better known in Canada, I find that more and more people are interested in the Flat-Coat to hunt over because of their versatility, and those who purchased a puppy in the past are eager to have another Flat-Coat to replace their hunting companion who is now ageing.

"I feel it is important to line-breed to produce healthy dogs with good breed type and temperament, that can not only satisfy the needs of the hunter but also do well in the Show Ring and/or Obedience Ring. However, North American Field Trials may not be the best indicator of a Flat-Coat's working ability. They are highly specialised events; many competitive trainers do not

Cyraine Dugdale pictured with Ch. Creekside Bubbles and Moira Jewell with Eng. Can. Am. Ch. Parkburn Brandy Boy.

LEFT: Am. Can. Ch. Parkburn Kountry Race WC, CD, bred by Moira Jewell, owned by Brent and Judy Byers.

ABOVE: The enormously influential sire, Can. Ch. Butterblac's Cruise Control WC: Winner of the 1980 FCRSA Field Trophy, multi-placed in Canadian Field Trials, No. 1 Flat-Coat in Canada 1979, 1980 and 1981. Bred by Doug Windsor, owned by Elaine Bourassa.

allow Field Trial dogs to be hunted over as they feel it can destroy their performance. I feel this contradiction is detrimental to the inborn hunting instincts of the Flat-Coat. The Hunting Retriever Tests and Working Tests are probably a better measure of the breed's natural abilities."

PRAIRIELIGHT: HANS AND MARGARETA BERIN
Hans and Margareta's first Flat-Coat was Glenbower Black Rose bred in Hampshire (England) in 1972, the year when the family and dogs moved to Canada. While on a visit to Sweden in 1984

Hans and Margareta Berin's highly successful Prarieflight Flat-Coats.

they bought Bhalgairs High Fidelity who was bred from in due course, but she is not regarded as the "foundation" bitch – this was O'Flanagan Terra Ignota (Imp 1989) (O'Flanagan Blixt and Dunder/NV 83 Nord UCh. IntUCh. O'Flanagan Rule Britannia). At the same time they brought in O'Flanagan What's Cooking (Ch. CD WC1 Am WC), both dogs bred by Lena Hagglund.

In 1991 Margareta and Hans' daughter brought over Ch. Almanza Wet or Dry at Prairielight, the highly successful No.1 Flat-Coat in Canada 1993, a son of SUCh. NUCh. IntCh. Almanza Larry O'Grady and Almanza Now or Never. They also have O'Flanagan Wheel of Fortune and two young home bred bitches. They are all very special, says Margareta.

Before leaving the Prairies, just a mention of Pat and Rick Lowe, whose interests lie mainly in the field. Rick organised the Working Tests at the 1994 Specialty at Calgary where the test dog was Wayne Sager's Ch. Eclipse's Black Lava CD WCX.

INGLIS: JUDY AND BRENT BYERS
They are currently on a high with Am Can Ch. Parkburn Kountry Race WC CD, No.1 F/C bitch Canada 1990 and her daughter Inglis Prairie Race sired by Ch. Almanza Wet or Dry at Prairielight and already making her presence felt in breed classes. Another daughter from the litter sired by Am Can Ch. Windwhistle Fraser went to Jeff and Jennifer Andrews – Am Can Ch. Inglis Victory Lane WC JH – she was Winners Bitch at the 1993 American Specialty.

ONTARIO
Travelling eastward some 2,000 plus miles, give or take the odd hundred we reach the wonderful city of Ottawa. The highest membership of the FCRSC is in Ontario (39) which at least gives scope for groups to meet for training (weather permitting) or even just socially. Most of these owners have three or four dogs as opposed to Kennels (with a capital "K").

There are of course some kennels of note. We have already come across some of Doug Windsor's Butterblac Flat-Coats which have contributed greatly in breeding programmes. Doug is a past President of the Society and has always had an active role in its development; he is also a breeder/judge.

There is also the Autograph Kennel of Joan and Fred Nettle, based on established American bloodlines, although one has to think of the very good dog bred by Doug Windsor, Am Can Ch. Butterblac's Excalibur Can CDX WC Am CD TT. He is the sire of Michelle Chiasson's Can Ch. Autograph's at Point Blank Range whose dam is Can Ch. Butterblac's Autograph Can CD.

The Flat-Coat owners in this area, I suppose in common with most supporters of the Breed, have enormous dedication and enthusiasm. Joan Schwartz and Linda Scully have three Flat-Coats, all champions, although, in a way, this is incidental to their role in the household. Joan was largely responsible for introducing "Morgan" (the dowager), largely Parkburn breeding; she was followed by Ch. Rupert of Casuarina CD for whom Linda has a great penchant; then the most recent arrival is Ch. Heronsflight Moss's Delight, for quite a time more usually referred to as "puppy from hell" – I think it is called energy!

Joan is the immediate past President of the FCRSC, to which role she brought her customary drive and motivation. Who else in the midst of organising the Specialty would come across Curly Coated Retriever owners and encourage them to set up a Club of their own, inviting them to the Specialty dinner so that they could see first hand what can be achieved?

Eli and Rick Brown have the nostalgic prefix, Ardrossan. Their main interests lie in field activities but they also enjoy shows. Eli is a pedigree freak; she is also membership secretary of the Society. Eli and Rick have the impressive male, Am Can Ch. Parkburn Jerome, the bitch, Ch. Riverly Run for the Roses (co-owned with Elizabeth Montgomery), and the young Ardrossan

Rosalind Pentecost's young achiever, Carronade Gentle Flowing Tamar WCX: All aged qualifier at just over two years of age.

Andalusian. Rosalind Pentecost is a typical Flat-Coat owner in that she is not a "Kennel". Rosalind had her first Flat-Coat in 1986 from Gillian Impey, solely with Obedience in mind, which she did, but then became enormously interested in Field events. The bitch was Can Am Ch. Quillquest Gentle Fancy Day Can/Am CDX WC1 JH (Ch. Heronsflight Burnet WC/Ch. Quillquest Artemis). Fancy Day was the first Canadian Flat-Coat to gain an American Hunting Test title.

A very typy bitch, she went BOS at the 1992 FCRSA Specialty – dual-purpose, even though Rosalind's interests do not lie in conformation. Fancy Day was bred once to Ch. Am/Can OTCH Hob-B's Knite Ryder MH WCX Hall of Fame (he is a son of Atari).

Rosalind kept the bitch Carronade Gentle Flowing Tamar (Scarlet). An intelligent worker, she achieved her Can WCX by the time she was two and by her third birthday was All Aged qualified in Canada and one of the only two Flat-Coats to run in Licensed Field Trials in Canada. Showing is minimal, she is half-way toward her Canadian (Ch.) title. At this age, with the needed luck and "a fair wind behind her", the future looks hopeful.

Rosalind also co-owns, with Gilliam Impey, Ch. Quillquest K Nine Kadet Can/Am WCX.

A very talented trio – well, quartet, as Rosalind's dedication is all-important.

Mary and Jon Scoates' interests lie very largely in field events although showing is taken in with the routine. Quillquest Jetstar Can CDX WC (co-owned with Gillian Impey) and Can Ch. Quillquest Eclipse WC Can CDX WCX have both furthered the cause of the breed in competitive events – "Jiggs" (Eclipse) in particular, a wonderfully kind temperament combined with very real ability fostered by Mary's skilled training. He had Junior and Senior legs in hunting tests. Sadly Jiggs died early in 1995, the type of Flat-Coat who is truly an ambassador for the breed.

Moving on to Niagara on the Lake to Heather Stewart who has two outstandingly able males – no doubt aided by Heather's own determination and dedication as a trainer. They are: Am Can Ch. Fleetwings Oak Brigadier Am CD Am Can WCX Can CDX SH (Briggs) (Ch. Bracken Hollow Oak Demon/Can Ch. Rockledge Fleeting Freesia Can CD), bred by Kathy Howland-Zavitz. 'Briggs' is a tough, natural retriever, outstanding in water. He has been Top Hunting Retriever with the Western New York Retriever Club and was the first Flat-Coat for many years to run in the Gold Whistle Indoor Retriever trial at the Toronto Sportsman's Show. A great pheasant-hunting dog.

Ch. Hardscrabble Hugga Mugga Max Can CD Can Am WCX (Rockledge Borago of Birdsong/Hardscrabble Tornfield WCX MH): another who adds to the credibility of Flat-Coats in competitive events. A consistent performer, he has been invited to take part in the Toronto Indoor Retriever Trials (no longer called the "Gold Whistle" – change of sponsorship).

FLEETWING: KATHY HOWLAND-ZAVITZ

The current President of the FCRSC is Kathy Howland-Zavitz who lives in Nova Scotia. Animals have always been a part of Kathy Howland-Zavitz's life. As a child, her family had Shelties and over the years she rescued many dogs from the dog pound, including a part-Setter part-Lab mix. It was this dog that actually started Kathy on the road to Flat-Coats when it was remarked by a breeder of Labs from England that the dog looked "just like a Flat-Coat". Research was done and, when the dog tragically died, Kathy's involvement with Flat-Coats began with the arrival of a black bundle of energy. Her name was "Daphne" Ch. Jantel's Barrnacarry CDX WC TT who was out of Levecque's Ch. Casuarina Nootka of Jantel and sired by Ch. Branch Alwood Feochan TT. Daphne was a small bitch with exceptional side movement and the most endearing personality at play and work. She became Canada's top Obedience Flat-Coat as well as obtaining group placements and being a superior marking dog in the field.

A beautiful bitch named "Maude" Ch. Rockledge's Fleetwing Freesia CD who was out of Pat Carlson's Am Ch. Summerhill October Treasure and sired by Am Ch. Hardscrabble Wingover Zip

A once in a lifetime pair: Ch. Jantel's Barrnacarry CDX, TT, WC and Ch. Rockledge Fleetwing Freesia CD TT, owned by Kathy Howland-Zavitz.

CDX WCX MH (HofF), arrived several years after Daphne. She was the most interesting and challenging Flat-Coat and her desire to retrieve was absolutely intense, sometimes uncontrollable. Over the years, interest in Obedience and the breed ring has expanded to include flyball and agility to satisfy the Flat-Coats innate playfulness and need for challenging activities. Flat-Coat affinity for agility was demonstrated time and time again by Maude when she would spontaneously run around, up and over the various obstacles while out in the yard by herself.

In the past 14 years Fleetwing has produced only three litters but these contained some notable dogs such as Can AM Ch. Fleetwing's Aurora, BoB Can National Specialty, Can Am Ch. Fleetwing's Oak Brigadier CDX WCX SH, Can Ch. Fleetwing's Crown Prince CD – and the current show dog at Fleetwing, Can Am Ch. Fleetwing's Caliope "Piper" who was Best of Winners at the Am National Specialty and top Flat-Coat in Canada for 1994.

It is firmly believed that the Flat-Coats at Fleetwing should be first and foremost family dogs, therefore there are never more dogs in residence than can be worked individually or live in a family situation. Grousemoor FW Chachalaca is the most recent arrival at Fleetwing. "Maggie" is out of Helen Szostak's Am Ch. Grousemoor Sweet Repeat WC and sired by Am National Specialty BoB winner Am Ch. Grousemoor Northern Song TDX CDX WCX MH (HOF). Kathy hopes that Maggie will contribute to the breed by proving herself a multi-talented bitch and producing Flat-Coats with correct type and temperament.

A future breeding between Maggie and Piper is anticipated.

THE FLAT-COATED RETRIEVER SOCIETY OF CANADA

With such vast areas to be covered the Society has an enormously important role to play in keeping members informed and forming a base for some cohesion. The quarterly News Letter plays a significant role in keeping communications open and has grown from being just a few pages to a comprehensive publication. Eli Brown has sent some information on the Society. There are 110 members, 75% of whom are actively involved in conformation, Obedience and Field. A Canadian Championship is obtained by gaining 10 points under at least three different judges.

A breakdown of the membership is interesting as it brings home the problems in, for example, putting on the Specialty (Conformation and Field events), with so few people to undertake a major task and with the distances involved.

Newfoundland	1
Prince Edward Island	1
New Brunswick	1
Manitoba	2
Saskatchewan	3
Quebec	4
Nova Scotia	7
Alberta	7
British Columbia	18
Ontario	39

There is a hard core of dedicated members such as, in the Ontario area, Ron and Miris McNicol from Penetanguishene, long-standing and respected Flat-Coat owners and competitors who are prepared to share their knowledge and skills, while newer members such as Val and Rod Davidson have less experience but have energy and enthusiasm. All recognise the need for extra "hands" for events in the area. Flat-Coat puppy owners are encouraged to attend classes even if only to learn basic commands and manners.

Approximately 8 litters are registered in a given year, about 75 puppies. With regard to Field training, Eli says that, given the climate, training can normally only be from April to November; usually dogs cannot be got into water until May. Most competitive Field Trial dogs have to be sent south for the winter with a professional trainer to ensure they will be ready for the start of the season. Sometimes owners go south with their dogs! Those training for Working Certificates usually try to meet up in groups for weekly training sessions using different locations, for example, to give the dogs experience of "stick ponds", which can be very tricky (they are created by beavers).

Discussions have been taking place and there are now plans to introduce a Canadian version of the American Hunting tests; obviously these would relate to many gundog breeds, not only Flat-Coats. As we have already heard, these are more akin to a true hunting/shooting-day situation and as such suit Flat-Coats very well.

Despite the small number of Flat-Coated Retriever owners and the vastness of Canada there is firm family feeling within the breed. This does not mean that everyone always agrees, what family does? But basically, the Breed is in good caring hands; this combined with enthusiasm must give confidence for the future. Highly appropriate to think that Canada again has a "Black dog".